This book is due for return o

Dale Spender, until she began research on language and sex, described herself as a person in search of a discipline. While gaining degrees in English, Education and Sociolinguistics she felt that there was a vast dimension missing. She is an Australian who prefers to live in London. She taught in Australian secondary schools for nine years and has been involved in teacher training. She is involved in the women's liberation movement and the Fawcett Library and is concerned with many aspects of feminist writing and publishing. She is a writer from choice and necessity and is the author of several books, including *Man Made Language* (Routledge & Kegan Paul, 1980).

Elizabeth Sarah, born in South Shields, County Durham, in 1955, has been a determined fighter for female liberation from the time she recognised (at a very young age) that boys got preferential treatment. After a degree from the London School of Economics she entered the classroom as a student teacher in the optimistic belief that some changes in traditional sex role learning could be achieved . . . against all odds. She has since decided to invest her energies elsewhere. She co-edited, with Scarlet Friedman, *On the Problem of Men* (The Women's Press, 1982) and contributed a chapter on Christabel Pankhurst to *Feminist Theorists*, edited by Dale Spender (The Women's Press, 1983). She has spent the last five years training to be a rabbi at Leo Baeck College, London, and will be ordained in 1989.

Edited by
DALE SPENDER & ELIZABETH SARAH

Learning to Lose

Sexism and Education

Revised Edition
with a New Introduction by Pat Mahony

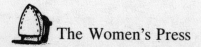 The Women's Press

First published by The Women's Press Limited 1980
A member of the Namara Group
34 Great Sutton Street, London EC1V ODX

British Library Cataloguing in Publication Data
Learning to lose.–2nd ed.
  1. Women. Education. Sex discrimination
  I. Spender, Dale II. Sarah, Elizabeth 370.19'34

  ISBN 0–7043–3863–7

Printed and bound in Great Britain by
Cox & Wyman Ltd, Reading, Berks.

Acknowledgements

Feminist writers have often exploded the myth that writing is done in isolation and is the product of individual talent, by acknowledging all the people who have made a contribution to their work. As writers who worked together in a group we wish to acknowledge publicly the help and support of each other, without which . . .

We also wish to acknowledge our debt to the women who comprise the women's liberation movement who have, directly and indirectly, inspired and sustained us. Because we feel strongly that we should like to repay our debt, the royalties from this book will go to the research fund at the Women's Research and Resources Centre, 190 Upper Street, London N1, so that other women who wish to explore and expose sexism may have some financial assistancee.

There are, however, two individuals who deserve special thanks. Firstly, Glynis Butcher who typed much of our scribble and tidied it up in the process. Secondly, we want to acknowledge the enormous effort made by Margaret Sandra in setting up the Working Party on Sexism and Education at York, 1978. Many of these articles were originally prepared for that working party and without Margaret Sandra's organisation and support we would have had no context in which to settle down, co-operate, and write.

Dale Spender & Elizabeth Sarah
London, 1980

Contents

Introduction to 1989 Edition

I first heard that *Learning to Lose* was out of print when a friend tried to buy her fourth copy (the first three having disintegrated through generous lending). She was indignant: 'It can't go out of print, that book changed my life.' And so it did in different ways for many women working within the education system. *Learning to Lose* was a crucial book in the development of feminist theory and practice of education. It burst upon a world in which feminist teachers, often in isolated circumstances, were struggling to articulate what was wrong with education and to deal with the unmanageable answer, 'everything'.

It brought together in one place strands of feminist thinking about education which many women were reading for the first time. Its copious references opened up that world further, and this was important in affording women access to a movement and in enabling them to feel part of it, thus strengthening their own voices. It encouraged women to speak of their own experiences, to seek change on the basis of these, and to recognise fully the importance of both change and experience. Finally it was (and still is) a treasure trove of 'firsts' which sowed the seeds of work to be continued by other feminists. The critique of co-education as progressive for girls, the recognition of sexual harassment as an issue in schools, the contradictions and dilemmas within Women's Studies, and even the accessibility of the language in which the book was written – all contributed to a sense of new and exciting possibilities for the future.

Of course, with hindsight and the benefit of more years which have seen the development of analyses of patriarchal education, it is easy to spot the limitations of the book. With its emphasis on the features of oppression which we share as women, there was little room to explore the issues which divide us. I have tried partly to rectify this by including three new contributions. Grace Evans writes about racial and sexual oppression, and Lorraine Trenchard discusses the importance of meeting the educational needs of young lesbians in school. And the new resource list and bibliography compiled by Sue Adler stands on its own as a testimony to the amount of work which women have done over the last seven years.

The importance of these new chapters cannot be understated. We cannot change the past but we can make sure we do not continue with the same limitations in the future. For white women this means understanding and deconstructing our own racism to the point where we feel an anger and disgust about it – directed at *change*, rather than guilt – equal to the anger we feel about our own sexual oppression: not from a position which presumes any moral superiority, but from the recognition of the debts we owe and of what we have yet to learn and give. Lesbians too are not fundamentally supported by liberal tolerance (though in the current climate some would settle for this). The importance for all feminists in identifying with the struggles of lesbians is that lesbians, by stating in the clearest possible terms a sexual, economic and emotional independence from men, underline the issues for all women: the right of us all to live free from the social control exerted by male authority. An anti-sexist education which is racist and heterosexist is not a feminist education, since it endorses and reproduces hierarchies of power to which feminism is fundamentally opposed.

It is crucial that we understand these links and never more so than now in the current political context of the New Right. The distaste of the New Right for liberal democracy, let alone feminism, will lead to an ever-increasing set of controls both outside education and within.* Some of these developments have very dangerous consequences for women. The reassertion of the patriarchal nuclear family as the social ideal, which was barely argued for even by the rhetoric of biological naturalism (maternal instincts in women and sexual aggression in men), is no longer to be treated as an interesting theoretical viewpoint. The preoccupation with the infertility of white middle-class married women and the vast sums of money spent on reproductive technology firmly establish motherhood as the centrepoint of women's adult identity. The reassertion of the power of the white male through the model of the white middle-class nuclear family is underlined by the way in which mothers outside this model are treated as problematic. Single mothers, according to Conservative MP Rhodes

*Since this was written the much-opposed Clause 28 of the Local Government Act 1988 has passed into law. The extent of its malevolent effects have yet to be realised.

Boyson, are the 'scourge of the 80s'. Lesbian mothers are subjected to appalling treatment by the courts; and, as the testimonies of black and working-class women show, the best the new technologies have to offer the unprivileged is contraception and sterilisation.

Control of sexuality is being exerted within the school too. Under the 1986 Education Act, governing bodies and head teachers have new responsibilities, to 'Take such steps as are reasonably practicable to secure that where sex education is given . . . it is given in such a manner as to encourage those pupils to have due regard to moral considerations and the value of family life.'

How far this will be open to interpretation remains to be seen. The signs are not hopeful that feminist morality and critiques of the family will accord with what the New Right and its propagandists, the tabloid press, have in mind. What *Learning to Lose* will mean in another seven years time is anyone's guess. One thing is certain – we have at present more need of a concerted push towards and for feminism than ever. This is why the book is worth re-reading and why the new contributions have urgently to be taken on board.

Pat Mahony
London, 1988

Introduction to 1980 Edition

The dissatisfaction with many of the existing critiques of education was the impetus for this anthology. As a feminist study group interested in the theory and practice of education we were convinced that the aim of removing sexism from the curriculum, while desirable, was sin itself, inadequate. We believed that if every possible recommendation for the avoidance of sexism in education were to be carried out to the letter, the position of women would not necessarily change. We were also convinced that education could not be held solely responsible for the reproduction of sexual divisions in society: women were learning to lose long before they had a right to education and in the past, it was the denial of education to women which contributed to the construction of inequality.

From these understandings we have attempted to develop a feminist critique of educational theory and practice. We recognised that the models of education were encoded by a select group of males (white, upper and middle-class) and that concepts of what constituted a good and sound education were formulated before women made their entry. Many of those concepts still prevail today, and they are still controlled by the dominant group. Utilising our own study group as a model of co-operative learning we have tried to develop an educational theory and practice which is not predicated on the construction of inequality. We have outlined many of the present deficiencies in the education system but we have also tried to indicate the way in which education could be transformed if the principles of the women's movement were taken into account.

Part One: Recollections

Pippa Brewster

School Days, School Days

This article has been put first for a variety of reasons. It is the starting point of many of the contributors to the book, it is about who we are and how, in some measure, we came to be what we are. But it is something else too: it is an attempt to put feminist principles into practice because feminism has adopted as a basic tenet that we should begin with ourselves. It has revalued the personal and given it a high priority and so it seems reasonable to make explicit some of our own personal experiences.

It is not simply because we are women that we begin with the recognition that subjective experience is important, it is because as human beings we have had the personal experience of discovering that many sanctioned 'objective' truths which have been applied to women are frequently little more than the expression of the misogynist or sexist bias of men. We have, therefore, become cautious about an 'objective' approach to the construction of knowledge.

We believe one of the weaknesses of the objective approach is that it deliberately excludes any reference to the personal, deliberately divorces itself from the subjective and categorises this aspect of the human condition as an 'irrelevancy or impediment to getting things done' (Hochschild, 1975; 281). We believe it was partly because women were not consulted about their own lived experience, partly because the personal was not taken into account, that the objective facts about women's existence — which are so distorted — were allowed to continue unquestioned for so long by the majority of people.

So, we value the personal. We have made it political. Our stance is not only chosen for its credibility but also for its challenge to the present male-dominated processes of knowledge construction (Smith, 1978); the status which feminists accord the personal is one means of redistributing power. In feminism personal experience can be raw material, the data for research. This is the origin of much of the knowledge generated by the women's movement. As a feminist study group we were no exception. Our analysis of education is deeply rooted in our own lived experience of education and it was because we wanted to structure and explore this experience that we wrote our educational autobiographies for the other members of the group. Like a variation on the methodology of oral history, our pasts became our present data.

When our experiences were shared we could not accept that it was mere coincidence we had so much in common. Certain themes recurred throughout our accounts. This was a little surprising as our education spanned the years from 1946-79 and occurred in different countries (Britain, America, Australia).

Parents feature prominently at the outset of most of the biographies, then seem to fade into the background, only to reappear with a different message for their daughters during adolescence. Terror and incontinence feature predominantly as children enter the educational system and learn they must conform to its rules.

My parents were very keen on education. They saw it as a way of giving us social mobility, of mixing with the right kind of folk. They didn't realise how strange and how unfriendly a school of this kind — a smart, cosmopolitan London prep school — seemed to a five-year-old who is not conscious at that age of the social differences between people, only that such a school can be very lonely and forbidding to a shy child. . . I can remember the first day vividly, blind panic, wet pants, an apple in my pocket.

Getting a good education seems to have been a constant theme in our household from as far back as I can remember. Neither of my parents left school with much in the way of qualifications and they seem to have been determined that their children wouldn't make the same mistake . . . I've never got over the shock of my first day at school. I wanted to go to the toilet. I asked but was told I had to go at break-time, a concept I didn't understand at three and a half. I couldn't wait and wet myself.

Incontinence was a common phenomenon but, I suspect, not exclusive to little girls. Nearly everyone linked their remarks about incontinence with parental emphasis on a 'good education'. School was not a place for play, but a place for serious aspirations and everyone mentioned arriving at primary school with strong motivation to succeed. Doing well at school was perfectly consistent with being a good girl at pre-pubescence.

I wanted to be clever at primary school. I took great pride in coming first in my class. That was partly for parental approval, I suppose.

I was always waiting for my report card to be sent home because I knew it would say glowing things which, of course, were not to be dismissed. Good reports often meant a present, a pat on the back and a feeling of confidence.

The strong tones of the parental voice are heard again in secondary education, but doing well at school begins to take on a slightly different aspect. Parents are beginning to urge their daughters to think of the future and the word 'security' seems to occur frequently. Education and work are circumscribed in terms of female future security.

Althought my parents knew I wanted to be a writer, they were very much in favour of 'having something to fall back on' and it didn't take much persuasion on my part to make them let me give up A-level history and do a secretarial course instead . . . Thus I left school with the idea of being a secretary to a great writer and not the great writer.

Without exception our autobiographies reveal an absence of aspiration in terms of work. It seems that none of us took it seriously. We found ourselves at work in our twenties but we were surprised by what we found ourselves doing. No one mentions making a choice about work.

I was twenty-three when I realised that I had become a teacher. I had never made any conscious decision to go into teaching. I had never felt any 'vocation' for it. I had drifted into it, carried gently on the tide of 'It's a good job for a girl. You get good money — it's equal pay. You can always go back to it after you have had child-ren'. I didn't resist the tide.

There was no doubt I would be a teacher. I am the fifth generation on my father's side to teach in the family. Most holidays had been spent with my father in school while my mother worked. I totally absorbed its atmosphere so it was not surprising that I entered college at eighteen . . . My first job was in Lambeth where my father and sister taught.

My first job has now become a career. As such it seems that I should be thinking about my future, and I find that I haven't had much practice at that. The moves through school and college seemed pre-destined. My family supported and encouraged me. Marriage seemed logical too and took away some of the responsibility for decisions. Divorce made me conscious of my responsibility to myself physically. Mentally, I'm only just beginning to come to terms with it.

Underlying all our educational accounts was the understanding that there was another job, besides paid work, for a woman. This is never lost sight of and it stands in sharp contrast to career considerations. Wherever there was conflict it seems that 'future security' demanded that it be resolved in favour of the feminine role. This shift, which occurred with all of us, has been variously described as female under-achievement, as lack of motivation, or as the emergence of the home-making instinct, but regardless of what it is called, it is quite clear that for all of us during secondary school, we came to be in a losing position in terms of our culture's criteria for achievement. We were conscious that it was occurring but were resigned to it.

I can remember that in primary school I was engaged in this constant exciting battle to come first. I always wanted to be first in arithmetic, the best story writer, the greatest actor. And I often was. It was an area primary school. It was unstreamed . . . By the time I was fifteen, I failed at school. And what I have to explain is not only that I didn't learn anything in secondary school but that I must have had to erase what I had learned in primary school, in order to be as poor a student as I was.

In explaining my declining school performance, my parents and my teachers spoke as if I had some sort of disease. I came to accept that I was infected by a virus that prevented me from succeeding at school. I didn't question the diagnosis, but internalised it, quite convinced that this was something quite out of my control. Never did I ask myself how I came to get this disease or how it could be cured.

Throughout my prep school days I was convinced that my parents thought I was stupid. The school couched it in educational terms. I was a 'slow developer' or 'most insecure'. Hardly surprising, if one is told that over and over again, I failed the examination to the main part of the school and no one was surprised.

Individual achievement at school, with some notable exceptions, Summerhill perhaps, tends to be gauged on the basis of competition and one thing which emerges from these accounts is that many competitive little girls (and it is debatable whether this is good or bad, of course) become non-competitive young women. Some might feel the need to explore the possible contributions made by instincts or hormones but it is not necessary to look to these factors in order to explain our changed attitudes. In a society where competition is mandatory, the penalties of withdrawing from competition, particularly in an educational context, become obvious. In the construction of a superior and an inferior sex there could be no more useful mechanism than that which convinces those designated as inferior that they should cease participating. It is much more 'civilised' if women withdraw freely. Enticed by the prospect of other, different rewards, too many of us became successful losers in the school.

I can remember being fascinated by physics and chemistry when we did the general science course in the junior school, but my maths wasn't up to it and I was steered away from that line of education. When I first went to this school, science had hardly been catered for at all — anyone who wanted to do A-level science had to go to another school.

I revelled in wearing the pyjama stripe uniform of my secondary school, boasting about my Latin and French lessons. Four years later, I was to fail both subjects miserably, having hated the lessons. Geography retained its early attraction, but I had to give it up in the third year, I can't remember why. I lost maths at the same time thank god, and went on with a curriculum of history, English, art, biology, French, Latin . . .

I left school qualified in the traditional arts subjects. No sciences other than biology were taught. No housecraft or any technical subjects. It wasn't possible to mix arts and science subjects, and so I didn't have any choice. Obviously, it was arts subjects.

There are leads here, but no explanations. The accounts at these points are littered with indications of disincentives, in both the simple non-availability of sciences in the curriculum and the unpalatability of sciences and maths which arises in the transition from primary to secondary school. We all have to live with ourselves, however, and we all had to make some 'adjustment' from competitive to noncompetitive, from relative success to relative failure. Two members of the group remembered their own avoidance tactics, their own accommodations when faced with the prospect of a science and a maths lesson.

The rest just frightened me, and I escaped into day-dreaming which reports described as laziness. I was so frightened of one lesson I poured boiling water on my hand and couldn't write for a week.

I was hopeless at maths and was taught by a woman who I can see now was a brilliant mathematician but who should have never been let near children . . . I was in detention most nights . . .

Here is another common theme. We were frightened of maths and science. The origin of this fear is a matter for speculation (see other accounts, particularly 'Gender and Marketable Skills'), though, in retrospect, some of us can see how it was manipulated.

I got two per cent for my O-level mathematics paper, and I had come top of the class in mathematics at primary school . . . I had more knowledge of maths when I was ten than I have had in all my adult years. I have to ask myself what happened in the interim. How does this make sense? I had the same maths teacher for all of my secondary schooling and he certainly didn't think too highly of females wishing to do mathematics. Whenever I asked a question of him the reply was generally 'Oh, you don't need to know that. You'll never use it. Do something easier.' No doubt he did play a big role in helping me to forget what I already knew and if it was just mathematics I suppose I could put it down to the teacher, but it wasn't just mathematics and I 'forgot' things in other subjects as well.

There is no clear and categorical explanation. One can only ask what happens to girls in secondary school that they should come to forget what they had already acquired at a younger age? What are the pressures on them to forget, what are the advantages of forgetting? I think the following extract provides some insight into this process.

For science we had this very young, attractive male teacher . . . My homework for science consisted of setting my hair, doing my nails, pressing my uniform . . . I bought a thick leather belt and I used to wear it under my school tunic so that when I put my tunic belt on, instead of there being a bulky look around my waist as the belt tied in the pleats, there used to be a nice flat look. I endured agony sitting in class with that leather belt pulled in so tightly around my waist. There were other girls who did it too.

Of course I was interested in boys but how could this interest have been the cause of my school failure? Sometimes I wonder what would have happened if anybody had sat down with me and asked me what it was that boys liked in girls. I know I could have given all the usual platitudes and I'm pretty sure I would have said that they didn't like girls who were too bright. But I know even that wouldn't have helped me greatly because if that was what boys wanted, that was what I was going to be. It was their approval I was seeking and if that meant being helpless and having them save me from the dreadful complexities of maths and physics, then that's what I did. During adolescence I simply changed my concept of success and I worked no less diligently at being feminine than I had done at being first in my class.

Nancy Frazier and Myra Sadker (1973) quote from the experience of secondary students in America. During adolescence when adult roles are being tested the dividends of femininity can appear to be much greater than those of 'the career woman'. The message of maternal fulfilment can appear much more seductive than that of the loneliness and even the despair of the 'old maid'. It is no accident that many young girls should be lured by one and frightened by the other. They are making a sensible choice in terms of social rewards and punishments when they opt out of education. It is often far more threatening to be unfeminine than it is to be an underachiever.

Science to me was an opportunity to be feminine. That meant posing around the experiments instead of taking part. It meant watching for the teacher's response and not watching the outcome of the experiment. It meant being foolish; making a big fuss when there was flame, bangs and so on from the things we were doing. It meant asking the boys or the teacher for help, gazing into their eyes and asking them to explain. That's what I learned in science and I learned it well. When I look back now I can see the gradual acquisition of femininity and that explains my school days. By adolescence I was interested in being approved of to the same extent as I had been in primary school, but I was looking in different places for my approval and I knew I got it for different things. It wasn't my parents any more to whom I went for the presents and the pat on the back. It was the males around me. Sometimes male students, sometimes male teachers. What did get me approval was being vague and dumb, letting them help me with my work, seeking their guidance.

Every society constructs its own rules and we can analyse the ways in which particular meanings have been constructed in our male-dominated society. Men have been in the position to legislate what those social rules will be (Smith, 1978) and it would be asking too much to have us accept as mere coincidence that there is no contradiction for men between masculinity and achievement. The *masculine* man is one who achieves, who is masterful; the *feminine* woman is one who underachieves, who defers. Our autobiographies are lived illustrations of many of the more theoretical claims that will be made throughout this book. Female educational underachievement is not just a concept, is not abstract; it is our personal experience.

Irene Payne

A Working-Class Girl in a Grammar School

Our education system positions the future generations according to both their class and gender. Within capitalism there is a limited amount of social mobility, but overall the education system perpetuates existing social relations, based on class and gender divisions. Males have to take on the behaviour appropriate to their future role in production. Females have to take on the behaviour appropriate to their future role in reproduction as well as in production. Paul Willis (1977) documents the ways in which working-class boys take on culture and values directly related to their future role as waged workers. He shows how their 'rebellion' against school has its roots in a realistic understanding of their own situation within capitalism. Angela McRobbie and Jenny Garber (1975) have conducted a smaller survey to show how a group of girls are positioned within both sexist and class ideology. Working-class girls need to learn their future position as low paid wage earners in the work force. However, there is a further dimension to the structuring of their material/social relationships. Girls must internalise their position in relation to men, through which process they will become domestic workers and child bearers and rearers. They must learn to give this labour freely, based on a notion of individual love.

My own experience of schooling, at a single sex girls' grammar school, is located within this context. I was one of a minority of working-class girls who went to grammar school. My experience was therefore not typical of that of most of my working-class contemporaries who went through secondary education in the 1960's. However, the way in which I negotiated my experience gives some limited indications of the class and sexist ideology within which it took place. I want to attempt to describe the difficulties which I experienced, as an indication of a more general picture. This can only be a very tentative offering.

The first problem after passing the eleven-plus exam was a material one because attendance at grammar school depended on money. School uniform and specified equipment made heavy demands on my parents' income. I can remember that many items had to be obtained on credit and that there was a definite sense of 'making a sacrifice' so that I could have an education. My family was probably what could be termed 'respectable' working class, that is, a particular segment who, for a complex of reasons, had taken on a certain set of beliefs about education. Their faith in education would not have been shared by many of the parents of my contemporaries. The material sacrifice necessary for a grammar school education would certainly not have been made by all working-class families. Thus any notion of equal opportunity, based on ability, is much too simple because of the complex forces at work which determine how people view the world. Working-class people have their decisions shaped by material reality. If education really did offer us all the same chances, how would the social relations of exploiter and exploited be reproduced? Attitudes to education are part of a whole structure of relationships to society, which have their roots in real material divisions.

There is a further element to this 'decision' about education, based on sex. I can remember the reaction to my own 'success' in obtaining a place at grammar school. Many relations and neighbours said that education wasn't really important for girls, as they only got married and had children. My brother's success was seen as much more crucial than mine. However, my own parents, and particularly my mother, never questioned the fact that I should be educated. It would probably be interesting to research more fully the experiences leading to this position, adopted by only a minority of working-class people. I can only speculate, on the basis of my knowledge of my mother's own educational experiences. She was regarded as able but couldn't take up any opportunity because of her family's material position and the patriarchal attitudes of her father. My mother certainly did not have a confident attitude towards education, but accepted the advice of some 'experts' who counselled sending me to grammar school. This passivity is, I think, a significant element in being 'respectable' working class. It goes hand in hand with a desire to conform. There was no element of understanding the educational system, let alone of actively using it, rather you took what the experts offered and just 'did your best' with it. My mother's relationship to schooling was very different from that of her middle-class counterparts. This inexperience and passivity had implications for the way I subsequently experienced education.

The major point I want to make, however, is that my education took place via a particular class/sexist ideology, which I experienced as a series of pressures in different directions. I want to examine the contradictions for a working-class girl being educated within a society which, by and large, didn't educate this particular segment of society. I want to examine the value system of my school in relation to the value system of my working-class neighbourhood. These school values are not always explicit but can be found in the total set of practices in the institution. It is useful to look at what I learned, both implicitly and explicitly, within this school.

The first clear set of values was characterised by the school uniform. The class roots of school uniform are fairly clear because their origins are in the public schools. Institutional colours, mottoes and crests were all part of a total image derived from the ruling class. The uniform represented a sobriety and discipline whose power extended beyond the school. I can remember that prefects had the responsibility of ensuring that girls wore their berets on the bus journeys on public transport to and from school. The power of the ideology showed itself in the fact that they meticulously performed their function and reported girls seen without their berets. The uniform was part of a process of destroying individual and class identity, in order that pupils would submit unquestioningly to school authority and what that represented. School control extended even to such hidden recesses as underwear and was enforced with a vengeance, by regular inspections. Punishable offences included wearing the wrong coloured knickers or socks. These practices were part of the process of enforcing a particular set of bourgeois values, based on ideas of respectability, smartness and appearances.

However, I think there was a further dimension to this, in terms of gender. The uniform couldn't have been better designed to disguise any hints of adolescent sexuality. I suppose the shirt and tie, the 'sensible' shoes, thick socks and navy blue knickers were part of a more 'masculinised' image. It was as though femininity had to be symbolically sacrificed to the pursuit of knowledge. Modesty was implicit as there were regulations about the length of skirts and the covering of your arms. Jewellery, make-up and nylon stockings were taboo. Ideas about dress were based on notions of 'nice' girls and 'not so nice' girls, with both class and sexual connotations. We were, after all, to be turned into middle-class young ladies.

I wore the uniform without too much suffering at school but it was the greatest source of embarrassment to me beyond the school gates. I can remember being terrified that someone from my neighbourhood might see me wearing it. I was worried that I might be regarded as a 'college pud' or a snob by my peers. If they saw anyone in school uniform they would usually jeer and hurl abuse. But it had sexual as well as class connotations. As I got older, I was particularly concerned that potential boyfriends didn't see me in this 'unfeminine' garb. The first thing I always did when I got home from school was dash to my bedroom to change out of my uniform. However, my rebellion against school uniform was never very strong as I wanted to do well at school and wearing uniform was part of the process of earning approval.

It is interesting, in the light of what Angela McRobbie and Jenny Garber's study reveals, that the rebellion against school uniform did take on a very 'feminine' form. Within the grammar school, there were groups of working-class girls as well as disaffected middle-class girls who were alienated from school and just wanted to leave as soon as possible. Their rebellion manifested itself in the usual things like smoking or being rude to teachers. However, it was also structured along 'feminine' lines, in opposition to the 'masculinity' of school rules about appearance. I can remember bouffant hairstyles, fish-net stockings, make-up and 'sticky out' underskirts being the hallmarks of rebellious girls. All of these stressed femininity and the girls involved were also noted for being 'experienced' with boys. The rebellion's ultimate culmination was in getting pregnant, which meant that a denial of sexual activity was no longer possible. Such matters were always carefully hushed up and the girl concerned quickly removed.

The school even had an 'official' attitude to boyfriends. I can remember the headmistress insisting that her girls didn't have time for boyfriends. This was another way of denying our sexuality. Social life was disapproved of and we were inundated with homework which made it difficult to do much else in your own time. I suppose we were being prevented from growing up so that we would conform to the demands of the school. Saturday jobs were totally disapproved of which shows the middle-class ideology of the school. I needed to work as my parents found it a struggle to keep me. These jobs also provided one of the few opportunities to participate in the adult world and gain some experience of work. Our horizons, however, were supposed to be narrowed down to working for school. All these practices were part of what it was to be a 'young lady'.

Another manifestation of these implicit values was in the whole area of language. Again, there were two dimensions to this. In terms of class I had to learn to 'speak properly', that is, like middle-class people, and in terms of gender I had to learn to speak politely, that is, talking like a

15

lady. This meant learning to speak both 'correctly' and 'nicely' and the pressure to conform can be quite inhibiting for a working-class girl. In our first two years of school we had speech training which was designed to teach us the correct way to pronounce words. I can remember thinking how 'posh' the teacher's voice was and she successfully instilled in us a belief in the importance of our pronunciation and diction. We were to avoid sounding 'common' at all costs. But as girls we had to consider more than these class factors: we had to try to be refined at all times and therefore such things as loudness of voice were discouraged as raucous and unfeminine. There was a total image to be borne in mind and to which we all aspired: we worked very hard to present ourselves as 'educated young ladies'. Any form of ostentatious verbal behaviour (shouting, arguing, challenging) was considered inappropriate and was often considered a punishable offence. One teacher gave us the following lines from King Lear to write out because we had been noisy: 'Her voice was ever soft, Gentle and low – an excellent thing in woman' (*King Lear*, Act 5, Sc 3, Line 272).

Implicitly and explicitly we were inculcated with our role in the 'art of conversation' which encouraged us not only to be correct (as no doubt working-class boys would be encouraged in the grammar school) but also polite and deferential (an attribute not necessarily encouraged among boys). My grammar school education reveals a class and a gender ideology at work on my language.

I managed to conform and meet the linguistic requirements of the school, but they could only be used within the school. I had to abandon them when I left the school gates and had to change my language for home. Such 'bilingualism' is not without its disadvantages and can work to make one feel inadequate and unconfident in all language use. Mistakes at school could be an offence, but so too could mistakes at home. I was in constant terror of being exposed as a 'freak'. My way of dealing with this threat was to over-react. In my home environment I made a concerted effort to appear as 'one of the girls' and to do this I felt obliged to be louder than anyone else, to swear more, just to prove I wasn't different and hadn't been corrupted by the grammar school.

It was like leading a double life, for neither side would have recognised me in the other context. I was straddling two very different worlds and felt considerably threatened by the fact that I didn't belong to either. I had a constant sense of being different, which I interpreted as inferiority. I was always aware of the possibility of making a mistake and being exposed as fraudulent. I could not relax in either setting. I had a sense of inferiority within school because I didn't come from such a 'good' background as most of the other pupils. I was always uneasy when people began to parade their status symbols and discuss their father's occupations and where they lived. At school I felt ashamed of my background and attempted to conceal it. My Dad was a manual worker and we were pretty poor and I didn't want my classmates to know this. Nor did I want them to know that I lived in a 'rough' area, in a house that didn't have a bathroom.

At the same time I didn't want my friends in my neighbourhood to know that I was considered clever at school. (It is not of course unusual for some working-class kids who have received scholarships to be diagnosed in this way. One 'clever' working-class student vindicates the whole system and attests to the myth of equality of opportunity. However, it places enormous demands on such students.) In order not to be dismissed by my out-of-school friends I pretended that school was unimportant; I gave the impression that I didn't care about it. This of course demanded many subterfuges on my part. Life was a juggling process. Homework, for example, was difficult for me as I did not want my friends to know that I did it (I could not have preserved the belief that I didn't care about school if I indicated that I conscientiously did my homework). Because I didn't want my friends thinking I was a 'swot' (and withdrawing their friendship as a result) I tried to get all my homework finished before they came to call for me.

With my girlfriends the problems associated with school success were class ones and so that I could retain their friendship I disguised my attitude to school. But there are gender as well as class dimensions to this problem for it wasn't just with my girlfriends that I felt obliged to hide my school achievements. The problem of being seen as clever was particularly acute when it came to having boyfriends. I thought that being regarded as intelligent would make me less attractive to boys. I was always careful, therefore, to make light of my grammar school education and to refrain from mentioning how many O levels I was doing. Again there was the fear of making a mistake for, to me, it seemed that it would be a mistake to be seen as being more clever than a boy.

The pressures on me were conflicting and varied. For quite a while I tried to negotiate two worlds, but the time came when such negotiation was no longer possible. The two worlds proved to be incompatible. The two sets of values ordained different futures and the point came where I had to decide which future would be mine. Eventually the pull of the school was stronger for it held out the promise of social mobility through higher education. Once I decided to stay on at school after the statutory leaving age my fate was sealed. I could no longer pretend that school was unimportant or irrelevant. It was clear to my friends at home that I had marked myself as 'different' and from this point our paths were to diverge. They entered the world of paid work and they left me behind; I could not disguise myself as one of them any more.

I think that my experience shows that working-class values are not readily accommodated within the middle-class culture of schools. It is not possible to incorporate both sets of values, for the conflict between them is too great. In trying to conform to the requirements of the school I ultimately had to live the ideology encompassed within the school and this meant rejecting many of the values of my home. This is not the experience of working-class kids in general because they are not singled out for school success. Realistically, working-class kids have few expectations of education as a means of transforming their lives. They continue to live out the values which will ensure their existence as workers for capitalism.

My experience as a working-class girl contained more contradictions than that of my middle-class peers whose culture more closely approximated that of the school. However, there were contradictions shared and the organisation of the curriculum provides an example of sexist ideology at work. In my school there was an academic ethos and this meant that practical subjects were accorded low status. While this is an aspect of bourgeois ideology which constructs the mental/manual division of labour, it is also an example of patriarchal ideology with its direct relationship to the sexual division of labour in our society. The least desirable subjects in the school curriculum were those associated with traditional female functions, for example, domestic science and needlework. These subjects were for those girls who were not considered to be very clever. Through this mechanism we learned that the skills which were associated with females were not valued. We internalised a hierarchy of knowledge and it was 'male' knowledge which occupied the higher rungs and which was our goal.

Achievement of such a goal, however, was not unproblematic. Certain sacrifices were demanded, among them our femininity. This was the price we had to pay for the acquisition of such knowledge. Those girls who were not of the élite, who did not do academic courses but who were supposed to be satisfied with the traditional female diet, were not required to make such a sacrifice: being good at needlework does not rob one of femininity This was their compensation.

Either choice can be seen as negative. When female skills are undervalued then being good at them does not necessarily count; but attempting to acquire male skills can also be negated because no matter how well a female does she can still be undervalued as only an 'honorary' male. Even within the area of 'male' knowledge, sexist ideology operates so that the female academic élite still learn to choose sex-appropriate knowledge. Although the majority of my teachers were female, the mathematics and physics teachers were, significantly, male.

The majority of the girls doing science 'chose' biology: fewer did chemistry and only a tiny minority did physics. In the lower sixth there were two English groups, each of nearly forty students, while there were only three or four students in the physics group.

The ideology of marriage was also a powerful force, even though there were a number of unmarried teachers on the staff. It was used as a rationale for counselling, particularly in relation to those girls who were not defined as academic. The lure of marriage often operated to obscure the female employment position. Those leaving school at sixteen were not encouraged to scrutinise women's employment situation and were given virtually no career advice at all. Marriage was implanted as their aspiration and the prevailing attitude was that 'any old job' would do in that fill-in time until their aspirations were realised.

Those of us who stayed on were pushed towards universities or colleges of education but, even here, the sexist ideology was not challenged. The possibilities for female employment were presented within the confines of what was appropriate to our sex. Limitations operated even for the academic élite, for the role of wife and mother was never lost sight of; it was always taken into consideration when discussing future careers. Those careers which were presented as possibilities were the ones most easily accommodated with the female reproductive role, and were often an extension of the female involvement with children, such as teaching, for example.

The curriculum, career advice and construction of the 'feminine' within the school all served to reproduce the sexual division of labour. The positioning of individuals is one of patriarchal capitalism's most important means of reproducing itself and my experience of schooling points to the ways in which schools function to reproduce existing social/material relationships via class and sex-specific ideologies.

19

Part Two: Feminist Educational Critiques

Dale Spender

Education or Indoctrination?

The distinction which is made between education and
indoctrination is often a strange and subtle one. Both terms are
frequently used to describe the process of the presentation of
information to the uninitiated. When this process is seen as desirable it
is usually called education, whereas when it is seen as undesirable it is
usually called indoctrination. According to *The Oxford English
Dictionary*, education consists of 'bringing up the young' while
indoctrination means 'to imbue with a doctrine' and although this
disctinction may not provide instant illumination (given that it is
hardly possible to bring up the young without imbuing them with a
doctrine) it does help to illustrate the way in which the two terms are
generally used within our society: education is a positive or neutral
activity whereas indoctrination is a negative one.

As a society we generally maintain that education is superior to
indoctrination and frequently make use of the rationale that education
permits choice. The belief that education presents people with a
diversity of world views, from which they are free to select what they
find acceptable, while indoctrination provides only one set of beliefs
which must be unquestioningly accepted, is one which can be found in
much of the literature on education. When the argument is stated in
this way it would be difficult to deny the superiority of education, but
belief is not always the same as *practice*. While anyone who is involved
in education may believe they are presenting diversity and providing

choice, it is quite possible that in practice they may be engaged in the business of indoctrination. Raymond Williams has stated that 'If we believe in a particular social character, a particular set of attitudes and values, we naturally believe that the general education which follows from these is the best that can be offered to anyone: it does not feel like "indoctrination", or even "training"; it feels like offering to this man the best that can be given' (Williams, 1975; 147).

In the nineteenth century, believing at one stage as they did in a 'particular set of attitudes and values', it was not indoctrination for educators to offer the working class 'limited literacy'; any more would have been inappropriate for their subordinate position. 'It is doubtless desirable that the poor should be generally instructed in *reading*, if it were only for the best of purposes — that they may read the Scriptures. As to writing and arithmetic, it may be apprehended that such a degree of knowledge would produce in them a disrelish for the laborious occupations of life' (Williams, 1975; 156, quoting a Justice of the Peace of 1807).

Today, when that specific set of attitudes and values no longer has currency, we find such explanations transparent. Some can even feel self-righteous and declare that such prejudice, such indoctrination, such oppression are of the past. Today, so the argument goes, we provide equal opportunity for everybody to partake of the fruits of education. There is no such thing as 'limited literacy' or its equivalent. It seems that we are just as deceived as our predecessors. We still adhere to a 'particular set of attitudes and values' which allocate people to their 'proper place' in society and we still insist that it doesn't *feel* like *indoctrination*. But . . .

. . . when the various mechanics of selection which operate in the educational system segregate and distribute children according to their estimated ability or potential (i.e. their predicted place in the class (*race and sex*) structure) in order that they can undergo different processes of training and preparation, *this is not some politically neutral exercise whose sole concern is the development of the child*. The necessary attitudes, skills and disciplines are being inculcated into the appropriate individuals in the appropriate proportions . . . (Ted Benton, 1974; 14; my emphasis and my addition of *race and sex*).

There have been some gains, of course. It is at least possible now to identify some of these indoctrination processes at work. While this view of education as a means of reproducing existing divisions and inequalities in society may not be shared by all members of society there is, nonetheless, a significant vocal and published group of people who do share it. The 'politics of education' has received more than scant attention and some aspects have been systematically and convincingly documented.

But even as the evidence has accumulated, there is still a serious omission. Many educationalists still assume that the world is comprised of men and still explain indoctrination not just in terms of men, but as if the male condition is the human condition. While this particular conceptual framework persists, the insights and understandings to which it gives rise are limited because they are applicable to only half the population. It is significant that Ted Benton omitted race and sex from his description of the oppressive practices of education. It is also significant that when he conceptualises *children* and the many influences which contribute to their formation as social beings, he states:

> If we consider the working-class child, these will include his family, the broader social relationships of his parents, the traditional practices, games and rituals of his neighbourhood gangs, which may in turn bring him into direct relation with the police . . . Even the geography of his area, the social relations reflected in the street design, the presence of the redevelopers, play a part in forming him ideologically . . . (Benton, 1974; 14).

What are the implications of treating this *representative* working-class child as male? The substance of Benton's analysis is considerably coloured by this consideration. Not only is it unfortunate that he should be so limited in his view of humanity, it is even more unfortunate that in his attempt to understand and clarify the way in which indoctrination operates in our society and education system he fails to notice one of its most oppressive and pervasive forms. The inclusion of sexism in his analysis would surely have provided him with greater comprehension.

Educational institutions play a major role in persuading people that they are unequal, but not just on the basis of class. They also persuade people they are unequal on the basis of race and sex. Of course Benton is right when he goes on to suggest that working-class boys do not *choose* to occupy the social position to which they are generally directed and for which education grooms them, but neither do working-class *girls* — or many other girls for that matter — *choose* the places to which they are assigned. We simply cannot accept that most men in our society choose to work outside the home and most women choose to work inside: we cannot accept that women choose to have less education than men and to work in less skilled and lower paid jobs (Byrne, 1978). We cannot believe that women choose to work — outside the home — for an average pay of £55.40 per week while men receive an average of £86.90 per week (*The Guardian*, 26 October 1978). If women are in this position it is not because they have freely chosen it from a range of options presented to them in education, but because education has played a major part in persuading them that this is where they should be.

It is unlikely that anyone presented with alternatives would choose the socially disadvantaged position which women occupy, and it is because they are precluded in many instances from making a choice, that education is required to make their lot more palatable. Education can assist in providing an ideological framework which justifies this disadvantage and helps make it seem reasonable. It uses propaganda to convince students that they themselves *desire* to occupy the position to which they were assigned.

The Cult of the Apron
Alleen Pace Nilsen coined the phrase 'the cult of the apron' to describe the depiction of women in school books. She analysed fifty-eight award-winning picture books in which only 'twenty-five had a picture of a woman in them. And of those twenty-five, all but four had a picture of a woman wearing an apron' (Nilsen, 1975; 199).

The books and materials used within our schools abound in crude and inaccurate images of women and men and are designed to *indoctrinate* children in sexual inequality. From the day they begin school children are confronted with images of human inequality and are exhorted to conform to them. From elementary reading schemes to A-level texts, these same biased images proliferate and convey the same sexist message. Image after sexist image functions to convince younger members of society that men and women are different — and unequal — and hence the possibility of choice is pre-empted. The process is a cumulative one. In almost every form of curriculum material there are more images of men than of women (Frazier and Sadker, 1973; Lobban, 1976; Maccia et al , 1975; Nightingale, 1977; Stacey et al, 1974) so that children cannot fail to understand that men are intended to be more prominent. Whether it be fairy stories or science textbooks, men are portrayed as doing more interesting things so that children can appreciate what their future role entails. Where women are included it is most often in a reproductive, child-rearing capacity so that children learn who is responsible for life-supporting tasks without necessarily learning to value those tasks. In six reading schemes analysed by Glenys Lobban (1976) she found that of 225 stories only two showed women who were not engaged in domestic tasks. Of the two women who were not cooking or cleaning, one was a shop assistant and one was a school teacher. This was in stark contrast to the portrayal of male occupations where a rich range of possibilities was presented. If children are using these images to build and project their future lives then it is evident that, for girls, there is little choice. Within our ideology of sexism the inequality of the sexes is subtly maintained by providing one sex with a few tarnished images with which to make sense of the world and their place within it and by providing the other sex with a range of glorified images. It is not surprising that the two sexes should learn the lesson and develop very different views of the world and very different self concepts.

Whereas women are portrayed almost exclusively in the home in curriculum materials, men are frequently portrayed outside the home, in the 'real' world, and one of the interesting images which Lobban found was that of boys watching older men in adult occupations. Boys could see themselves in books as learners actively engaged in a positive role of acquiring important skills. This was not the case for girls. They were just there, usually in a passive role. In all the 225 stories which Lobban analysed, the most active and strenuous things which girls did was to hop and skip. Obviously, some explanation is required to account for the grossly distorted picture of the world we place in front of students virtually every day in their school lives. It would be a mistake to assume that these rigid and exaggerated images are receding. When Nilsen examined the books which won major American prizes as good children's books from 1951-70 she found that rather than inequality being eliminated it was actually becoming more pronounced. The number of women characters was actually decreasing.

Years	% of female characters
1951-56	46%
1956-60	41%
1961-65	35%
1966-70	26%

Glenys Lobban's more recent analysis of sexism in British curricular materials suggests that the practice of providing few, and inferior, images of women persists virtually unchecked. She gives examples of new materials to illustrate that 'rigidly different roles for the sexes' are still depicted and that they portray 'males as superior in everything except the ability to cook, dust, clean and smell flowers' (Lobban, 1977; 105). When such images are the content of reading schemes, their purpose is not solely to teach children to read, claims Lobban: 'Such reading schemes do not mirror real differences between the sexes, they are part of the process whereby artificial differences are maintained and perpetuated. Such schemes do not just teach children to read. They convey a subtle and pernicious message that females are inferior, and do untold psyche damage to the self evaluation of girls particularly' (Lobban, 1977; 106).

One important lesson which girls learn from these images is that it is desirable to be small, an image which fits comfortably with social values in which physical strength is seen as positive and as the prerogative of men. Although pre-adolescent girls are often bigger than pre-adolescent boys of the same age, in children's books boys are invariably shown as bigger and taller. The real world may not always accommodate our sexist rules but instead of dismissing the rules as inappropriate when we encounter tall women and short men, we tend to think it is their size which is wrong, rather than our prescribed rules that men should be tall and women short. We do not make our rules from the evidence produced by the population but, rather, make the rules and then require the population to conform at both the physical and psychological level.

The message is that boys do all the interesting things while girls, when they are not doing household chores, just fill in the background. They are the foil for male endeavour. And once this message has been learnt, the children reproduce sexual inequality. Boys begin to extend their horizons, to grow in self-esteem. Girls, however, learn to reduce their expectations, to lower their self-esteem. They have been persuaded to distort their own being in order to be consistent with the distortions which surround them. There has been little *choice* in the matter. Having been subjected to this constant barrage, they are lucky if they can visualise any alternatives to the advantaged male and the disadvantaged female.

> Adventure books written especially for boys have a wider scope than those for girls. Boys' books are about subjects like trapping, sailing, smuggling, mining, the wild West, cops and robbers. Scenes are set all over the world from Alaska to the South China Seas. The boy heroes need not only physical courage, they need to know what they are doing in great technical detail. Books like these are there to expand a boy's horizons. Read a corresponding book for girls and you will conclude it is expressly designed to dampen down any spirit a girl may have left. They are set in ballet schools, and pony clubs, in the mild English country side. The books are really about the social side of life, the only life girls are now supposed to be interested in (Nightingale, 1977; 98).

The images confronting children in their books at school frequently fail to match their experiences in the world. For example, not all fathers work. 'The percentage of men who work full time is not, incidentally, 100% as most of us think', states Ann Sutherland Harris, in reference to the United States, 'but 69.4% of all men of working age' (Harris, 1975; 163). As unemployment increases this figure is likely to decrease so that for many children the images of a working dad and a domesticated mum will not be consistent with their lives. But education has rarely made use of the lived experience of students within the curriculum. Society could be threatened if, within education, students were required to scrutinise the realities of their lives. Even the image of the nuclear family is no longer appropriate for many people. *Ms. Magazine* (March 1978) stated that the nuclear family in the USA is now a minority arrangement and that among the working women of Britain 'nearly one fifth . . . are the breadwinners' (Byrne, 1978; 72), a statistic which stands in complete contradiction to the images presented to children in school. When over 40% of women work outside the home (Lindsay Mackie and Polly Pattullo, 1977) and when only two out of 225 stories in reading schemes recognise this, then it can be seen that curriculum materials are presenting *fewer* choices and not more.

As Glenys Lobban has pointed out, the images we present to children in school are not images of the real world, but distortions which show 'a world more rigidly patriarchal than the one we have at present' (Lobban, 1977; 104). In the real world children may well be driven round by their mothers and have their meals cooked by their fathers but such images cannot be accommodated within education where the practitioners, who learned well what they themselves were taught, maintain a system which makes people unequal on the basis of sex. Although it is possible to press for a transformation of the official version, to point to its inadequacies and inaccuracies — as in this book, for example — the more common response on the part of students is to opt to change themselves. The contradiction can be resolved if they strive to be unequal. Educators may not always note its significance but they are constantly in the presence of students who are trying to transform their own lived experience to make it more acceptable in terms of sexist ideology so they are not left to live with untenable contradictions. From the young girl who says 'women cannot be doctors', even when her own mother is a doctor, to the boy who says 'women cannot be astronauts' when confronted with the Russian woman astronaut (see 'Teachers and Students in the Classroom'), children are trying to deny their reality when it conflicts with the legitimated reality. Such denial can become a habit, and perpetuate sexist ideology.

Sexist ideology is not, of course, confined to reading schemes and children's books — though these provide some of the most blatant examples — but permeates the entire curriculum (see 'Teach Her a

Lesson'). History, for instance, also provides examples of sexist ideology at work and contributes to the structuring of inequality. School-taught history is composed of selected items and as such reflects the interests and bias of the selectors. When we accept that history has been selected by a group of predominantly white, middle-class men it is not surprising that we should find the favoured images in history those of white, middle-class men who have looked at the past civilisations and have seen only wars, male politics and male achievements:

Often pages will be devoted to discussing the details of various battles in various wars, but intellectual, cultural and social achievements in which women have traditionally been involved will be totally excluded, or glossed over. . .For example, in its discussion of the frontier period, one (American) high school text spends five pages discussing the six shooter and scarcely five lines on frontier women. . .The most glaring omission of all is its lack of a single word about birth control, the fight for its acceptance by Margaret Sanger and other physicians, or the impact it had on the lives of women. Moreover, there is incredibly little information on prejudice that is still going on — for example, the legal challenges to discrimination in hiring, promotion and equal pay (Frazier and Sadker, 1973; 116).

When women look for their own reflections they find that the images of women are elusive, and are

. . . to be found in the lives of the obscure, in those almost unlit corridors of history where the figures of generations of women are so dimly, so fitfully perceived. For very little is known about women. The history of England is the history of the male line, not of the female. Of our fathers we know always some fact, some distinction. They were soldiers or they were sailors; they filled that office or they made that law. But of our mothers, our grandmothers, our great grandmothers, what remains? Nothing but a tradition. One was beautiful, one was red haired; one was kissed by a Queen. We know nothing of them except their names, and the dates of their marriages, and the number of children they bore (Woolf, 1929; 141).

In science, sexist ideology plays its part in terms of illustrations as well as instructions to the students (see 'Teach Her a Lesson'). A picture of Madame Curie with her hand on her husband's shoulder, while he looks down the microscope and she looks at the photographer, allows her contribution to science to be trivialised. Illustrations of the laws of gravity and force depicting women with brooms and men with crowbars and levers, associated with technological advances, reinforce the message that for men the doors of science are open, while for women, that way is inappropriate.

Mathematics textbooks play their part too. The mathematical challenge for girls is encompassed in doing the shopping while boys are pictured in a much wider range of problem-solving situations. Marsha Federbush comments on the frequency with which girls are shown as helpless while boys are shown as helpful: it is always the boy who is portrayed helping the girl in mathematics textbooks. 'The expression on girls' and women's faces are sometimes the model of bewilderment as they struggle to find a way to put order into a seemingly chaotic or even simple numerical situation' she says, and such images are not 'intended to help girls feel mathematically competent' (Federbush, 1974; 180). When it comes to the history of mathematics we are led to believe that women have not participated in mathematics. Few mathematics students have heard of great female mathematicians such as Hypatia or Emmy Noether. It is no accident that they are deprived of the knowledge that there have been competent and brilliant women mathematicians.

From literature to history to science and mathematics to sex education, the curriculum is permeated with images that help to promote sexual inequality. The primary concern is not the *accuracy* of information which is transmitted, for much of the educational curriculum would be abolished if this were the priority. It is about reinforcing belief in a 'particular set of attitudes and values' which prescribe particular places for people in society. These indirect images of sexual inequality transmitted at school are reinforced by very direct ones. The important positions in the school are usually occupied by men, the authority figures studied are usually men, the authors of educational books are predominantly men. Even when it comes to English literature where women have achieved success in the real world, their success is not carried through to the educational world. Anna Walters (1978) documented the sex of authors of the prescribed A-level texts in English literature for 1977-8 and students were unlikely to see from these examples that writing is something which women might pursue.

	Women Writers	Men Writers
London University A-level	1	26
Associated Examining Board	0	15
Metropolitan Examination Board	1	10
TOTAL	2	51

Elaine Showalter (1974) reveals that the pattern is no different in American universities: in one typical English department there were 313 men who were considered suitable for and worthy of study and only seventeen women.

By providing an abundance of images of positive males and a scarcity of images of females (and negative images at that) we do both sexes a disservice. We distort the humanity of both men and women. But distorted, unreal and offensive as these images may be, they do function quite efficiently in the maintenance of a sexually unequal society. Sexual inequality, and the ideology which sustains it, is neither incidental nor accidental. It is as much a part of the politics of education as the indoctrination which reproduces the class division in society. Sexual inequality cuts across class and race divisions and is given substance in what has euphemistically been termed education and distinguished from that less desirable form of 'indoctrination'. Such a distinction, however, is not a real one. The education system is not primarily an agent for the promotion of greater choice among students. It can only be said to provide equality of opportunity for people to fulfil the expectations which the dominant group in society has already laid down. It is when students conform to these expectations that inequality is perpetuated. While the prevailing belief is that women are inferior, and while this is taught within education with all the 'massaging' of the evidence that such teaching requires, women will continue to find themselves devalued, in the lowest paid, least skilled jobs, with least power to change those conditions.

Now feminists are insisting that sexism is part of the politics of education, and that girls and women are being moulded to occupy a particular and pre-ordained place in society, this in itself is evidence that changes are occuring. That we can partially identify the means by which girls and boys are indoctrinated for sexually differentiated positions of power and influence not only helps to expose the benign clichés behind which education frequently hides, but also helps to provide us with targets to attack. In recent years *sexism in education* has moved from being an idiosyncratic belief held by a tiny minority to being a fact that must be taken into account in any discussion of ideology and indoctrination within the education system. We have by no means succeeded in our aim of eliminating sexism from education or society but we have moved a considerable distance from thinking that within education 'we are offering to this man the best that can be given'.

Irene Payne

Sexist Ideology and Education

In our society girls are socialised into the expectation that their primary role will be one of wife and mother and once this expectation is accepted and internalised, the continuation of the existing sexual division of labour is ensured. The results are observable. Girls *expect* to be wives and mothers, they make decisions about their lives in the light of this expectation and they *become* wives and mothers, thereby providing the evidence that the primary role of girls is to become wives and mothers.

But this is to observe what is happening, not to explain it. We can see the manifestations of sexist ideology (which expects women to be defined as wives and mothers) but not its origins or its processes. The internalisation of sexist ideology begins in the home (and there are many accounts of socialisation, of the way in which children are taught their gender roles, see Oakley, 1972, for example) but it is also reinforced through state agencies like the school. There can be little doubt that despite the belief that women enjoy equal opportunity, they continue to take their place as low paid workers. The expectation that girls will be wives and mothers is fostered within the school and this determines many of the decisions which are made about the education of girls.

Some research has been done into the way schools operate to fit working-class children into their prescribed roles in the labour force (Whitty and Young, 1976; Willis, 1977) by setting up 'appropriate expectations' and helping the children to achieve these desired ends, but as yet there has been little research undertaken on the way girls are fitted for their prescribed role. But just as people are assigned to a particular category with specific expectations, based on class and regardless of any other considerations, so too they are assigned to a particular category — with specific expectations — based on sex and regardless of other considerations. The ideology that women are wives and mothers first, that they are the appropriate domestic workers, is crucial in categorising *woman*.

As a feminist teacher I want to challenge the generally accepted notions about being male or female and try to understand how children and adults can accept that masculinity and femininity are 'natural' even when they are confronted with contradictory evidence. We must work towards some understanding of how ideology works if, as feminist teachers, we are to combat it.

Any notion of ideology as a system of 'false beliefs' perpetuated by the ruling class to exploit the working class seems inadequate. For one thing, such theories fail to explain how and why such beliefs can persist even when they are not 'true' and when the discrepancies or contradictions are obvious. These theories do not help me to account for the way little girls, for example, accept that they are weaker and more fragile when they are surrounded by empirical evidence that prior to puberty they are often stronger than boys of the same age. It is not enough to say that the girls (and the boys) have acquired 'false beliefs': the question is, how do they maintain them, and even accept the 'naturalness' of them?

There are also limitations within Marxist attempts to analyse ideology and consciousness.[1] Because there has been no adequate analysis available one of the major preoccupations of the women's movement has been the attempt to find an explanation, to formulate a model of the way in which ideology works. Feminists realised the significance of consciousness. The women's movement has been built on changing consciousness, on 'consciousness-raising', in an attempt to expose the dominant ideology in relation to women. But frequently such change is at an individual level and I am cautious about making too many claims for its success. I readily recognise that individuals can change their consciousness, that they can see things in a new way, that the old ideology is exposed and appears as most 'unnatural' (Jo Freeman, 1975; 118). However I agree with Charlotte Brundson when she says of female oppression that 'remaining at the level of the personal will not fundamentally transform this subordination' (Brundson, 1978; 23). If explanations in terms of individuals are inadequate we are still left to face the question of how then does ideology operate? How are ideas and practices constructed within the social and material world? If there were simple answers to these questions then I am sure they would have been clearly stated before now. All I can do is raise some questions and indicate some of the material that I have found helpful.[2] We are taking on a whole system of beliefs when we question the dominant ideology and there is no single issue, no simple approach to the problem. It seems to me that one of the fundamental questions we must ask is, how do students learn. If we can appreciate how they come to accept certain meanings (and I am not thinking of the conventional learning theories posited by psychologists) then we have a basis for helping them to learn different meanings. I think it is a top priority for feminist teachers to address themselves to questions of learning.

We must try to appreciate the individual and social forces at work in the learning environment of the school. As teachers we are concerned with both processes. If we aim to transform the consciousness of our pupils so they can recognise the divisions ideology has created between race, class and sex then we will frequently find ourselves in conflict with the wider function of the school as a state institution serving the needs of our society — which means the needs of a capitalist and patriarchal society. We are faced with the problem of how to change consciousness within such a framework. It is not just the institution of the school with which we must contend. Children bring experience with them into the school, and this experience may also be structured by ideology which sustains patriarchal capitalism. We must also ask ourselves how children internalise new knowledge. Can they accept it or reject it and what is the basis of any such decision? If feminist teachers present them with new knowledge which contradicts and challenges their beliefs, then we should try to understand what forces are at work from the point of view of the learner. We have all seen students capable of 'switching off' from the presentation of traditional knowledge and there seems little reason to suspect that they will necessarily be more favourably disposed to the presentation of feminist 'knowledge'.

Another question which we can ask is whether information must be directly transmitted in order for students to learn. Do they acquire their beliefs through explicit or implicit sources? I think there are reasons for suggesting that ideology is transmitted indirectly. If the crucial part of any socialisation process is the internalisation of 'appropriate' behaviour then it is necessary to analyse the sources from which children learn such behaviour. Obviously, they must look to the adults around them to see what is done and what is not done on the basis of class, race and sex, and there are adults in the school to whom the students may look for role models. The organisation of the school can show in microcosm the way that society is divided on the basis of gender: it can show the economic relations of gender. Any examination of schools reveals a general pattern: women are over-represented in nursery and primary schools, where they are often perceived more as child minders than educators. The low status of these jobs is indicated by poor conditions, low pay and the virtual absence of men. But the situation changes markedly as we look up the educational ladder. There are fewer women in secondary schools, but it is their distribution, rather than their number which is significant. It is men who dominate in the decision-making posts in the schools. They also control subject areas such as maths and science where the status is greater and where the subject matter is considered to be a rational body of knowledge associated with abstract thought. It is no coincidence that there are more women teachers in subject areas like English and the humanities, for these are seen as areas of knowledge which have more connection with the 'personal'. Defined as less abstract, they are therefore thought to require a less demanding process of initiation (they can be referred to as the 'soft' options, a description not without its significance). The lowest status of all secondary school subjects is assigned to domestic science and needlework where the teachers are exclusively women. These subjects are seen as an extension of the 'natural' female function as housewives and they are tied up with the idea of training girls to fulfil this role more efficiently. This aim is explicitly stated in government reports (Dyhouse, 1978).

The ideology behind the sexual division of knowledge in schools is not usually so explicit. Few teachers directly teach that women are suited to one area and men to another, but the model is there for the students to emulate. Ann-Marie Wolpe (1977) has documented this process in school (also see 'All in a Day's Work' and 'Feminist Practices in the Classroom') and she makes it quite clear that it serves a double function: not only are girls trained in skills appropriate to the division of labour, they are also trained in accepting that this division is legitimate, that it is natural. Examination of the rest of the school structure shows the same sexist ideology in operation. The school caretaker will undoubtedly be male and he will control a predominantly female work force. Cleaners, helpers and secretaries will be almost exclusively female and they will have less status and less pay than teachers. One of the first jobs which a feminist teacher can tackle is making these 'hidden' values of school organisation explicit to the pupils. Where ideology operates through the provision of possible models for the students to emulate, the feminist teacher can point to the inadequacies of these models and, in doing so, undermine the ideology.

As teachers, our own consciousness has a crucial part to play in any process of change. We also transmit ideology; we also have sexist expectations of our students. Ann-Marie Wolpe (1977) has shown how teachers expect different things of boys and girls according to their own internalisation of the female and male categories. She shows how sexist ideology is transmitted almost unconsciously, even in seemingly neutral subject areas. The ideology of women as homemakers and men as breadwinners comes to the surface much more directly when secondary school pupils have to make their subject choices at the end of the third year. It is at this point that the links with the sexual division of labour can be most clearly seen. Assumptions about future roles of girls and boys are made much more explicit. This process of subject choice has been documented in *Teaching London Kids* No 10. For feminists, the problem is how we can change the expectations of our pupils so that they don't follow a predetermined path. We can work with our students to begin to suggest alternatives but our scope is very limited, given the power of the labour market. Our work must therefore take us outside the schools to fight for fundamental social change. Our focus needs to be a total one, encompassing the demands of both the women's movement and the socialist movement.

There are some specific tasks which feminist teachers can undertake. The sexism in children's books has now been well documented (see 'Education or Indoctrination') and attempts are being made to write material which contains more positive images of women, but this is only a partial strategy as we are surrounded with sexist imagery and some slight changes in educational materials will not necessarily alter our world view or even undermine sexist ideology. Language is also a crucial area and although the elimination of sexist language will not mean the end of a sexist world, it is quite clear that sexism will not disappear while sexist language continues to be used. Feminist teachers can become aware of their own language and that of their students and in the process can challenge sexist ideology.

I see positive female images as important to changing girls' self-image and to altering boys' conceptions. However, I question the assumption that a non-sexist literature could exist if only we tried hard enough. The cliché that we can't reconstruct the image without a transformation of what produces that image points only to the tip of the problem. I see developments like Women's Studies courses as important steps in the complex process of changing consciousness but not as solutions to the much bigger problem of changing capitalist society. Women's Studies courses are inadequate to combat sexism in the same way that Black Studies courses are insufficient to fight racism. They do encourage oppressed groups to understand the basis of their oppression and to acquire a sense of collective identity and strength. They provide ways of redefining reality and of redressing some of the sexist bias within education.

However, the capacity of capitalism to incorporate ideas threatening to its existence should not be overlooked. There is a contradiction between the political roots of both Black Studies and Women's Studies and their practical realisation within state institutions like schools. For example, there is a danger that such courses can become a way of hiving off potential struggle: teachers may feel that sexism and racism are being 'covered' and therefore will view these areas as being outside their immediate concern. Sexism and racism are, however, lived experiences and confronting them should be part of our total practice as feminists and anti-racists. We need to argue our case convincingly, and to communicate our beliefs to other teachers too. The complexity of ideology should be tackled at all its levels. We cannot wait for a revolution to answer our problems but must take part in the 'battle of ideas' now, and in any way possible.

Notes

1 The attempts of Marxists to analyse ideology and consciousness have suffered, in the past, from crude economism. That is, society was conceptualised into base and superstructure, with the economic base as the determining force. Manifestations at the level of ideas and practices were thus referred back to the relations of production. Marx's *Preface to a Contribution to the Critique of Political Economy*, 1859, has been taken as a source for such a conceptualisation. However, Marx stressed that the relationship between base and superstructure was dialectical and criticised the separation of areas of thought and activity. Engels was even more explicit. In *Correspondence*, Vol 2, 1887-90 he states: 'According to the materialist conception of history, the ultimately determining element in history is the production and reproduction of real life. More than this neither Marx nor I have ever asserted. Hence if somebody twists this into saying that the economic element is the only one, he transforms that proposition into a meaningless, abstract, senseless phrase.'

2 A model of ideology which I have found useful is the one posited by John Mepham in *The Theory of Ideology in 'Capital'* (1974). For Mepham, the structure of language is central to understanding how beliefs are socially constructed. He argues that the particular mode of production in any society gives rise to a particular form of social life and provides the conditions for specific forms of language. He

demonstrates how real social relations become distorted through a complex set of language structures. He traces this through a process of real relations — phenomenal forms — ideological categories — discourse and practice. I have found it a useful way of understanding how real female/male relations become obscured through a complex yet structured process.

Dale Spender

Educational Institutions:
Where Co-operation is Called Cheating

Formal education, like all other social institutions, has been defined by men, and while women have begun to participate, their contribution is still very different from that of men.

> Though women's participation in the educational process at all levels has increased in this century, this participation remains within marked boundaries. Among the most important of these boundaries, I would argue, is that which reserves to men control of the policy making and decision making apparatus in the educational system (Smith, 1978; 287).

In Britain, Eileen Byrne (1978) has provided statistics which leave no room for equivocation about the contribution women make in policy and decision making. Byrne calls this area the 'government of education' and indicates that it is almost exclusively comprised of men. She sees this as one of the reasons why girls receive an inferior education which then consigns them to an inferior place in society. This different, often inferior education which girls receive is 'planned perhaps with no conscious ill-intent by the men who represent ninety-seven per cent of the government of education, but which nevertheless gives no foundation for a later career in either work or government' (Byrne, 1978; 15). Byrne sees a 'cause and effect' relationship between male policy and decision makers and female educational 'underachievement' and the predictable consequence of low social status.

The limitation of Eileen Byrne's thesis is that the problem can be solved by males without necessitating any changes in the power structure. Yet while men remain in the policy and decision making positions the model of education remains male. Any unique contribution women may make which could lead to a substantially different model of education will continue to be denied expression. Although it is no simple task to locate the distinguishing features of the male view of the world it is useful to speculate. It can bring into focus the links between men's version of experience and the education system as it has been and bring into question what has previously been taken for granted. It can also reveal the way in which education could look very different if women's experience were to inform educational models. There is, however, no need to postulate a conspiracy theory, for men have simply tried to make sense of the world by imposing some form of order upon it. What has happened in patriarchal order[1] is that men have had the power to insist on their definitions, in which they are central and differentiated from women, as the only legitimate definitions. Alternative definitions have been suppressed, treated as *non-data* as Mary Daly (1973) calls them. Men have assumed that the male-is-the-norm, the paradigmatic human being, and have imposed their view on women for whom this may be an alien understanding in terms of our own existence but one which we must internalise if we are to function in a male defined reality.

Stratification is fundamental to the male view. On the stratification of men and women rests the claim to male supremacy and the construction of a male supremacist reality. With this basic premise of inequality hierarchies emerge as a logical social arrangement. Competition is a by-product of these arrangements. When only a few can get to the top — and this is seen as extremely important in our system — there is a struggle for the coveted positions. There is also a need to rationalise the outcome and to be able to justify the results. The rationalisation which is often used and seen as acceptable is that of meritocracy which asserts that initial inequalities — such as class and race — can be ameliorated by 'equality of opportunity', ostensibly allowing all those who participate to enter the race, without handicaps. In those terms the winner deserves their victory and hierarchy and competition are sanctioned in the process. It is this view which has, embedded within it, principles of duality, hierarchy and competition that have formed the parameters for the specific educational models which we confront.

Yet even the male educational model now has its male critics, many of whom have specifically focussed on the hierarchical and competitive arrangements within education as the source of much educational failure (Barnes, 1976; Britton, 1975; Freire, 1972; 1973; Ilich, 1971;

Whitty and Young, 1976; Young, 1975; Williams, 1975). However they are often more critical of what they regard as the misuse of hierarchy and competition than they are of them per se. They are critical of the way in which students are obliged to compete in a race that has been rigged, rather than being critical of competition itself. Ted Benton (1974), Charles Husband (1974), Chris Searle (1973), Michael Young (1975) and Raymond Williams (1975), for example, have objected to the unfair means by which students are stratified and have indicated that it is not coincidence that white middle-class students are disproportionately successful in educational terms. The solution to this problem – according to some male educationalists – is that the various class and ethnic groups should be proportionately represented at all levels of the hierarchy (sex is not usually referred to as a variable). Among many men educationalists, stratification itself and the concomitant utilisation of hierarchical structures appear to be either 'taken for granted', and therefore to go unquestioned, or else to be acknowledged and accepted as inevitable. Raymond Williams (1975) is an exception – as are other Marxist educationalists – and they have developed a persuasive case for the undesirability of stratification in all forms of social organisation.

We do not know what women could bring, as women, to our forms of social organisation – including education – because we have had few, or no, opportunities to give substance to our view of the world. When women did begin to fight for education in the nineteenth century, there were arguments as to whether the male model was suitable for women.[2] Primarily because a different form of education for women would have run the risk of being 'ghettoised' and devalued – so the argument went – the priority became that of ensuring that women excelled in male decreed educational terms. Even at a time when some men were critical of the male model of education, some women made the commitment to reproduce the male model in order to gain acceptance.

While feminists have now begun to generate educational models which are given form in Women's Studies, we continue to confront problems similar to those of our foremothers. There are some women who believe we should develop our own structures and not compromise; there are others who feel that expediency demands that we be seen to be respectable, that we prove that we cultivate what the male model has decreed to be 'high standards', valid knowledge and legitimate methodologies and teaching/learning practices. We, too, worry about exclusion from the male circle and entertain the possibility of ghettoisation rather than autonomy.

However, instead of insisting on women's right to share equally in male defined success, to have an equal education with males and to occupy an equal number of high and low status positions on the hierarchy — a not uncommonly proposed strategy — we can begin to question the efficacy of hierarchies and the desirability of stratification. This is a specific contribution that feminism can make in an analysis of educational theory and practice, and a crucial area for a feminist critique of male-defined education.

Perhaps one of the most fundamental dichotomies that has been called into question and that we continue to question is the separation of educational knowledge from knowledge acquired through living. Because of the way education has been structured '. . . it is not surprising that we tend to think of this institutionalised education as *the* basis and form of education. It is easy to use education as something you *go to* school or college *to get*, rather than a continuous *process* which is present throughout our everyday routine, of work and leisure' (Husband, 1974; 149).

Douglas Barnes (1976) has also commented on the false, destructive and unequal division which would have us accept — with predictable consequences within a stratified society — that the only knowledge which counts is acquired within educational institutions, regardless of how inaccurate or irrelevant it may be. With the distinction once made between knowledge acquired institutionally and knowledge acquired personally it has been possible for 'experts' to be created to judge what counts and what does not. They reinforce the duality of right/wrong and, of course, the duality of winners/losers. It would be extremely threatening to educational order to dispense with these dualities, for a considerable part of the educational edifice is built upon them: they are a means of discriminating. Everyone has personal knowledge which is valid and there would be no way of classifying this. There would be no ready-made means of determining *failure*. This is, of course, where a feminist educational model is crucially different from the institutional model. It is precisely because personal knowledge and experience does not readily accommodate failure, and does not promote stratification, that it has been valued and employed.

Another basic (and false) dualism prevalent within the present model of education is that of teaching/learning. Until relatively recently it was assumed that teaching and learning were separate activities and that there was a one-to-one correspondence between what teachers taught and what students learned. This was accompanied by yet another division where the role of the teacher was an active one while that of the student was a passive one. These divisions have also been challenged and the term *hidden curriculum* has been coined to overcome the deficiencies inherent in the original classification (see Douglas Barnes,

1976; 17 for his section on the hidden curriculum). The conceptualisation of teaching as the transmission of ready-made knowledge to the 'empty vessel' of a learner no longer suffices for it is now readily acknowledged that learners play an active role in the process of learning, selecting information from what teachers intend to teach, and what they do not. This understanding can pose a serious threat to educationalists who, when they recognise the independence and autonomy of the learner, are somewhat at a loss to know how to handle it. To treat students as autonomous human beings capable of constructing their own knowledge is to blur the unequal relationship of teacher/student and to seem to invite anarchy, for it would undermine teacher authority.

Within feminist contexts (such as learning groups) such a distinction is frequently abandoned on the grounds that it is artificial, unproductive and serves only to divide and stratify people. Feminists attempt to engage in learning as a co-operative venture and to ensure that everyone makes a contribution comparable in some sense to that of the traditional teacher and also to that of the traditional learner. Again, the duality which fosters stratification appears to have collapsed. Where feminists have set up their own educational groups they appear to have evolved a model in which the traditional distinction between teacher and learner no longer applies. Similarly the distinction between *objective* and *subjective*, a distinction which is becoming patently inadequate to educationalists, and the dichotomy of reason and emotion are also being called into question and it does seem absurd that numerous learning theories have been constructed on the premise that emotion plays no part in the process. Even the increasingly discredited dichotomy of hard and soft data (see Bernard, 1975; Oakley, 1974; for further discussion) is becoming difficult to sustain. Males have not only inappropriately dichotomised and polarised but have also stratified the objects and events of the world. What they have appropriated for themselves (objectivity, reason, right, etc.) is seen to be more valuable.

Feminists can demonstrate that the dualism of educational knowledge and personal knowledge, of teaching and learning, and all the concomitant divisions, are not an integral part of education itself. We are engaged in the task of reconceptualising and restructuring the social order itself and this must qualify as an intense learning experience. For this we have not needed to make use of stratification in the same way: the establishment of hierarchical structures is one of the most salient features of institutionalised education and, in itself, constitutes a lesson in 'the way the world works' for all its members. Apart from the initial stratification between teachers and students there are also hierarchical structures within these two discrete groups. Students are stratified on the bases of age (even when it is recognised that this is not a particularly useful or valid index and that it is likely there are more students considered advanced for their age, or immature for their age, than there are those who conform to the decreed norm), and of ostensible ability and allocated, covertly or overtly, to streams. Further stratification usually occurs in terms of aspirations, attitudes and behaviour.

Teachers are also located hierarchically, from university professors to head teachers to teachers' aids, and, of course, the teaching staff itself is distinguished from the non-teaching staff. It would not be possible to pass through our conventional educational system and remain oblivious to hierarchies and their implications for structuring our lives.

> One consequence of having been through the educational system is the development of an easy acceptance of specialisms, specialists and professionals. There are teachers who specialise in maths, those who specialise in English. Some children excel at technical drawing and others at foreign languages . . . Throughout the educational system, in subject after subject, there are acknowledged experts, and students learn to respect expertise and experts.
>
> At junior school the expert may be the teacher whose authority is based upon the assertion that 'I know best' . . . or at university the expert may be a current academic guru whose writings are *in vogue* . . . Despite the varying justifications of expert status there is a common theme throughout the educational system in that there are always experts to whom one should defer (Husband, 1974; 149-51).

If students deny their own experience and accept that of the experts then hierarchical structures are strengthened on many fronts: if, however, they do not accept the judgement of the experts, then a novel form of interaction between those traditionally classed as teacher and student can emerge. This has become the basis of understanding within consciousness-raising groups. No member of a group is vested with authority which automatically makes her personal experience better – or worse – than anyone else's. This is part of the feminist model of teaching/learning and even though there have been many obstacles, it is considered desirable in the organisation of Women's Studies courses (Mack, 1974; Howe, 1977). In order to construct knowledge and to engage in teaching/learning it is not necessary to have the services of experts.

There remains one of the most significant stratification procedures which feminists have had to confront – that of imposing a hierarchy on knowledge itself. This can be used to deny knowledge to students (and thereby reinforce the hierarchy). Students are often informed they are too young to know or too old to be told again. The following example reveals the absurdity of the practice.

> You know in Canada they don't go to school till they are six? Well that was just too long to wait, so I sent him to nursery school when he was four. But, by law, nursery schools are not allowed to teach reading or arithmetic because, evidently, the teachers would have nothing to do when the kids arrived if they could read and do arithmetic. It caused lots of problems, partly because he was well on the way to reading when he went to nursery school. But he knew they weren't supposed to learn to read and we had some real problems. He went crazy when I asked him to read his books to me. 'I'm not allowed to read', he'd shout. 'You know I mustn't read till I go to proper school.' Well, what do you think of that? That's education for you (private discussion, Toronto, 1978).

Each division of education fits into a hierarchical frame and within each division knowledge is stratified according to a rather inexplicable plan. Generally speaking one cannot go to secondary school unless one has been to primary school; one cannot go to university unless one has been to secondary school. And this is not necessarily because there is any logical progression, a fact to which both students and teachers will frequently testify. Students have been known to complain about the lack of continuity from one level of education to another and teachers have been known to declare to their new intake that the students must 'forget everything your teachers taught you in that last place': this applies even at university where it is not uncommon for lecturers to instruct their students that they must start from scratch for the knowledge and the methods of enquiry they learnt in school are inadequate, if not wrong. Apart from contributing to the vulnerability of the student, this helps to enhance the superiority of the new institution and its staff. The educational hierarchy is jealously guarded by many of the practitioners. Their rulings on what counts as knowledge and what does not, what is more important and more complex, are presented as superior rulings.

Where feminists have evolved an educational model, however, this form of stratification does not seem to apply. There is no need to pass a qualifying examination in order to participate in the production of woman-centred knowledge,[3] there are no entry qualifications and no hierarchical orderings of knowledge, no one is required to wait until they are older or better informed before being permitted to present their own personal knowledge. All this would seem to suggest that these divisions are not inherent in the process of learning but are mechanisms which have been imposed upon learning. Many of them actually function to inhibit learning and to deny access to knowledge for the learner. This would seem to suggest that it is not learning which has a high priority in educational institutions but conditioning, whereby people imbibe and reproduce the social hierarchical order. In order to reproduce that social hierarchical order, a fundamental educational principle demands that most people fail — sooner or later. At one end of the system is the junior school and at the other end the university and, although theoretically one hundred per cent of the population attend junior school, only fifteen per cent (in Britain) attend university or higher education. This means that eighty-five per cent of the population must be eliminated from the system. In a society where there is a positive correlation between educational achievement and employment, this process of elimination must be presented as desirable in order for it to be acceptable. When only the few can get to the top, and when education is perceived as a distribution agency allocating people to their places, then many must be classified as failures. Through their barrage of marks, grades, tests, examinations, streaming, traditional educationalists promote the belief in the necessity of failure and the inevitability of inequality. For a system which relies so heavily on assessment, some might find it surprising that so little research has been undertaken on the inadequacy of the tools employed, from IQ tests to teacher marking.

There is more than differential individual ability involved when it comes to educational failure:

There are 300 of us in first year and only 200 places in second year. That means 100 of us are failures, it's just that the system hasn't put its mark on us as yet. And there is no logical or reasonable way of sorting us. We might be 300 committed, hard working students but the system demands that 100 of us fail and so fail we will. Then next year, well, they could have 300 lazy students who aren't at all interested in the work, but 200 of them will *pass*! It really is quite crazy, isn't it? Success and failure is built into the system. It's got nothing to do with the ability of the students, even if you could measure it. We are all competing with one another just because that's the way it has been set up (eighteen-year-old polytechnic student).

The argument which is invoked for this practice is the preservation of standards but, as this student indicates, the standard also fluctuates from year to year. Besides, standards, evaluations of excellence, are usually in the eye of the beholder and not supplied by the material itself (a phenomenon which can be observed when the same piece of work is assessed by a variety of·markers, or by one marker over a period of time, and where the work can be graded from excellent to reprehensible). They have their origins in a culturally specific view of the world. Standards are not there waiting to be 'discovered'; we have constructed them with particular principles in mind.

But education does not have to be structured in this way: the competition and failure endemic to education are little short of ridiculous. The feminist world view has had no recourse to competition and failure in the production of educational models. These are viewed not just as unnecessary but as inhibitors of learning.[4] Feminist education is a co-operative venture (Howe, 1974, 1977; Mack, 1974; Reubens, 1978) whereas in the male view of the world, co-operation constitutes cheating. This is a logical outcome of a system predicated on isolating students and measuring them against each other, for if they collaborate they are defrauding the system.

Traditional educational institutions have 'proven' by the competitions which they have structured and fostered that some people are successful and some are failures: feminist educational ventures have 'proven' by the co-operation they have structured and fostered that the concepts winners and losers are meaningless and useless. If the traditional educational system is as inadequate as some critics claim and most evidence suggests, then there is an alternative model, which stresses co-operation, available. Such a model will not, however, reproduce the existing divisions and inequalities within society.

As women we have entered education after the structures have been laid down and consolidated. We were denied access to the formulation of that model in the past and are still largely excluded today. But feminist educational models, where women come together to learn, whether in a consciousness-raising session or for an MA in Women's Studies, can serve as a living critique of the existing male educational model.

Notes

1 How patriarchal order arose in the first place is another issue and one for which there is no satisfactory explanation. Margrit Eichler (1979) has pointed to the inadequacies in all the current explanations for the origins of sexual inequality.
2 This is well documented by Sara Delamont and Lorna Duffin in *The Nineteenth Century Woman: Her Cultural and Physical World* (1978), and by Rita McWilliams-Tullberg in *Women at Cambridge: a men's university – though of a mixed type* (1975). See also 'Co-education and the tradition of separate needs', this volume.
3 Where Women's Studies courses are located within the traditional educational structure, such as the MA in Human Rights at the

University of London Institute of Education, there are qualifying requirements imposed by the university. But frequently even these have been resisted, an argument for their undesirability presented, and modifications have been made.

4 This is the case in many feminist study groups and also in courses in Adult Education where the need for educational qualifications, for 'certificates of entry' to another level in the hierarchy, are not so pressing. In these contexts it is often assumed that learning is an end in itself and not a passport to a particular place in society.

Patricia de Wolfe

Women's Studies: The Contradictions for Students

Little has as yet been written about the confusions and
contradictions which may arise out of teaching Women's Studies as an
academic discipline, and what little there is tends to have been written
from the viewpoint of those teaching Women's Studies courses rather
than from that of the students taking the courses (e.g. Wolff, 1977;
Tobias, 1978). I wish to outline here some of the problems which may
confront students who take Women's Studies as part of their degree, as
it seems to me that these problems may be considerable.

I do not want to argue against the inclusion of Women's Studies in
degree courses, but I think it is important to recognise that even after
the battle to get Women's Studies recognised as 'worthy' of inclusion in
academic courses has been won, a large number of difficulties remain
unresolved. This is because in several respects feminist philosophy is
incompatible with existing methods of teaching and learning. It
challenges generally held assumptions about the way in which courses
should be organised and assessed, about the way in which boundaries
between disciplines should be drawn, and about the validity of received
knowledge. The difficulties arise out of the fact that when Women's
Studies is accepted as a component of a degree, nothing else changes,
neither what is presented as 'knowledge' on the rest of the degree
course, nor the methods of assessment which are used to grade students.
Students may, therefore, find themselves trying to meet two sets of
standards, one which stems from their understanding of feminism and

of its implications for learning, and another which is imposed by the regulations and the ideology of the university.

Women's Studies and Assessment: A lower second in Women's Studies?
The women's movement has always stressed the importance of shared experience and co-operative learning in a situation in which there are no leaders and no experts. Moreover, because it has been 'proved' so many times that men are academically more competent than women, feminists are particularly wary of systems of grading which establish some students as clever and others as mediocre. This emphasis on co-operation and on anti-hierarchical learning produces a number of problems when Women's Studies is an assessed course.

Assessment is linked to an ethos of competitive individualism: it is assumed that students vie with each other for places along a scale of marks, and that each student is therefore the adversary of all the others. For this reason, the insistence on individual assessment may seem not only inequitable, but absurd, when many of the ideas which students use in their work emerge out of group discussion and out of suggestions put forward by other students. When concepts and lines of enquiry arise and evolve from suggestions and reinterpretations contributed by a number of women, it is incongruous for each one to produce an individual piece of work, and receive an individual mark, for it is impossible to attribute any one idea to a particular person. Individual assessment is liable to ensure that the highest marks go to students best at ordering ideas and presenting them on paper, perhaps at the expense of students who may have raised thought-provoking issues and set the discussion in motion. The production of joint pieces of work is not allowed on most courses and, even if it were, it would probably not provide a solution because writing in conjunction with other people is a skill in itself, and one which students do not have the time and opportunity to acquire.

The allocation of marks can disrupt the work of students who study collectively: however much students may try to persuade themselves that marks are meaningless, it is in practice almost impossible to avoid regarding oneself and others in terms of one's place in a hierarchy of grades. Thus grading may introduce elements of competition and envy into previously harmonious groups of women students and, ironically, for those women who do badly, Women's Studies may become a mechanism for convincing feminists of their own inadequacy.

Marking leads not only to tensions among students, but also to mistrust between students and teachers. If the marking of students' work labels some students as better than others, it also implies that best of all are the lecturers who have the power to assign the marks. Thus teachers who may at first have been perceived as participating in a common process of learning may suddenly be transformed into judges.

Another problem concerns academic standards. It is hard within any discipline for students to know what constitutes a 'good academic standard' in the mind of the marker, and this difficulty is compounded in the case of Women's Studies. Women's Studies, after all, does not simply denote a subject area; it embodies a political perspective according to which women are oppressed. It therefore becomes necssary to consider the question of whether a 'good' essay on a Women's Studies course needs to show an awareness of the oppression of women and of the need for social change, or whether it is sufficient for a student to be able to give an account of feminist thinking. To put the question in an extreme form, could a good mark be given to a biological determinist who summarised feminist theories, or feminist critiques of non-feminist theories, and ended with a neat, 'balanced' and 'informed' dismissal of feminist views? If the answer to this question is 'yes', does it really mean mean that such a student has gained a better understanding of feminism than someone presenting a more disjointed or rambling essay from a feminist viewpoint? All this raises not only the vexed question of 'academic standards' and its relationship to Women's Studies, but also the question of the relationship of Women's Studies to the women's movement, and the attitude which feminists should adopt towards Women's Studies. For if Women's Studies as an assessed course can disrupt solidarity between women students, and can encourage the production of 'academics' rather than feminists, perhaps committed feminists should oppose the inclusion of Women's Studies as assessed components of degree courses, and should advocate their restriction to adult education classes and informal discussion groups where students could develop their ideas and learn from their teachers and from each other without having to face the difficulties arising out of assessment.

But the avoidance of assessment on Women's Studies courses would not necessarily be in the interests of Women's Studies students. If a Women's Studies course is not for assessment, students may be placed in the unfortunate position where the work in which they are most deeply involved and for which they have expended the greatest amount of effort is not counted as part of their degree. Moreover, courses which are not assessed have little status, and such a devaluation of Women's Studies would not only give credence to those who believe in the intellectual inferiority of women, but would also reinforce the notion that sexual divisions in society are a side issue irrelevant to serious academic debate. So while there are dangers that feminist philosophy will be undermined if Women's Studies is integrated into the formal curriculum, there are strong reasons for insisting on this integration if

51

the invisibility of women, as students, as teachers, and as subjects in history and society, is not to be perpetuated.

Women's Studies and Patriarchal Knowledge

Apart from the difficulties associated with assessment, there are other reasons, this time academic ones, why Women's Studies cannot easily be integrated into existing degree courses. This is because engaging in Women's Studies does not simply mean 'adding women in' to the existing body of knowledge (for example, producing studies of women at work, women criminals, women's culture, to supplement existing studies of men at work, male criminals and male culture), although this additive process may be useful as a first step. Feminist research involves a radical questioning of the concepts which have been used to make sense of society and to explain social events. Social explanation may look quite different if women and their activities are included in an account of how and why particular social events (wars, revolutions, industrialisation) took place, and the social events themselves may look quite different if we start to consider their consequences for women as well as for men. An example of this change in perspective can be seen by looking at the periodisation of history. Labels attached to historical periods invariably refer to what happened to men, without regard to the fact that something entirely different might have been happening to women. Thus, in the so-called Dark Ages, women enjoyed a relative measure of equality and freedom (Power, 1975), while the Renaissance and the French Revolution, both of which saw an increase in freedom for men, and are accordingly regarded as times of progress, were times of diminishing powers for women (Kelly-Gadol, 1976). Considerations like this give rise to the need for rethinking basic concepts in many disciplines. Thus feminism raises all sorts of questions about the objectivity of 'social sciences' which assume that men both make and constitute history, and that the male necessarily subsumes the female.

But while students on Women's Studies courses are encouraged to examine the patriarchal bias in the construction of knowledge and to formulate new ways of collecting and ordering data, this kind of questioning and reconceptualisation is not always received with enthusiasm or understanding elsewhere. This means that while a feminist perspective is accepted, and even expected, on Women's Studies options themselves, students may find it almost impossible to reconcile this perspective with what they are taught on the rest of their degree course. This difficulty remains even when students are assured by 'liberal' teachers that it is quite acceptable to 'do something on women' on courses other than Women's Studies. The presuppositions of these courses, the ways in which problems are posed and conceptual frameworks for their solution presented, are usually incompatible with a feminist analysis. Students, therefore, have two choices open to them: either they can undertake a feminist critique of the concepts used on these courses – and this is often an immense task – or they can write within the existing boundaries, and thereby almost certainly opt for a better mark, at the cost of academic schizophrenia.

In the same way, feminists can find themselves bewildered and tongue-tied when offered a 'seminar on women' on a course concerned with, for instance, Marxism or industrial society. Apart from the clash of theoretical frameworks just mentioned, such seminars hold an additional difficulty when it is assumed that all relevant information relating to women (of all classes, ages, races, etc.) can be neatly packaged and dealt with in the space of, say, an hour and a half. Given the hostility and neglect which feminists often encounter, it can be hard for feminist students to prevent themselves from gobbling up these liberal crumbs with pathetic gratitude. It might be better, however, if they were to decline the offer of 'seminars on women' on the grounds that the issue of sexual divisions is fundamental to an understanding of society and should, rather than being confined to one seminar, become a recurrent theme throughout the course.

Implications and Strategies

I have concentrated on the difficulties on Women's Studies courses, but this is not to deny their value or to underrate the achievements of those who have set them up. Women's Studies courses have an important part to play in making women visible and in helping us to understand the nature of our oppression and the mechanisms by which it is perpetuated. Because it has implications for political action and for social change, such knowledge is, in a sense, power. They also have an important part to play in challenging and transforming patriarchal knowledge. It is, therefore, essential that Women's Studies courses should be available to students, despite the fact that they contain contradictions and imperfections. To demand a perfectly integrated Women's Studies course is probably to demand a non-sexist society, and if we waited for the ideal conditions for these courses, they would never be started at all.

What I am suggesting, however, is that some of the difficulties I have mentioned should be brought into the open and discussed as part of the curriculum of Women's Studies. If this is done, some of the problems may be alleviated. For example, if there is a clash of frameworks between Women's Studies and the rest of the degree, it may be possible for those teaching Women's Studies to liaise with feminists teaching other subjects, so as to try to raise issues relating to sexual divisions in areas other than Women's Studies, and thus create links between

Women's Studies and other degree components. If there are no other feminists teaching, students may at least be helped to formulate critiques of the theories they are taught on other courses. In this way they may become better able to pinpoint the differences in perspective between Women's Studies and other disciplines and, therefore, be able to arm themselves with coherent arguments rather than floundering around with a deep sense of unease which they cannot put into words. There is no easy solution to the problems which arise out of assessment, but these problems can, if made explicit, give rise to discussion about the nature and organisation of Women's Studies, and about the strategies for furthering feminist methods of learning in institutions geared to very different ideals.

If the problems are not brought into the open, the dangers are two-fold. The first is that feminist theory will be hived off into Women's Studies options, leaving unchallenged the bulk of 'knowledge' produced by academics and presented to students. Women's Studies thus runs the risk of becoming another quirky subsection of sociology, rather than a radical challenge to the whole of patriarchal learning. The second danger is that Women's Studies will become increasingly remote from the women's movement. If such issues as the political implications of theory, the 'objectivity' of academic standards, and the ways in which assessment creates hierarchies are treated as unproblematic, feminists themselves may soon come to regard Women's Studies as irrelevant to the liberation of women, and as easily accommodated within the status quo. The women's liberation movement has given rise to an enormous amount of intellectual activity over the past few years; it would be a pity if the knowledge thus gained lost its usefulness to and its connection with the movement that mothered it.

Elizabeth Sarah,
Marion Scott & Dale Spender

The Education of Feminists:
The Case for Single-Sex Schools[1]

Educational sexism is a multifaceted phenomenon which
operates on many levels — both inside and outside educational
institutions — and, consequently, it must be confronted in a variety of
ways.

Having examined the problem throughout this book, we attempt
in this section to outline some of the methods adopted by feminists to
resist patriarchal education: the introduction of feminist materials
into the classroom (see 'Feminist Practices in the Classroom') and the
construction of a Women's Studies curriculum are strategies designed
as correctives to existing education. On their own, however, they are
insufficient. While any modified curriculum which eliminates some of
the gross distortions of the present system is desirable and necessary,
it still functions within the existing framework of male defined
educational models; it still takes for granted the acceptability of
mixed classrooms, for example. It simply seeks to teach the students
something different, to promote a different emphasis, while
operating within the existing structures. Even the alternative
curriculum, often the province of adult education, runs parallel to,
or is complement to, the established educational system and is only
available to *some* women who have, for the most part, already
completed their secondary education. Without wishing to sound
pessimistic — and we think there is more cause for optimism than
pessimism — we think that it is necessary to acknowledge the

limitations of many of our current approaches and then to focus on more fundamental areas in our quest for an end to women's oppression. We need to be more radical.

We must begin to think about challenging the dominant educational environment to which the majority of pupils are subjected. We must ask ourselves whether it is possible or feasible to make significant alterations or corrections within the patriarchal structure of education. And this makes explicit a question which has hovered over many of the discussions in this book: when males are dominant, is it sensible/useful/desirable for women to be educated with men?

Whether women should cultivate their own space — and their own strength — outside the influence of men is a question which has been addressed in most feminist contexts: what we are dealing with here is the educational aspect of that question. Let us look at the general thesis of women's autonomy or separatism and examine the reasons that are put forward in favour or against. Many feminists have suggested that the oppressed have a different version of oppression from those who are the oppressors (Miller, 1976; Rowbotham, 1973; Smith, 1978) and therefore the oppressed must speak for themselves (Leonard, 1979). As it is difficult for women to speak in the presence of men — some might say almost impossible — then it becomes mandatory for women to talk to each other, without the presence of men, if they are to articulate and develop their understanding of their oppression and the means to combat it (Spender, 1980). In patriarchal society women are 'programmed' in myriad ways to defer to men and to the male version of reality and one way of circumventing this is to exclude men, perhaps as a temporary strategy until women have constructed their own theories and are prepared to confront, rather than to defer to, men.

This 'solution' to the problem is by no means unanimously accepted, however. In 'The Politics of Education Conference' transcript, there is a heated debate as some women insist that because men dominate and take it as their right to determine the parameters of the discussion then there is little alternative but to exclude men. But other women, one in particular, view it as totally counter-productive to exclude men, and would argue that it is precisely because men do have the power that we should be addressing them. The general response is that this is little short of delusion because without our own power, without the opportunity to talk and to be taken seriously by each other, women will not be able to persuade men of anything, and especially not of something detrimental to their power position. Within this debate, most of the major arguments for or against the exclusion of men are aired. The consensus is that men should be excluded so that women are free to develop their own models, to find their own analyses and solutions to their oppression. This also seems to be the consensus within the women's liberation movement where it has been accepted that in our own interest women have the right to organise autonomously.

If we accept this principle then it has many implications for education. The feminist experience of separation from men — both in organisational and social terms — in order to develop the collective strength of women and to generate and reinforce a female view of the world demands that we ask whether single-sex education is desirable. Single-sex education has not always been seen as undesirable; in fact its fall from grace is a relatively recent phenomenon. In popular belief, *co-education* has been one of the most progressive developments in educational policy in Britain this century. Single-sex education, as the product of a traditional social structure in which the two sexes inhabited entirely different social worlds, is deemed inapporiate in a modern pluralistic society. To be more specific, since society has ostensibly ceased to be segregated on the grounds of sex then the school must be co-educational if it is to be 'consistent' and constitute a 'normal' social environment (Dale, 1969; 1971; 1974). Moreover, in much educational writing it is the *social* aspects of co-education that are vested with importance. Dale also claims that there are advantages for the girls because when they are together boys and girls compete with one another and work harder (Dale, 1974). When outlining the advantages — for girls — Dale conveniently avoids dealing with the outcome of this competition (commented on at greater length later in this discussion) and stresses that it is because mixed education constitutes an approximation of 'the real world' that it is desirable. The rationale for mixed education reveals the operation of the assumption that the two sexes are different, that on their own they are limited or unbalanced, but that together they are complementary. The early champions of mixed education recognised that boys and girls would bring into the classroom different sets of social experiences and they *hoped* that this would prove to be beneficial: what was not considered was the possibility that one sex would derive more advantage from this situation than the other. That it has been boys who have received the greater benefits from mixed education is perhaps one of the reasons that educational theorists and practitioners have been slow to reappraise the efficacy of this arrangement.

Currently, the issue of co-education is not one which arouses great debate. When the practice is challenged, it is in the interest of girls. To our knowledge there has been no recent discussion arguing for a return to single sex education *in the interest of boys* and the absence of this argument is significant: from this we can conclude that co-education is working well — for boys. This does not just mean in simple terms that boys are doing better at the traditional tests according to the traditional measurements, although there is considerable data which supports this view (see Byrne, 1978, for the statistical analysis of boys' greater success); it means that in many subtle ways boys are deriving benefits from an educational system deliberately established to replicate inside the school the 'normal' social environment which functions outside the school. In concrete terms, male superiority can be realised within the co-educational system: in the presence of girls, boys from the earliest age have someone to be superior to, and Katherine Clarricoates (1978) notes that teachers are often more than willing to reinforce this division and inequality.

Just as it is no longer feasible to maintain that in society the two sexes can be different but equal, so too is it difficult to hold such a position within education. Teachers — and students — may profess such beliefs, but their actions often belie their words. The power relations of domination and subordination between the two sexes — characteristic of patriarchal society — are reproduced within co-education. It is interesting to note that Dale was aware that boys were likely to achieve better academic results in a co-educational context but that he still maintained that the *social* advantages were more important. One can only ask: *social advantages for whom?* Obviously depressed academic performance is no advantage for girls and one wonders what possible social compensations they could receive.

Having established that boys do better in mixed schools it is necessary to examine the means by which this is achieved. Part of the greater success of boys could perhaps be attributed to the self-fulfilling prophecy: boys are *expected* to achieve better results than girls and they fulfil this expectation. While the expectations of others no doubt play a role, it would be too superficial to account for differential performance simply in terms of social expectation. What might also play a role — but what has not been the focus of systematic research — is the level of confidence which learners have when they embark upon a task, and the expectations they have of themselves. It would seem plausible that those who approach educational tasks with the expectation that they will do well are more likely to experience success than those who expect to do poorly. Margaret Spencer (1976) has indicated that the self-concept of the learner plays a crucial role in learning to read: for example, those who think they will be readers, that it is their 'right' to read, experience much greater success than those who think that reading is not for them. In both cases the students are confirming their own expectations of themselves although the outcomes are vastly different. Perhaps this principle of *self-*expectation (which is socially derived) applies across the curriculum and not just to reading and, if so, boys are in general in an advantageous position. They can expect to be more successful than girls.

In her study of maths anxiety, Sheila Tobias (1978) has also suggested that self-expectation is a contributing factor in explaining their own performance to the two sexes. While both sexes may obtain the same high or low results, they are likely to interpret them differently. Girls don't think they should be good at mathematics and they can maintain this belief despite their results: if their marks are good they have been lucky, if they are bad, they have been 'caught out'. And boys who expect to be better at mathematics can also maintain their beliefs — despite the results: if their marks are good, they have deserved them, if bad, they have been unlucky. Confronted with the same low mark, a girl could interpret this as a sign of her inadequacy while a boy could simply use it as an indication of the need to do a bit more work. One interpretation inhibits learning while the other can promote it.[2] Numerous studies have indicated that boys demand more of the teachers' time and it is perfectly obvious that, in a class of thirty, boys will have greater access to teacher attention even if they comprise only half the class. As has been pointed out (see 'Teachers and Students in the Classroom') *any* form of response from a teacher can serve as positive reinforcement to boys' behaviour and can be utilised by boys to enhance their own image and confidence. Because boys can manipulate the classroom activities by these demands on teachers they ensure it is *their* interests which are given priority in the classroom (that they may not do this intentionally is not at issue here). Boys can establish the *norm* in a co-educational classroom and it is one to which girls are required to conform. Jenny Shaw (1976; 137) indicates the outcome of this monopolisation by boys when she states that 'mixed schools are actually more like boys' schools rather than being somewhere in between all-male and all-female schools'. Similarly, Sheila Wood has said that 'We think too many schools are boys' schools with girls in them' (*The Times*, 25 April 1973). When girls and boys are brought together there is *not* a merger of two equally balanced groups but a submersion of one, while the other can remain virtually unchanged.

While the interests of girls are passed over in this way in mixed schools we are not only witnessing the reinforcement of female subservience, but also the construction of a male oriented curriculum. Girls are being told that they and their experiences do not count. This would not be the case in a girls' school where the girls could not be required to act as a 'negative reference group' for boys in the classroom (Shaw, 1976; 57) nor required to serve as a foil for male achievement. Such curtailment does not operate in single-sex schools where it is possible for a variety of roles to be open to girls and this can have the effect of opening up possibilities that might be inconceivable in mixed schools. In mixed schools it seems that the stereotypes can be even more rigorously enforced than in society in general. Rather than breaking down the gender demarcation lines, mixed schools seem actually to strengthen them: '. . . the social structure of mixed schools may drive children to make even more sex-stereotyped choices, precisely because of the constant pressure to maintain boundaries, distinctiveness and identity' (Shaw, 1976; 157).

There is evidence that girls are more likely to be coerced into adopting the feminine stereotype in mixed institutions. Florence Howe (1974) refers to their options to be 'silly or silent' in a mixed educational environment and, in her study of women's preference for single-sex education, says that it is not uncommon for women to state they felt less inhibited when men were excluded. Anxieties about clothing, hairstyle, and proper demeanour were absent with the absence of males. Women did not feel it necessary to appear as feminine to each other, and where femininity is antithetical to educational performance — as it frequently is with its emphasis upon passivity, deference, conformity and foolishness — this must represent the removal of a considerable handicap.

Elizabeth Fennema (1980) reveals that there is another potent factor operating in a mixed classroom and that is the attitude of the boys towards the success of the girls. When asked whether girls could be good mathematicians, the girls generally believed that they could be; girls saw no reason for girls faring worse at mathematics. But this was not the case for the boys; boys believed that girls could not do mathematics, that they would not be successful at it. Of course how far the attitude of the boys influences the girls is another matter, but what can be asserted is that the influence would be minimal in a single-sex school where girls were not obliged daily to encounter the lack of faith in their ability by the boys.

Sue Sharpe (1976; 135-6) found that girls were inhibited by the presence of boys: 'The majority of Ealing girls agreed that boys do not like girls to do better than them in school work. The implication is, therefore — if you want to attract boys — don't start by showing them how clever you are.'

The advantages which boys may derive from having a deferential and 'dumb' audience have not been investigated but it would seem that where girls are required to hide their talents boys are encouraged to parade theirs. In single-sex educational institutions this pattern could not easily emerge. In her assessment of the pros and cons of mixed versus single-sex education Rosemary Deem (1978; 76) suggests that 'we ought to give some thought to whether the "normal social adjustments" which mixed schools are argued to give pupils, does not in fact encompass the worst aspects of sex stereotyping'.

When teacher attention is focused primarily upon boys (Sears and Feldman, 1974), when the curriculum is directed primarily to boys (Clarricoates, 1978), when boys are permitted to talk more and encouraged to challenge and question more (Parker, 1973) it becomes clear that girls suffer considerable disadvantage in the mixed class-room. When we add to this the fact that girls in mixed educational environments are likely to be presented with little evidence that women can overcome these handicaps because 'in all co-educational schools almost without exception girls will see a community where responsibilities are held by men' (Wood, *The Times,* 25 April 1973), it becomes clear that the *social* aspects are those which foster female inferiority and dependence. If we have a serious commitment to the elimination of sexism in education then we must begin to study single-sex education as a viable alternative to the present system. The question we have to confront is: what sort of learning situation best serves girls — particularly during adolescence when the pressure to conform to the feminine stereotype seems to be greatest?

One of the main arguments put forward against single-sex education — especially as regards girls — has been that it frequently dictates a considerably narrower range of subject choices than in the mixed school. Indeed, the reason Eileen Byrne gave for supporting co-education was because she felt that it would 'widen access to subject areas not available in single-sex schools' (1978; 133). But such optimism was misplaced: while physics and chemistry facilities may be better in mixed schools (where boys' interests predominate) girls do not necessarily avail themselves of these greater opportunities.

> While the chance of a subject being (technically) available is greater in a mixed-sex school than in a single-sex school — boys are more likely to be *offered* biology and music and girls physics — in fact *pupils make more sex-stereotyped subject choices in mixed sex schools* (Leonard, 1977; 21; see also DES 1975, *Education Survey 21*).

By ensuring that the school replicates 'the real life' situation of the outside world, we have created a climate in which girls might learn *at a younger age* that physics and chemistry (or even careers) are not for them. While they are 'taught' within the school that (a) they are supposed to be feminine and (b) this entails keeping themselves from taking on the roles traditionally reserved for men, the girls can almost invariably be relied upon voluntarily to avoid them.

This gives rise to an interesting observation. While girls who are educated in single-sex schools may ultimately discover numerous obstacles in the path of entering male areas (from the accusation of loss of femininity to the very real discrimination which can be exercised against them) they may at least be in a position to choose such a hazardous course, for at the end of their schooling they may possess the necessary qualifications to enter this territory. But girls who have attended mixed schools, who have been directed away from qualifications which lead to traditional male roles, may not have this choice. Poor physics and chemistry facilities can still lead to furthering one's studies in science (even with its concomitant problem) but A-level English cannot!

Rosemary Deem (1976; 75) has summarised the case for separate education for girls:

Although girls in single-sex schools may have less choice of subjects, they are likely to be much freer to choose which ones they take than in a mixed school where they will be competing with boys for resources and also perhaps subtly encouraged to fulfil their traditional sex roles.[3] In addition, the emphasis on academic learning in a single-sex school is not likely to convey to girls the impression that it is unimportant whether girls do well at school or not, a message which may already be conveyed to girls by their socialisation and culture and not always contradicted in mixed schools. Furthermore, girls in single-sex schools are more likely than girls in mixed schools to be taught maths and science by women and hence are less likely to think of these subjects as 'masculine'.

The testimony of many women who have attended single-sex schools supports Deem's thesis. One woman PhD science student has said,

'I went to an all-girls' school and most of my teachers were women. They were in positions of authority, they taught science, and I never questioned the idea of women having careers and making decisions. It seemed quite normal to me.'

Other women have made similar comments about the *positive* reinforcement they received in all-girls' schools. In the article 'Girls' Schools Remembered' women indicate what an advantage single-sex education can be: '. . . there are values around in the school that weren't around at home, for instance, the idea of women having a career, which was something absolutely fundamental to the ethos of the school' (*Women and Education*, 1978, No 13, 4).

There is a class dimension here: it is one which Irene Payne has documented (see 'A Working-class Girl in a Grammar School') and it can be the source of many problems. Most single-sex schools for girls were founded in the nineteenth century for the daughters of the bourgeoisie with the purpose of offering girls a comparable education to boys ' and one which would provide them with the basis of an independent life style' (Deem, 1976; 7). In the girls' grammar and direct grant schools 'the stress was very much on academic education for girls' (*Women and Education*, 1978, 4) and although the experience of girls in secondary modern schools has been demonstrably different, the fact remains that it is *only* in girls' schools that we will find conditions that are not a replication of 'real life', that is, *patriarchy*. The social conditions of the girls' school may be artificial but, when male supremacy is seen as 'natural', the creation of an artificial environment for girls has its advantages. '. . . It was only when I got to university and on to my degree course, and discovered that there were only two women among twenty men, that it ever occurred to me that maybe as many girls didn't do science as boys. That was the first time it hit me' (*Women and Education*, 1978, 6).

If educationalists had made any serious or systematic attempt to investigate the consequences *for girls* of single-sex versus mixed schooling they would not have ignored what appears to us to be over-whelming evidence in favour of single-sex schools for girls. We believe that one of the findings that would have emerged is that within single-sex environments girls can develop a sense of solidarity; just as *sister-hood* grows from women working with women outside the school, so too it can flourish inside the single-sex school: 'It was just so much easier being with all females . . . we related to each other so differently. We weren't forced to compete with each other when boys weren't around' (discussion with a woman who attended both single-sex and mixed school, London, 1979).

Florence Howe found these sentiments commonly expressed by the women who attended Goucher, a single-sex American college: 'Their dependence on male approval came out particularly in discussions of co-education . . . close to the surface and freely aired was the question of dressing for boys. It was a relief, students said, to be able to live whole days at Goucher in jeans and no makeup. And they joked about looking very different — sometimes unrecognisably so — when they left the campus for a date or a weekend' (Howe, 1974; 72).

Then they ceased to be women relating to women and became women relating to men. Clothing is only one index of the metamorphosis that this demands.

If we were to argue for the replication of the 'real life' situation of women talking to women within the school — and for many women in the women's movement this *is* 'real life' — we could hope to find women developing co-operative and collaborative processes. 'I actually learned to like the society of women', says one woman, commenting on her experiences in a girls' school (*Women and Education,* 1978,7). Irene Payne has told us that she has observed similar developments in her own classroom where she has been able to arrange to teach the girls separately some of the time. 'The sense of solidarity they can build up when the boys aren't around is quite remarkable', she says, 'and it runs back over into the mixed sex classroom. The girls will often act as a group and challenge the boys when they feel they are getting too much their way.' In mixed classrooms girls may never have the opportunity of relating to each other as a group and may never know the strength that can come as a result of collective action. In Irene Payne's classes where they are given this opportunity the results are quite startling and encouraging (it certainly demonstrates that one teacher can be extremely effective in reversing some of the most disadvantageous aspects of sexism).

Single-sex schools, with their positive experiences, are rapidly becoming a thing of the past. As they reminisce about their all-girls' education, the two women in 'Girls' Schools Remembered' reach the conclusion that their experience of separate education has been crucial to their development as feminists, and ask:'What will happen to feminism in the next twenty-five years, if the next generation of women hasn't had the same kind of school experience?' (*Women and Education*, 1978, 8).

While we would not want to suggest that the only route to feminism was through an all-girls' school (though, surprisingly, all the contributors to this book spent at least part of their schooling in an all-girl environment[4]) we do want to emphasise that some of the values of single-sex socialisation do not flourish in many other institutionalised contexts, and this may in fact mean that one of the very few facilities provided by society for women and girls to meet and work together is eliminated. Though we may mount a long term campaign for the return of single-sex schools, we also need short term strategies. Within mixed education there is good reason for us to create a separate space for girls, though we are willing to predict that there will be protests from the men and the boys. It would be sexist to assume that it must be the girls who should be regularly removed from the classroom: it could be the boys. Establishing a 'girls only' lesson period could give the girls some opportunity to develop confidence in themselves as individuals as well as a group, with the result that when the boys return they are not likely to find the girls so ready to be 'silly or silent', to be divided and deferential.

To suggest that all girls be educated in an all-female environment is a *radical* proposal: at the same time, it is not a utopian ideal. We are not assuming that universal single-sex education for girls would completely resolve the problem of sexism in education, but in an age where co-education is heralded as a symbol of progress, it must be made clear that while it may represent progress for boys, for girls it represents a defeat rather than an advance.

Of course, single-sex education for girls can be used, and has been used in the past, to furnish girls with 'accomplishments' suited only to a subordinate role in society. Indeed, cross-cultural comparison indicates that this is the main purpose of a segregated learning environment for females in other more overtly patriarchal societies (for example, the Islamic societies). However, this state of affairs is not *inevitable*. When girls learn *with* boys in a co-educational environment, they learn in a most immediate sense about the socio-political relations of domination and subordination in patriarchal society. When girls are educated in a context in which boys are absent, in which they are encouraged to grow and develop their human potential, then they will be in a much stronger position to resist oppression in the wider society.

There is one major dimension of the educational value of separate schooling for girls which we have not mentioned directly but which has been implicit in our argument, and that is the *subversive potential* of *women learning from one another,* rather than from men whose authority and power is thus reinforced by the process. In a crucial sense it is this characteristic which defines the *feminist* response to patriarchy. This is not the explicit policy of girls' schools today but as long as female members of staff are involved in exercising some authority on their own behalf and that of other females, namely their pupils, the experience of the girls *as girls as human beings* is receiving some validation.[5]

Notes

1 Since writing this article, we have found Jill Lavigueur's M.Ed thesis (University of Sheffield), entitled 'Equality of Educational Opportunity for Girls and its relation to co-education'. Chapter Four is 'Co-education and the tradition of separate needs' and it indicates that many of the reasons given for mixed education have

been sexist. Because of the light that her work throws on the debate of the single-sex versus co-education, we have received permission from Jill to reproduce her chapter as an appendix. We do recommend that people read the entire thesis.

2 This is called 'Attribution Theory'; to what do students attribute their success or failure? Elizabeth Fennema (1980) has also discussed attribution theory in relation to women and men's explanations for mathematical performance, and her findings are consistent with those of Tobias.

3 Caroline Benn and Brian Simon (1978) discovered that 50% of the mixed schools in their English survey restricted some subjects to boys, and 49% did the same for girls. In Scotland the figures were even higher with 70% limiting some subjects to boys and 68% to girls. The most common reason given for this was that the teachers of boys subjects refused to include girls in their classes (Shaw, 1976; 135-6).

4 In the process of discussing, reading and writing this article we have become even more aware of the predominance of single-sex-educated feminists. Although we began convinced of the merits of single-sex education we held a 'balanced' view that, of course, it wasn't *solely* responsible for launching women into feminism. But it seems to have been a fertile recruiting ground. We are now constantly asking feminists, 'Were you educated at a single-sex school?' The answer is almost invariably positive. It would be useful if this were to be systematically researched: a suggestion for the EOC?

5 At the Sex Differentiation in Schooling Conference, Churchill College, Cambridge, 2-5 January 1980, it was considered a matter of urgency that research should be instigated into the advantages and disadvantages of single-sex schools. The claim for single-sex education for girls as a means for overcoming some of the problems of sexism in education was considered legitimate and sensible, in the light of evidence presented at the conference.

Part Three: Women Teachers

Katherine Clarricoates

All in a Day's Work

This is part of a larger piece of research on primary schools, funded by the Social Science Research Council.

Women who have two jobs — that is, an unpaid one within the home and a paid one in the workforce — have many demands made on them and only twenty-four hours a day in which to fulfil them. Some of the demands can be not only time consuming but also conflicting. Because I was interested in finding out how women teachers coped with these demands, and because I wanted to see if comparable demands were made on men, I interviewed forty teachers (thirty-three women and seven men) during my observational research in four different primary schools. I asked them about their personal lives at home and their educational objectives at work. (Readers will note the emphasis on women teachers. This is because I have a commitment to feminism; most primary school teachers are female; and I found the male teachers I interviewed did not encounter physical and emotional conflict in their lives to the same extent as the women.)

I asked them questions about their family commitments and tried to find out whether these had changed over the years along with their main objectives for teaching. The interviews were tape-recorded and were conducted during lunch-time and after school. They lasted from twenty minutes to over one hour. The teachers' replies are treated confidentially and are used in a way that permits no particular identification.

Demands of the Paid Working Day
Most of the teachers I interviewed had an honest if tentative faith in the education system, seeing it as a benevolent preparation of pupils for a

complicated, technological society, despite evidence to the contrary (Wolpe, 1977; Shaw, 1976; Lobban, 1978). My question was 'What do you think are the main aims of the Education System?' and I quote some of the responses:

> Hopefully to turn out a better society or a . . . good . . . working . . . capable set of people with as wide a knowledge as possible . . .

> To educate the children to live a better life . . .

> I think primarily educating them and also to help the child make it in school; to extend his character obviously, so the teacher's got to be sympathetic to the child.

> To make sure they are literate. And I think to a certain extent to develop them to their full potential.

> Equip the child for life. With education . . . schooling should give a child a good background for the world.

> A general education for a start . . . you know . . . literacy, numeracy . . . and to prepare them socially for going out into the world.

> To provide the children with a basis for life. To teach them all the things they need to know to get on and learn.

Primary school teachers are in sole charge of twenty-five to thirty children (in some areas this is more, in rural schools it is fewer) for six hours a day, five days a week, forty weeks a year, teaching a wide range of subjects. Unlike the secondary school, the interaction between teacher and pupils will be prolonged at least for a year, with one particular teacher in charge of one class all day, every school day. It has long been accepted that teaching guaranteed a livelihood to women entering the profession and it was seen not as a contradiction but as something complementary to their 'usual' and 'natural' role of wife and mother. Teaching allowed teachers leisure hours which corresponded to those of the children, which society assumes they will have. To the question 'If you have a family how does your teaching career fit into the overall scheme of things?' the teachers' answers certainly indicated that they shared this assumption:

> It fits in very well. Obviously the shorter hours and the holidays fit in very well . . . really I should think it's one of the best professions in that respect.

> Perfectly well because when the youngest child started school I went back into teaching and I have the same hours as they do . . .

> All in all it's worked out pretty well really especially with the school

holidays; you see I have the same holidays with the children which is just fine . . . it works out OK.

Very well . . . but of course they have the same hours that I have.

Anybody who teaches or who has taught at some time in their life (or observed classrooms on a day-to-day basis), is well aware of the physical and emotional output of energy required from teachers in the ever-changing organisation of our education system. They have to teach children to a limited 'required standard' and these children — who come from varying social backgrounds and who bring their individual problems to the school — will be *labelled* within the ability range from the remedial child to the future university candidate. This, together with the need to attend staff meetings and be present at extra-curricular activities (sports events, open evenings, concert arrangements), besides the very necessary preparation of classroom material, makes enormous demands upon the teacher. This further increases the burden of the other job of wife and mother.

Demands of the Unpaid Working Day

To the question 'Do you find it difficult to meet your domestic obligations along with a full-time career?' only one married teacher, with no children and with a master's degree in science, had come to the decision that she had no domestic obligations. For the rest of the teachers their days were fraught with the physical and emotional problems of teaching all day and going home tired; but tasks in the home made still further demands upon them. Efforts to ease the burden varied from person to person (some ignored some tasks completely, waited for holidays to catch up, worked part-time) some said that their husbands were good at 'helping'. One teacher had hired help:

Yes it is very difficult. I sometimes wonder what on earth am I doing driving myself into the ground, but in the end I suppose it's all worthwhile.

At first I found it very difficult, but I'm finding it a lot better lately as I'm beginning to work out a pattern. But my husband helps me a lot as well.

Yes I do. My husband doesn't help much . . . well I suppose if you sort of ask . . . But you know I can't help feeling resentful . . . if he was at home and I was at school he wouldn't think of cooking tea although he'd probably make a cup of tea but that would be all.

Very well at the moment because I'm only part-time. When I'm teaching full-time I find it very difficult.

Yes but it's just a case of having your priorities right. Some people would think my house was a dump but as long as we have got clean clothes and food on the table it doesn't worry me; I prefer to have a career.

Sometimes yes. It's tiring, especially if you're working flat out here and you get home tired . . . and after you've had a meal . . . well that's it you know. But some nights . . . especially during the week-end you're working full out to catch up with your work, you have to. But it's best to leave the big chores . . . you can catch up with those during the holidays.

No, because I have someone who comes in to clean for me. And I have somebody who comes in and does the gardening.

I sometimes go home . . . you know . . . sort of . . . exhausted and fall asleep for an hour, and then have to carry on and do little bits about the house.

The overall pressure to be proficient in all aspects of their lives is generally felt by the teachers, who strive to work out patterns and rigid routines in their attempts to 'fit everything in' and 'get everything done'. Some teachers told me their husbands felt that the 'quality of home life' had deteriorated since they had started or resumed teaching. Instead of questioning this presumption they felt they had to justify themselves and offer excuses as to why they couldn't excel at being *both* the perfect wife and the perfect teacher.

It took me about a year to adapt to coping with a job as well as housework, and I'm not as good a housewife as I used to be. I often wish I could do more . . . particularly with the children . . . I mean I've stopped reading to them . . . but they've adapted quite well.

I'm not interested in a career as such, my main job is my kids, my family . . . I've got enough . . . my boys come first, that's how I wanted it to be and this is what my husband wanted it to be as well because he said the quality of our home life went down because there wasn't the time . . . he was having to help me more. Not that he objects to that, he's very good in the house. But, for instance, one of our pastimes is caravanning . . . but we can't go now as much, except during the holidays because I haven't got the time to do all the things that I would do to get ready for the caravan, to go away.

Too Many Demands Equals Guilt
Despite the fact that most teachers told me that they had 'helpful' husbands, they did concede that the ultimate responsibility for house-work and childcare was theirs and this was recognised, opportunistically

so, by their male partners. Many felt varying degrees of guilt over their inability to cope with the impossibility of the demands.

> My one worry is that I can't get things done that should get done . . . say the bedrooms once a fortnight and my windows don't get cleaned as often as they should . . . in fact they haven't been done for weeks.

> You know in some ways I suppose I don't do a 100 per cent good job at home because of my school ties and I feel I don't do a 100 per cent good job at school because I've got so much to do at home.

Maintaining impeccable houses while achieving the 'true feminine ideal' is the goal most women try to attain.

> Housework presents a whole world of rules and pressures from which men are wholly exempt but which can drive normally sane women into absurd depths of guilt. It is a tight, inescapable world in which every housewife is imprisoned, whether she works outside the home or not (Comer, 1974; 93).

And the guilt is real enough. Television and other media advertising extol the qualities of household aids, portraying women swooning over the whiteness of their wash, portraying clear complexions, the hairlessness and odourlessness of their bodies and the softness of their hands, despite having just done a pile of dirty dishes:

> The rules of housework are determined by what is socially acceptable, and what is socially acceptable is displayed in every magazine, some of which, like *Living* and *Family Circle*, with the largest circulations of all women's publications, are entirely devoted to urging women to greater and greater heights of house-pride (Comer, 1974; 93).

For married women teachers the sense of continued responsibility is carried over to the home when their school day is at an end. The imposition of a host of other duties will once more fall onto their shoulders. Very rarely do men experience the pendulum-like swing of concentration from one world into another.

> You try to find the other character, that of a teacher, before you get to school . . . and sometimes you feel that really is quite a task especially if you've had a bit of an upset with one of your own children . . . how you are going to find your other self. It's very near schizophrenia . . . you fulfil your role as a mother, carry on your own hobbies, if you've got time for any . . . and then you teach children what to do. Even at school there's no getting away from it

. . . you know you dash off to the shops at dinner-time to get something for tea . . . it never ends.

Teaching is the kind of occupation that can be seen as an extension of traditional women's roles — certainly at the primary level — and perhaps this is the reason primary teaching attracts women who seem less likely to oppose traditional sex-stereotypes. Their replies to the question 'What made you decide to become a teacher?' were many, but the main reason was that they liked children.

I really like children. I've always enjoyed explaining things to them.

I like children. I like working with them and discussing things with them.

Because I enjoyed being with children and to be quite honest most of my friends were doing teaching as well.

I like children and my temperament being what it is I knew I could be a good teacher.

Just to work with children. I started as a teacher's aid and eventually decided I would go to college for a course in teacher training.

I suppose any job that I thought of would have been connected with children.

Consider these answers from men, typical answers in my research.

Don't really know. I know when most people were evacuated during the war we were without staff so I did a bit of teaching then, so it probably developed from there.

I don't really know.

Pure luck I think. After the war there was a good deal of sorting out to be done and clearly all the guys who were leaving the service had to find jobs. Not quite knowing what to do this appealed to me and so I decided I would apply.

I don't know, I just did.

I thought I'd like to try my chances at it, so I did.

All the teachers seemed to agree that female teachers were 'child oriented'. From the replies above, it does tend to point out that men and women choose to go into teaching for different reasons and these reasons are frequently bound up with traditional stereotypes. Some women also informed me that they either drifted into it or felt pressured by their own teachers or well meaning parents to 'have something to fall back on'. Another main reason was that it was a worthwhile job for women (see 'It's a good job for a girl (but an awful career for a woman)'):

> I didn't particularly want to be one, I just sort of drifted into college because I didn't get into university. Fortunately I quite enjoy it.

> I wanted to be a teacher like my Mum and I think it's a worthwhile profession to get into, a good job for women.

> It was decided for me actually. My mother and father decided it was a good profession to be in. Being ordinary working class the teaching profession was an improvement.

> Pressured from school to have something to fall back on when I needed it.

> When I was in the sixth form at school I didn't particularly want to do a lengthy study and so it seemed natural that I should do teaching as it was an easy course, or so I thought.

The pressure of social prejudices about women having a 'natural' leaning towards the care and education of small children, and the fact that they will also have to take into account their future or present roles as wives and mothers, weighs heavily upon them in their decisions to pursue teaching careers.

> I think at the time I was orientated towards teaching because of the fact that I had young children and I thought it was the sort of job that I could do, and do justice to teaching and the family as well without either of them having to suffer . . .

But, again, all agreed they had consolidated their ideas about teaching since their entry into the profession and had high job satisfaction and enjoyed their work despite the many problems.

The primary school teacher is a very important figure as the first adult, other than parents, that most small children will attempt to identify with (Belotti, 1975). Studies undertaken in Britain, Italy and America have clearly shown that primary school teachers are crucial in replicating the sex-role stereotypes that pervade our education system (Frazier and Sadker, 1973; Belotti, 1975; Lobban, 1978; Clarricoates, 1978). The very content of teacher training would seem to prepare teachers as conveyors of patriarchal ideology. Lee Comer states:

> Attitudes to sex-roles are as entrenched in the colleges of education as they are in the schools themselves. The emphasis, even in the most liberal of institutions, is always on exploiting the child's 'natural' and innate abilities; the abilities of children are assumed to correspond exactly to the abilities they will need as adults. In the class-

room, this turns out to be preparatory work for adulthood and in the infant class, where the pattern for their entire school lives is first laid down, girls are pushed to express themselves in domestic play, in the Wendy House, while the boys practise their mechanical skills with bricks (Comer, 1974; 24-5).

Some teacher training colleges are remote and run on very strict lines of sex-segregation with many repressive and trivial rules. It is not my intention to imply that primary school teachers are lesser teachers than those in secondary schools. The former qualify with a teaching diploma (for the most part) whereas the latter are mainly university graduates and hence have higher status. But their intellectual preparation is approximately as long (graduates do an extra year for their post graduate certificate of education) and probably just as exacting. The significant difference is that graduate teachers do not initially perceive their profession as that of teaching but set out to study subjects such as politics, English, sociology, foreign languages or science, for example, and during their course of study it is likely they will have come into contact with much more radical and challenging ideas than their colleagues in the rigid and traditional teacher training colleges.

Defined as 'mother'

Most of the teachers I interviewed could be regarded as good teachers and successful wives and mothers.

> If the career woman is married with a family she is especially vulnerable to suspicions and accusations. The demands of a career are commonly supposed to conflict with those of a family. She may be a success in her job but she's failed at the one which counts. Dodging accusations of this sort is hard work and it is no wonder that, to avoid being neatly packaged away under the label 'career woman', the woman who happens, like a man, to be committed to her work as well as to her private relationships, has to bend over backwards to prove to the world that she is first and foremost not herself, but her husband's wife and her children's mother (Comer, 1974; 46-7).

They are constantly dogged by the haunting spectre of 'maternally depriving' their own children and this is revealed in their answers to the question, 'What kind of problems do you find exist in being both a parent and a teacher?'

> That's a bit difficult. Mainly, I think, a guilt problem. Because Susie's so dependent, and she's been at the nursery ever since she was old enough to go and I find it very difficult expecting to do a full day's work and then feeling I can cope adequately with her when I get home.

You don't have enough time for everything you want to do. I supposed my family suffers from lack of attention because I'm so fed up with the day I've had perhaps. In some ways my kids get left out of it when I've had a bad day, and I don't want to know when I get home.

Sometimes I go home and you know these children here are very demanding. They sort of drain you to the limit. Then if you go home and sort of meet any problems with your own children you don't feel inclined to sit down and discuss it with them . . . you know you're tired and then you end up feeling a bit guilty and wish you had done.

I sometimes feel as if I don't spend enough time with my own children . . . I don't think I let the children down in shool but I feel very guilty about my own two children . . . I feel as if I ought to be spending more time with them.

These women, like the rest of society, are deluded into believing that it is men's place to work and pursue a career with what is assumed to be a single-minded dedication, whereas women experience having to divide their time between their paid and unpaid jobs, thus 'subtracting' time, stamina and love from their families. Hence the guilt. I am appalled at Belotti's accusation, 'These are timid creatures who have chosen a profession which shelters them from many things in life which might be traumatic as well as stimulating and exciting' (Belotti, 1975; 127).

'Timid creatures' they are not! From tending aged parents to single parenting to caring for four children under the age of ten . . . these teachers have surmounted obstacles and problems and coped with personal tragedies which most men would never dream of in order to pursue and continue their teaching careers.

I wanted to be a teacher and go into college when I was eighteen, but I had to leave school at sixteen. You see my father died and my mother wasn't well so I had to leave school and get a job. And then I waited till my own family had grown up before I went to college.

I always knew I wanted to teach but then I had to leave school because my mother had a nervous breakdown and I had to look after the home being the eldest girl of the family. And then the war came along . . .

I matriculated at sixteen but, of course, my father was a widower and I was one of four children, not the eldest, but the only one who was willing or able to look after the others and so I was landed with

77

the job. but I knew if I waited long enough . . . do you know I had to wait twenty-two years before I could finally do what I wanted . . . teach.

The major predicament most teachers were apprehensive about was if members of their family became ill. It is expected that women, whatever their job, will stay home when their husband or children are ill. Some were even more wary of becoming ill themselves.

> I really dread getting the flu or something that forces me to stay at home. My husband really does help me a lot but . . . if I ever get poorly . . . you know you can see the house literally coming down about your ears. The pattern . . . the routine you've built up to keep one step ahead of everything just falls apart. I've always believed that no one is indispensable but sometimes I wonder . . . and he can't understand why I get so 'het up'. All he says is 'Leave it until *you* get better'. I know it sounds ridiculous but I just can't afford to be ill.

The male teacher's view
Of the seven male teachers I interviewed, six were fathers and all but one saw the conflict between being a parent and a teacher differently from their female colleagues. They tended to see it as a *professional* conflict rather than a *domestic* one.

> It's very hard to stop being a teacher. I'm often asked on open nights if I help my children or if I correct my children's homework and so on . . . but I try not to carry on being a teacher once I'm at home.

> You're over-critical of your own children. But I think it mainly works out very well because knowing what stages there are, you can monitor their progress yourself without having to be always running to school . . . You know the problems of teaching and you are also in the position to help to answer one or two problems that may occur. We're lucky that way.

> I think at times I expect too much of my own children but apart from that, none.

> I'm fairly strict on discipline in the home and at school so I find no conflict between the home and the school.

> With my school being the only one in the area my kids attended it. And I think the main problem was that the kids were in the same school as the one I had authority in. Particularly when they were in my own class I leant over backwards to try to display . . . to demon-

strate if you like . . . that I wasn't favouring them and as a result you tend to be a bit harder with your own kids.

Only one male teacher with two small children stated he 'experienced' problems similar to those of female teachers; but even here, there is a difference:

It's quite a conflict really to sort out time given to teaching and time given to my family . . . you know you've only a few hours in which to teach . . . it's hard to decide − well − how many hours can I give to school and how much time do I give to the family.

Increasing the Demands: Promotion
Geoffrey Partington (1977), in his book *Women Teachers in the Twentieth Century*, quotes Dr Alexander who believes 'the salaries of women teachers are already high enough to make it difficult to induce women to apply for headships of schools and other posts of responsibility'. Indeed a statement made by a teacher to me would tend to support such a hypothesis. It indicates that it can be both men and women who operate a double standard with regard to women's pay: '. . . let's face it, as far as a woman's job is concerned it's fairly well paid for the hours that you do, and there are always the holidays to catch up with everything in the house.'

But Partington, along with Alexander, makes little of the enormous burden of the double workload which women teachers are required to shoulder. When this immense burden is allowed to remain invisible it is hardly surprising that those same sociologists and educationalists should explain women's lack of promotion in terms of the 'apathy' of women. They do not have to take the impossibility of increased demands into account and so they reinforce an ideology which expects women to do two jobs, and then self-righteously explains that it's women's own fault if they don't *choose* to increase their workload even more.

Why do so many more women than men choose to go into teaching, particularly primary teaching? Caroline Joll suggests part of the answer:

For one thing the proportion of all female teachers who are graduates (16%) is half the proportion of men and such qualifications are more important for entry into the secondary and further education sectors (Joll, 1976; 8).

Furthermore:

Apart from the generally lower level of expectations and career orientation of women, the fact that substantial numbers of married women who used to be secondary school teachers choose to re-enter teaching in the primary sector illustrates the fact that women's domestic commitments may induce them to choose a less well paid job because it has shorter hours or is nearer (Joll, 1976; 8).

It is not too radical to suggest that guilt can erode self-confidence and as male and female teachers bear very different loads of guilt it should not be surprising to find they have developed very different patterns of self-confidence. Until the *double* workload which women undertake is made visible and is taken into account women will go on assuming that the inability to meet all the demands placed upon them is evidence of personal inadequacy rather than the inadequacy of social arrangements. In effect this means that there are two obstacles between them and promotion: the first is that positions of responsibility often demand more time, a commodity which they simply do not have, and the second is that they use this as evidence of their personal inability to tackle the task. Already more demands than can be reasonably accommodated are made upon them and this is particularly well illustrated when it comes to the sickness of children. Women are expected to reconcile children's illnesses with their paid work and often take the only course of action which is open to them: they stay at home and mind the children. Rather than entertaining the possibility that social arrangements could be made for the care of sick children when their parents are in the work force, women teachers frequently seem to internalise the contradictory demands which society makes upon them. They therefore rule out promotion possibilities because they (realistically) assume they would not be seen as plausible candidates for promotion when it is recognised they could not leave sick children to fend for themselves. (There were ten women teachers in my sample with young children who, when all the time off 'in the interest and welfare of the children' was added together, had had fifty-eight-and-a-half years' break from teaching, so it can be seen how great is the demand for facilities for children when parents are expected/required/forced to work.)

Added to these difficulties are the mobility problems which women teachers can encounter. For example, women are generally expected to move with their husband if his job demands it but are frequently unable to move themselves when promotion requires it (see 'It's a good job for a girl').

For women teachers there is usually a great deal more 'in a day's work' than there is for their male colleagues. Women who fulfil two jobs are obviously working harder than the men who have one. But most women teachers have more demands made on them than they can reasonably meet, feel guilty, and have their confidence eroded, and these factors combine to keep most women teachers on the bottom rungs of the teaching ladder.

Lou Buchan

'It's a good job for a girl' (but an awful career for a woman!)

Although feminism has questioned the desirability of the male-defined hierarchy of which careers are a part (see Arlie Hochschild, *Inside the Clockwork of Male Careers,* 1975), there are still substantial feminist reasons for many women entering the higher levels of employment. As distinct from assuming that the male pattern is the acceptable pattern, many women assume that one way of changing the pattern is to do so from inside. (In Australia we have a term which covers this process — it is 'whiteanting' and it means precisely what it says: eating away at the foundations from inside until they finally crumble.) If we wish to see demonstrable changes in politics, in law and education for example, then one strategy is for feminist women to enter these areas in increasing numbers and for them to begin to aspire to some of the influential jobs which have traditionally been reserved for males. This may appear to be a logical approach, but for women in education in Australia (where women are well represented, but at the lower levels of the hierarchy) there will be many obstacles along the way. In the absence of legal/official disqualifications of women from influential positions (it is only thirty years since most women were required to resign when they got married) the education system has developed sophisticated and pernicious mechanisms for disqualifying women. They are sophisticated in their subtlety and pernicious in that they work to 'blame the victim': women find that they are often not promoted and are encouraged to accept that it is their own fault.

There is a convenient slogan, 'women are their own worst enemy', which is often used to explain the absence of women from the upper levels of the hierarchy: as one person who did try to enter the male preserve I can testify that the explanation lies not in some denigrating evaluation of women but in an educational and social system which works against women being anywhere else *but* in the home.

There seems to be an element of farce in educational research which has as its priority the establishment of the reasons for women's 'failure' to take up promotional possibilities. I know why I didn't (and I assume the situation is the same for many women) but I cannot believe that educationalists would find my analysis acceptable and would be enthusiastic about adopting the necessary changes in order to ensure that in the future women would not encounter such obstacles.

The idea of teaching being 'a good job for a girl', has not been publicly challenged. It is still believed that if you can get your qualifications (relatively easy) and a teaching appointment (much more difficult owing to the self interest and lack of foresight of public education authorities), then you have instant access to a good job and even a good career. Unfortunately, the idea is a myth.

Adria Reich (1974) has looked at the processes which led women into teaching in America, and in Australia they were remarkably similar. From the point of view of the authorities, she refers to the economic expediency of using lower-paid women, traditionally, to answer the needs of an increased population. She points out that it was 'natural' to place women and children together. From the teacher's point of view, she notes that teaching is considered a 'profession' and therefore carries some prestige and job control. It was, and still is, one of the few professional areas available to a B.A.

These characteristics, combined with the increasing social acceptability of women pursuing work outside the home as well as raising a family, have contributed to the general view that teaching is the ideal job. In Australia, the hours and holidays allow women to return to work after their children are themselves at school. They even enable women with pre-school children to hope that they will not feel guilty about leaving them for such a short time. Compared to other positions that women occupy in large numbers (office work, nursing, factory work), teaching seems to offer the most manageable opportunity for combining job and family.

However, should a woman wish for more than a job and aspire to a *career* in teaching, the opportunities are not quite so available and the situation is far from ideal.

The following is the chronological review of the progress of a typical Australian school teacher. It is an autobiography of my 'career' in education in two states in Australia. It helps to illuminate the discrepancy between the belief that teaching is a good job and the reality that it is a poor career. I think it provides part of the answer to the conventionally framed question of why women don't seek promotion but it will probably not be the sort of answer that educational researchers are accustomed to: but then, it is possible that they are not asking the right question.

Born in 1946 of middle-class parents, who learned from the Depression the importance of an education and a secure job, I was encouraged and stimulated to achieve at school. As a conventional female child, I co-operated and received approval from both parents and teachers. In 1962 I completed my Leaving Certificate and was awarded a Teachers' College Scholarship to university. I wasn't really aware that I could have gone anywhere else. The only paid working woman role-models that I had encountered were the female teachers who had taught me. I had a vague notion about some exceptional women who became doctors or lawyers, but they had nothing to do with me. As the scholarship offered tuition fees and an allowance, I moved willingly to the university to study for a B.A.

Of course I took the 'soft' subjects . . . English, anthropology, education and psychology. By 1967 I had completed a B.A. and a Diploma of Education. I had succeeded! I was on the way to having a 'good job'.

During my first two years of teaching, in a country high school, I focused on learning how to teach, a task for which my years of higher education had not equipped me. I enjoyed this learning period. I was well paid in comparison to my counterparts in offices and factories; my hours and holidays, always partly devoted to the preparing and marking of papers, were seen as enviable privileges and often evoked critical comments, even from my parents. I was aware that as a new teacher and a female I was protected from the authorities by a 'Subject Master'. Fortunately (and from what I can gather it occurs mainly in the Humanities), he was genuinely interested in my progress and did not protect me merely to protect himself.

After two years of teaching, and not consciously aware that the job involved anything other than face-to-face teaching and pupil-teacher relationships, I was sure I had my good job sufficiently under control to take on another one. I got married. By having two jobs I believed that I had immediately doubled the possibility of rewards. With a little organisation I managed quite capably to run a house and teach. It did occur to me, but not with hostility, that the males with whom I was teaching had the same potential for rewards without quite so much organisation and juggling with time. But I was satisfied.

The English master suggested that I apply for inspection for the First List (i.e. a test which, if you pass, allows you to do another test several years later but ensures that you don't get there too quickly)[1]. In doing so, I became aware for the first time of the politics involved in promotion. As a female, I had to be super-prepared to face an inspector and so, willingly enough, I became involved in producing the school play (after school hours), organising and coaching the debating team (during lunch time) and I joined the professional English Teachers' Association, of which I became Secretary. I began to take an interest in organisation, planning and professional development but, as a junior staff member, there were few opportunities for that within the school. The only extra jobs available were organising staff lunches (and washing up afterwards). There was no place in the school system for my efforts to be really productive.

I passed my inspection and afterwards found that teaching without the added pressure was rather deflating. I started an M.A. course, two nights a week, and for two years managed to keep busy running a house, preparing and marking school work, co-producing the school play and attending university and studying. I completed the M.A. in 1971. I received no additional pay or responsibility and again felt that I needed to be doing something more. I wanted to have more say in what I was teaching and how it was being taught and spent many hours devising programmes which were never used and making resource lists which were filed for future reference. In 1972 I resigned (I was not eligible for Leave of Absence as I had not completed the obligatory five years service) and spent a year in Europe.

Early in 1973 I was notified of an appointment to a teaching position and returned from Europe to find the position withdrawn — there was a surplus of English teachers even then. I waited for a month for another appointment and was sent to a city school as a Supernumerary (or an extra with no real teaching timetable) to be employed at the Master's discretion. He used me by including me in a Senior Programme as a team teacher. I had ample time for preparation and marking and thoroughly enjoyed the work. However, halfway through the programme I was transferred to another school to take up a full teaching load.

The new school was an inner-city girls' school where most of the staff had been comfortably ensconced for many years. I was given all junior classes and some remedial work. There was no access to the power group who decided which staff members taught which classes and, partly through dissatisfaction with my 'good job', I decided it was time to take my next step and have a baby.

I was away from teaching for five months and although I had previously taught with the Department of Education for four and a half years and had returned to Australia over twelve months before to take up a non-existent teaching position, I found I was not eligible for accouchement (maternity) leave or pay. My child was born two weeks short of my being re-employed by the department for a period of twelve months. I was granted Leave of Absence without pay.[2]

I was annoyed by the seemingly pedantic rules which excluded me from one of the much publicised benefits of the job and this led to some discussion with female colleagues. I found that surprisingly few of them had qualified for full accouchement leave benefits. Apparently if your child arrived either before or after the date indicated on your application for leave, you lost a certain amount of your pay. The idea of accouchement leave is a very attractive one, but not if it involves an induction of birth in order to qualify.[3]

I began teaching again in June 1974. My child was three months old and safely, I hoped, in the care of a trained nurse. Her fees were a little higher than the usual rate and she insisted on being paid through the holidays when she was not caring for the child, but she had been recommended as 'loving' and 'thoroughly reliable'.

At the school I again started from the bottom. Junior classes and low stream groups were my lot for the year. I obviously had to prove that I was not going to have time off when the baby was sick; that I was not prone to monthly absences; that I was serious enough about my work to take over the debating group (after school hours). There was one female in the school in an administrative position. She was a List 2 and was acting as Girls' Supervisor. She suggested that I try for my Second List during the next year and also suggested that, if I did, I should start finding out who ran the school and I should start cultivating good relationships with the clerks and cleaners as they would provide the only help that I would get. I found her attitude rather cynical but did get to know the cleaners and the clerks. Later, I was grateful for the hint.

When I informed the Headmaster that I wanted to be inspected, he neither encouraged nor discouraged me. He did check with the English Master that I would not be making a fool of myself or the school and did assure me that he would familiarise himself with my accomplishments and support me all he could. He also always called me by the wrong name.

The Deputy Headmaster suggested that I apply for an internal appointment as a Form Mistress in order to prove my organisational ability. This I did, and was notified at the end of 1974 that my application had been successful and that I would commence 1975 as Mistress of Form I. Although this position carried the largest workload early in the year, I gather it was seen as appropriate as I could provide a 'mother image' for the new students. Also, there are traditionally fewer discipline problems in Form I.

I started the 1975 school year enthusiastic about the challenges that lay ahead. I was to produce the school newspaper (as it would impress the inspector), start a drama group (to cover the fact that no school play had been produced for two years) and continue with the debating group. I also had to learn how to run a Form Meeting, alone in an auditorium with 280 students, and have all relevant information on each one available for parent interviews and teacher enquiries. Apart from this, I had graduated to senior classes, which I thoroughly enjoyed, and spent a great deal of time marking and preparing their work. Out of school, I deposited and collected the child, shopped, cooked, cleaned and managed some sort of social life. I thought it flattering when one of my senior students informed me that the class referred to me as 'Superwoman'.

About halfway through the year, and just before inspection time, I discovered that some staff members had objected to my appointment as a Form Mistress on the grounds that I was working for a second salary and many of them were single income families and could have better used the money. The source of this information also persuaded me to make some enquiries about my extra money and I found that the administration had solved the second salary problem by paying me at a lower rate than was usually paid to the Master/Mistress of Form I. Those in charge of Forms I, IV and VI were awarded a higher rate because of the extra work involved in those forms. I had been given the lower rate and the higher rate was paid to the Master of Form V. He had been paid the higher rate in the previous year and the payments had continued, unchanged.

I confronted the Deputy Headmaster with this, a little embarrassed at what could be seen as quibbling over a few hundred dollars. He assured me it was merely an error and would be rectified. He suggested that I approach the other teacher involved about the money that had already been paid. The other teacher was more senior than me, a male, and 'had dependents'. It was an awful situation to place me in and, of course, I never mentioned it again.

Thus with little support from above and with no access to the inspection talk that went on in the local club after school while I was shopping, collecting my child and organising dinner, I prepared for my inspection. My female colleague had been right about the clerks and cleaners. My typing was always done when I needed it and my classrooms were especially clean, a sign of a good teacher from the Inspector's point of view. I passed the inspection and was invited to join the other successful teachers for a drink after work. After a series of phone calls, I managed to meet them for an hour and was aware of a certain hostility embodied in comments such as 'He (the inspector) must have liked your legs'. I was also aware that had I known what they knew about inspections, and had the support that they provided for each other, the ordeal would have been much easier. For my part, there was a certain amount of satisfaction in knowing that I had done it on my own, but also some resentment that the accumulated knowledge of past experiences had been kept from me. It was no longer because I was a junior teacher — it was simply that I was a woman.

It is easy to see why women rarely seek promotion within the Department of Education. Research has indicated that 'Women are trained to accept a sexual identity that corresponds to what society says is an appropriate sexual standard, and the female sexual standard has not included power positions' (Fennema, 1976; 345).

It has also revealed achievement-related conflicts in women and a 'motive to avoid success' (Horner, 1974). Simply summarised, this means women learn to lose, not just as the students in the classroom but as the teachers on the staff. The day-to-day comments on mixed-sex staffs in the school embody the same values as the wider society. Efficient and competent females are constantly diminished. Seen as threatening, they are the target for denigrating comments about their femininity. There are numerous overt and covert pressures designed to encourage women to step gracefully aside and let men move up the ladder. Such pressures are not identified, let alone examined, in the mind set that 'women are their own worst enemy', but they undoubtedly work.

If you add the findings of Matina Horner to the reality of a situation where the decision to move upwards is made in a male-centred environment, with little or no support, it is obviously difficult to give up the security and rewards of face-to-face teaching for the doubtful privilege of becoming an authority figure and standing alone.

By the time I acquired my Second List (and a great deal of insight into the politics of promotion) my future career in teaching was theoretically assured. No doubt, had I been male, I would now be considering my Third List and an appointment as a Deputy Head-master. As a woman though, there have been other contingencies . . .

Early in 1976 my husband was transferred interstate and I had the choice of remaining where I was until a suitable appointment was available (perhaps three years) or going with him and teaching in another state. I chose the latter and in doing so, negated my hard-earned 'victories'. I was informed by the administration that it was most difficult for them to replace me after the school year had commenced and that this was the whole problem with female teachers: they were unreliable. Rather than contributing to 'a change in the belief of men and women concerning the abilities of women' which Elizabeth Fennema (1976) says 'is of primary importance', I apparently reinforced the idea that women cannot make good, professional teachers.

Such thinking is of course symptomatic in a system which serves society and reflects its values. (It is possible to imagine what the comments would have been had I chosen career in preference to husband. They would have been vitriolic). There is no recognition that it is society which has ordained that women should be responsible for child care, that men's jobs are more important, that the wife should simply follow her husband's career path. But when these social values intrude into education, women are not only the victims, they are also blamed, held responsible for being the victims.

I did start teaching in the new state, but as I was given no credit for promotional status, I started from the bottom. I taught subjects that I had never encountered before (e.g. Consumer Education) and to junior classes. I had no say in what or whom I taught and, with little hope of change in the next year, I left and took an appointment with a private girls' school. There I was accorded autonomy within my subject field (Speech and Drama) and found the attitude of the predominantly female staff more accepting and supportive. However, after many years in state schools where the most rewarding aspect had always been the positive relationships with students, I found it disconcerting to be seen as a paid servant by both the pupils and their very involved parents. My first parent-teacher night was spent defending my methods and stating my qualifications.

At the end of 1977, I withdrew from teaching. I gave up my 'good job' and still think unkindly of the originator of the dream that 'It's a good job for a girl'. Until this myth is dispelled and the reality of teaching in a male-dominated school system is exposed, women will remain primarily in low-key positions or, like me, will withdraw to seek more rewarding and autonomous jobs.

Notes

1 In Australia teachers are eligible to be inspected for the First List after approximately four years of teaching. Once on the First List they are then eligible for promotion. If and when they are inspected for their Second List a few years later, and are successful,

their names are literally placed on a list. Once a name works its way to the top of the list, that person is offered a Head of Department position, whenever one becomes vacant. It is a slow process. It has little connection with ability to perform the job and a lot to do with staying power. After being promoted to Head of Department in this centralised bureaucracy, teachers are eligible to apply for inspection to be placed on the Third List, from which Deputy Heads are appointed. Although officially termed 'promotion by seniority' this practice is unofficially termed 'promotion by senility'.

2 Maternity Leave, or accouchement leave as it is called in New South Wales, is only paid *after* women have been teaching for twelve months. I had only been re-employed by the Department of Education for fifty weeks and so was not eligible for maternity pay.

3 Further enquiries into the status of women in teaching revealed that the compulsory Superannuation payments could not be assigned to family members if you happen to die before retirement. They reverted to the state. If you withdrew from teaching, your contributions were returned, minus administration costs. As far as I know this situation still pertains.

Anne Whitbread

Female Teachers are Women First:
Sexual Harassment at Work

In examining the situation of women teachers in terms of satisfactory work experiences we are confronted by the negative consequences of women's dual roles and of the low position and status occupied by women in the teaching profession. (See 'All in a Day's Work' and 'It's a good job for a girl'.) However, there is another dimension of the oppression of female teachers at work which has been given very little consideration, namely, sexual harassment.

Lin Farley's book, *Sexual Shakedown: The Sexual Harassment of Women on the Job* (1978)[1] makes it quite clear that not only is the sexual abuse and intimidation of working women a widespread phenomenon of western capitalist society, both currently and historically (see pp 14-15 for a definition of sexual harassment), but it is also a crucial aspect of the social control of women by men in a patriarchal society. Apart from describing the ways in which sexual harassment operates and presenting the evidence, so far gathered, of the extent and significance of the phenomenon in the United States today, as well as its historical antecedence, Farley also considers the information which has emerged concerning the response of women workers to sexual harassment. Overwhelmingly, if they do anything at all, women leave their jobs rather than lodge a formal complaint. In my opinion, this form of response has as much to do with the fact that women experience harassment as an individual problem as it is a consequence of the fulfilment of sex-role conditioning. The latter explanation is also problematic, in so far as it excludes the possibility that women make a conscious realistic assessment of their powerlessness in the work situation and act accordingly.

As long as women take up individual and passive solutions to sexual harassment, the widespread phenomenon of sexual abuse and intimidation will go largely unnoticed, and will indeed continue 'as normal'. However, on the basis of my own personal experience, I believe that a collective response is possible and that it can be quite effective in modifying the full onslaught of male aggressive behaviour.

The following account concerns sexual harassment at a boys' comprehensive school in North London and how the twelve women teachers (including myself) acted collectively to deal with the problem.

The Sexual Harassment of Female Teachers in a Boys' School
New members of staff and students on teaching practice were the principal targets of sexual abuse. This is not surprising. As Farley points out, women in low status positions are more likely to be treated as mere objects for male titillation than women with more authority in the work situation. The general tactic employed by the boys was to 'make a grab' while milling around in a group on the stairs or in the corridor, and then to run, leaving the victim unsure of the identity of the offender and frightened to make a false accusation. Equally humiliating were the obscenities shouted from a distance or the appraising remarks exchanged within hearing.

Amongst most of our male colleagues the subject of sexual harassment was either a joke or an embarrassment. After all, more than a few of them considered it perfectly within their rights to pat or pinch female staff at will and if the women were complaining about the boys doing the same, where did this put their behaviour? Even those men who were genuinely sympathetic could do little more than offer strong arm support as a deterrent. This seemed unlikely to attack the real root of the problem which we saw as the image of women generally in the eyes of the boys. It became obvious that if this kind of abuse was a strictly female problem it needed the women to come together to work out a proper solution. None of us had organised before, as females against males, and yet as soon as we began to confide in one another, it seemed an obvious step to form a women's group to begin to confront sexual harassment.

The first staffroom announcement of a meeting for women teachers on the subject of sexual harassment met with a mixed reaction from the male members of staff. There was approval from some who felt that such a move was long overdue, incredulity from others who could not see the point and dismay from those who did not want to acknowledge

91

that there might be a need. Jokes were made about the separatist and sexist nature of the group. This attitude, coming in a school that prides itself on its record of multi-racial education, was surprising in itself. No one would have denied the black staff their right to reinforce their identities positively by separate meetings, but white middle-class men happy to espouse the black cause looked askance at our efforts to support ourselves.

Our first meeting was not automatically smooth. We had all been isolated individuals much too long for instant harmony, but it was notable for being the first occasion in which, as a group, we had sat down together to discuss the problem of sexual assault and our various reactions to it. It was very reassuring for the student teachers and younger staff to hear that the older staff had also suffered similarly in their early days and to realise that it was not a personal failure on their part. Unanimously we decided it was a problem that must be taken seriously and that we should never allow the slightest untoward touch to go unnoticed, even under the cover of a group, but without undue histrionics we would roundly address all present as to our feelings about the matter. Nor should we be afraid, if the offence warranted it, to dispense punishments. After all, why should school shield the boys from the reality of the consequences of such behaviour in the outside world, where arrest could follow? We were aware, of course, that the same behaviour which may be unlawful on the streets *is* allowed to continue, without legal intervention, if it takes place inside the home or the workplace. (Wife battering is only one example of the indifference of the police to violence which does not take place in public.)

Although we felt we should largely deal with such offences ourselves, in the case of a serious abuse to a new or student member of staff, we made the decision to refer the offender to a senior female member of staff. One of the perennial problems faced by women teachers in a boys' school mainly staffed by men is the belief among the boys that women are 'soft' and can't control classes without a man to help them and back up their disciplinary measures. In the overtly macho world of adolescent boys this 'control' invariably means physical force — if not the reality, then the threat at least. It follows from this that the successful control of experienced female teachers is often discounted because it does not look like the paralysed silence of the disciplinarians. To overcome the image of women's helplessness it seemed particularly important, in the case of sexual abuse, that women were seen to be supporting each other and capable of dealing with the situation without male help, however sympathetic and supportive. Not that we had any reason to believe that the male members of staff were on our side. An incident which had taken place a few months earlier was not quickly forgotten. Two boys had been sent to their housemaster for persistent remarks about the size of a student teacher's breasts. They had been told 'If we can't, you can't'.

We reported the discussion and decisions of our first meeting back to the Staff Council. The intention of the closed group was not, as some colleagues thought, to discuss the particular failings of male staff in their absence but so that women, very much the silent minority in most large meetings, should feel free to speak. Our strategy was supported, verbally at least, and a general discussion of sexism within the school began. To be fair, it is temptingly easy for a man to achieve instant camaraderie with a class of boys on the level of sex when it might be hard to unite with them on issues of race or class. It is easier for the boys too. Similarly, it is more difficult for a man to overcome the boys' expectations that he will, ultimately, use physical force to control them, even though in succumbing to this demand he will make it doubly hard for a woman to teach after him using different methods of control. (The two popular forms of abuse in the school are 'woman' and 'poof'.) The hidden curriculum is all-important here and it is difficult to change attitudes reinforced since birth. Only when the majority of the staff are as consistent in their attitude toward sexism as they are to racism is there any hope of affecting the pupils.

Our women's group has continued to serve a vital function in bringing together the female staff and reinforcing a group identity within a predominantly male environment. Women strengthen their confidence to speak up at school meetings and the group is also a protection against the tendency to become estranged from other women and even to take on the sexist attitudes of the pupils. One woman confessed that she had chastised her class for bad behaviour by calling them 'silly girls'. Taking on honorary male status and values, and becoming female 'uncle Toms' can only demean us as women.

The group has also developed plans for introducing feminism in the curriculum without undue alienation and we are contacting women's groups in other boys' schools to share experience and ideas.

The initial impetus for the group arose out of a determination on the part of the women teachers to act collectively to confront sexual harassment. Our work has only just begun and because the group exists the problem has not been 'solved'. Sexual abuse does continue but it is worth noting that the boys are decidedly less bold and more wary of treating their women teachers disrespectfully than they were previously. They are aware there is more than 'a piece of skirt' to a female member of staff and that their chances of 'getting away with it' are slimmer than before because the women are fighting back.

Understanding Sexual Harassment

Lin Farley's study argues that sexual harassment of women is a general phenomenon in patriarchal societies. Is it possible to draw on my particular account of sexual abuse in a boys' school and develop a better understanding of sexual harassment in general?

To begin with, there is the question of whether the situation I describe is peculiar to a boys' school. Is sexual harassment a perennial problem for *all* female teachers in any educational environment in which males are present? Certainly the minority position of female teachers in a boys' school does make them more vulnerable to sexual intimidation because their marginality, and therefore their powerlessness, is particularly acute. However, given that we have reason to believe that the manifestation of sexual abuse is probably less contingent upon the dynamics of any particular situation than on the subordinate position occupied by women as a group in society as a whole, then one can assume that as long as the social context includes *some* men, women will be subjected to sexual assaults of one form or another. In an important sense, to speak of sexual harassment is to refer to the way in which men *typically* relate to women in a patriarchal society.

My account of sexual harassment in a boys' school can be understood as a particular illustration of a more general phenomenon. It also suggests what women can do about it. Far from being helpless victims women can make a collective challenge to sexual abuse. Indeed, I would argue that collective action is the only viable option available, because, unlike individual forms of response, it has the potential for modifying the asymmetrical power relationship between males and females which gives rise to sexual intimidation in the first place.

The main obstacle to collective action is that women continue to perceive sexual harassment as an individual problem and so, inevitably, look for individual ways of coping with it. It follows that it is the task of feminists to raise the issue of sexual abuse in order that it may be seen as a *general* phenomenon which affects *all* women. Then, perhaps, women will be more likely to consider the possibility of *working together* to confront it.

Notes

1 See also *The Secret Oppression: Sexual Harassment of Working Women*, Constance Backhouse and Leah Cohen, Macmillan, Toronto, 1978.

Part Four: Curriculum

Marion Scott

Teach her a Lesson:
Sexist Curriculum in Patriarchal Education

Working-class girls will most typically 'endorse the traditional female role and . . . femininity, simply because to the girls these (seem) to be perfectly natural'.[1] The 'naturalness' of such a role is not universally self-evident (as Margaret Mead, 1971, has indicated, where different cultures construct different beliefs about 'natural' femininity) and for it to be perceived, and accepted, it is necessary to develop a complex and extensive apparatus. In order to associate the social role of women with the biological fact of childbirth so that it appears 'natural' for women to be engaged primarily in housework and childcare, many connections are required. It is the strength of these subtle and pervasive connections, and the role that they play in perpetuating patriarchy and capitalism, which is frequently *not* taken into account in an analysis of sexism and education. The complex relationship between schooling and capitalist patriarchy is frequently neglected.[2]

Sexism in the curriculum cannot be eliminated easily because it is not a superficial overlay, a result of mere ignorance and oversight. Sexism is integral to our society, necessary to our system, and advantageous to men. It occurs at every level of experience within schools and serves a purpose. All educators should acknowledge this, and it is within this framework that I shall examine sexism in the curriculum and its relation to society.

Within capitalism, schools play a major part in the reproduction of the productive forces. Whereas in the past people frequently acquired skills and knowledge within the workplace itself (with teacher-education itself being one such example), today other institutions have taken over this function. The school has become an influential agency in dividing people and assigning them to an appropriate workplace (via the means of assessment) so that it is actually in schools themselves that children begin to learn the severe lesson of the division of labour. It is partly because this is an unpalatable fact that the myth of the 'equality of opportunity' has been created to mask the practices of the school (see also 'Educational Institutions: where Co-operation is called Cheating', and 'Education or Indoctrination'). When we acknowledge the work destinations of the majority of working-class children we can see that it is not 'equality of opportunity' which prevails in our schools, but quite the reverse: the pattern of success/failure is invariably consistent and it serves to help that particular group which is currently successful to perpetuate its own success.[3]

When we speak of skills in the late twentieth century we must be clear that in the majority of cases we are not referring to the specialised manual techniques and knowledge of materials and processes, learned and controlled by people of the past. In the twentieth century there has been a 'degradation of work'. We have witnessed the 'breakup of craft skills and the reconstruction of production as a collective or social process' (Braverman, 1974; 443). Now control over labour processes develops through scientific, technical and engineering knowledge, and this knowledge is concentrated in the hands of a few. The skill which is left to the workers is 'degraded', often being merely a matter of speed, simple dexterity and limited and repetitive operations.

Ironically, at the same time as the level of skill for the ordinary person has decreased, with the specialist taking more and more of the responsibility, the length of time spent in school has increased. Sometimes this *has* been because the educational requirements of the production process have necessitated it. Often, however, other factors have been significant. In the thirties and the seventies unemployment reached such proportions that it has served a useful purpose to keep young people in school rather than in the dole queue (compare this to the fifties and early sixties when a whole generation was lured towards jobs).

Two points emerge from this: firstly, we have a meritocratic society in which only a *few* can succeed, but, secondly, *all* share the ideology of the society. At present employers are in a position to ask for qualifications that are not *essential* for the job, but 'could be useful'. Although educational qualifications are no longer a job guarantee we must remember that the average number of years spent in school is the same for the employed as the unemployed. Education may be purveying a particular ideology which is accepted by *all* the students, but not all students will find that ideology equally applicable. For as well as creating a work force, with a particular level of skill (or lack of skill), schools also help to inculcate a certain frame of mind, a particular set of expectations, a 'common sense' knowledge of society. The organisational structures of schools and the presentation of knowledge within different subject areas make a crucial contribution to the patriarchal and capitalist divisions of labour: the division of the school curriculum into the broad areas of mental and manual is preparation for the divisions in the 'real' world outside the school. There are further divisions in the fragmentation of knowledge as academic subjects are divided from each other, and arts are separated from sciences. This reflects and reinforces the differentiation of the work place.

But where do girls and women fit in? So far my discussion is reminiscent of much writing in the area of education, ideology and capitalism. It has not dealt specifically with women. But whereas much of the literature *stops* at this point I propose to *start* at this point.

Currently there is much discussion of how to integrate a Marxist analysis of capitalism with a feminist analysis of patriarchy.[4] While the Marxist approach to work and education can be very fruitful it has had difficulty in accommodating the unique position of women 'within and without' the relations of production. Not only do women enter the workforce (and in increasing numbers)[5] under the constraints of their *femaleness*, defined and constructed by patriarchal, capitalist society, but they are also a part of the economic system as reproducers and nurturers of the workforce (and others) within the family. Stated bluntly, this means that many women are required to do a double shift as they enter paid employment but continue to remain responsible for housework, childcare and, unavoidably, childbearing.[6]

The justification for women's role within the home is well entrenched. The never-ending and immeasurable task of home-making is bolstered by an ideology which would have such service classified as a 'labour of love' or 'natural'. Women service men (as well as children, the sick and the elderly) in return (theoretically) for economic support and security. But this entails *dependence*. 'Women are trapped into a material dependence upon a man by our lack of access to a decent wage, the absence of services to make full-time waged work and childcare compatible, the ideological and social pressures to marry, and the almost complete absence of any alternative to the family as a way of life, a learned sense of inferiority, and the personal affects of isolation and overwork . . .'[7]

Within the family labour is replenished, sexuality is controlled, and sex roles are acquired (Belotti, 1975). It is a powerful institution and the site of women's subordination. The family is seen as an *economic unit*. The male wage is calculated on the basis that a man has a family to support while the female wage is calculated on the premise that she receives part of her means of subsistence from the man's wage (with little thought given to the number of women who are *not* in this category). In this way the circle of dependence is set up and although this dependent relationship of women is not the result of capitalism alone, it is a relationship which is supported by capitalist ideology, by the state and the market.

When a woman does enter the labour market this forms a contradiction with her (potential or actual) role as wife and mother. And because of a woman's position within the family (and the work which she performs), an area of paid work comparable to the work performed in the home becomes, by analogy, *women's work*. And women frequently find themselves in these low paid, low status 'appropriate' jobs. These jobs often relate closely to those tasks which are considered 'natural' for them. (Also, women are often in unskilled work and thus are intimately involved in the deskilling process of capitalism, see Wolpe, 1977.)

In the sale of their labour attractiveness plays a role for women. In the way they are treated at work, the self-image and consciousness they have of themselves as workers, the role work occupies in their lives in relation to their work in the home, women are different as workers. (The way in which women are expected to be attractive was illustrated when receptionists in New York went on a smile boycott: it produced considerable hostility because, as receptionists, women are expected to be smiling and attractive.) These entrenched ideologies of domesticity and femininity will not be easily changed.

Schools play a key part in the construction of this ideology which relegates girls and women to a unique place in the family and a specific place in the workforce. Schooling contributes at the level of *material skills* (see Byrne, 1978) as well as at the level of consciousness and ideology. While it is not difficult to expose the sexism of the education system (particularly in the curriculum) it is difficult to expose attitudes when they are considered to be 'given', 'pre-ordained' and 'natural'. Although the school alone will not change patriarchal capitalism it can, however, make a contribution to such a change.

Ideological Justifications: official policy and ordinary beliefs
Sexist ideology is to be found in virtually all of the education reports and bulletins this century, and no less so since 1944. In 1943 (127) the Norwood Report argued:

The grounds for including domestic subjects in the curriculum are variously stated in the evidence submitted to us: briefly, they are, firstly, that knowledge of such subjects is a necessary equipment for all girls as potential makers of homes; secondly, that the subjects have the advantage of offering a practical approach to theoretical work; thirdly, that for girls who are likely to go on to Domestic Science Colleges . . . they are necessary subjects and should therefore be taught at schools.

Later the Crowther Report (1959; 112) said:

The passionate interest that many girls feel in living things can be as strong an educational incentive as the love of machines. It is not for nothing that biology is the main science taught to girls, as physics and chemistry are to boys.

Then, in 1963 (37) the Newsom Report stated:

For all girls, too, there is a group of interests relating to what many, perhaps most of them, would regard as their most important vocational concern, marriage . . . many girls are ready to respond to work relating to the wider aspects of home-making and family life and the care and upbringing of children.

Ann-Marie Wolpe (1977) has examined these official statements (and the theories of other educationalists) and has documented the 'institutionalisation of the dominant female role' (see 'Education — the road to dependency' 1-19). She found that whenever boys and girls are explicitly considered as educationally distinct there are specific and traditional assumptions made about the future roles of the schoolgirls in question. These assumptions are consistent with the ideologies of domesticity and femininity and help to perpetuate the conditions under which women enter the labour force and live their lives. The school in effect *believes* the girls will be primarily wives and mothers and 'educates' them accordingly so that the girls find themselves equipped (materially and psychologically) to be primarily wives and mothers. In this way the role of women is perpetuated.

The educational assumptions about girls can be broadly summarised: that the main priority in the girls' lives — especially 'low ability' girls — is to marry and raise a family; that paid work will play a non-essential part in their adult lives; that they will enter paid work only in limited fields; that the work they perform in the labour force is not important to society and only necessary to women as 'pin money'. These assumptions are clearly discernible in past educational reports and Wolpe (1977) has clearly outlined what was *implicit* in an *explicit* way.

It is to be expected that these educational reports reflect the dominant institutional arrangements. If we look through (or deconstruct) the ideology we can see that women do not need to be defined primarily as wives and mothers (and consequently coerced towards providing cheap labour). Even if women do marry, marriage, and children, need not of themselves prevent women from working (although the lack of services in terms of caring for children, the sick, the disabled and the elderly make it difficult for this to be otherwise), but, more importantly, marriage and children will not remove the *need* for paid work which some women face. But it is unlikely that government reports would take this into account for to do so would be to widen radically the vistas and extend the possibilities for girls in education. Educational reports are unlikely to acknowledge openly that work is a *necessity,* not a 'pin-money' option, in most women's lives, married or not. To recognise this reality would be to state explicitly the discrepancy between the dominant ideology and the reality for most women.

It is true that middle-class girls can break through many of the barriers, but this is limited progress. In 1963 the Robbins Report described girls' educational achievement, but directed its suggestions towards middle-class girls of high ability. Later the Plowden Report (1967) showed that differences in the activities provided for boys and girls in primary schools had decreased, but was still able to indicate different achievements in the school performances of boys and girls. These reports do show an 'official consciousness' of the issue of sexism in education and even in 'official ideological' terms there has been some improvement. The Sex Discrimination Act (1975) specifically outlaws subject provision for one sex only within a school and the Equal Pay Act (1975) can, in a limited way, lessen inequality in the wage structure. However the former is not always evoked where it is applicable and the latter does not affect those areas of work where there are no comparable male workers, or work can be downgraded when taken on by women. The long-term influence of these two acts cannot yet be judged, but their limitations are already apparent.

In 1975 a Department of Education and Science report discussed some of the features that the Sex Discrimination Act was designed to change. It pointed out that girls and boys were generally still choosing very different subjects.[8] It did *not* discuss the factors which were influencing these choices (for example, teacher expectation, course content or organisation of the curriculum) nor the out-of-school influences which operate (for example, parental attitude, peer group expectation and approval, and the media) to persuade the sexes about 'appropriate' choices (DES Education Survey 21 *Curricular Differences for Boys and Girls, 1975*). In a Green Paper in 1977, the Department of Education and Science was even less serious about sex discrimination and differentiation and was claiming (without providing convincing evidence) that such distinctions were disappearing (Harman, 1978; 12).

We cannot deny that legislation and organisation inside and outside the educational system have improved the situation for girls. We do have a Sex Discrimination Act; schools are beginning to run craft courses for girls, and this must represent a gain. However, the depth of this change in terms of general attitudes is much less certain. In 1978 *The Times Educational Supplement* reported on newspaper responses to a situation where a Devon mother wanted her son to do more English rather than take a 'soft craft', which had to be either cooking or needlework. Attitudes indicated a basic conservatism on the part of parents, press and civil servants. Local and national headlines read: 'A school recipe to "turn boys into pansies" '; 'Beginning of 1984'; 'Parents don't want sons to be fairies'. A working party, headed by Jocelyn Owen, Chief Education Officer for Devon, had drafted a council report on sex-stereotyping in primary schools. This had recently been rejected by the Education Committee, lead by Ted Pinney, who said to reporters 'If boys are to be turned into fairies and girls into butch young maids, it should be for parents to decide and not the education authorities or schools . . . If parents wish to bring up boys as boys and girls as girls, this would seem to be *highly desirable and fundamental to family life'* (my emphasis).[9]

This type of response evades the fundamental question of sex roles and their naturalness or inevitability; it ignores issues about skills, learning and behaviour which are considered appropriate to each sex; it fails to account for the cultural specificity of family life as we know it. Interestingly, however, this example does show that opinions range from reactionary and traditional to radical and liberal at *all* levels of education. Sometimes it is the classroom teacher who is convinced that change is undesirable, unnecessary, or both, when education authorities are pressing for reform and for curriculum development which minimises discrimination. More commonly, however, conservatism which exists at the grass-roots level of the teaching profession is bolstered by a lack of strong directives or a lack of concern within the reactionary and sexist hierarchy. Concern, where it can be found, usually rests on a rather narrow conception of how education should function to serve society and this is often incompatible with intentionally educating women so that they are *not* primarily defined as wives and mothers (many would no doubt argue that such policy would not serve the needs of society at all!).

In the same *Times Educational Supplement* article it was reported that the EEC Education Commission was concerned about the 'under-achievement' of girls as a result of rigid sex stereotyping. To speak in terms of underachievement of girls is to suggest that our education system operates fairly and without discrimination and that girls do not avail themselves of all the opportunities. Such a suggestion is false, not only for girls but for working-class and black pupils in general. But there is also another subtle dimension to this categorisation of girls as underachievers; for if girls do underachieve then it could be argued that it is wasteful to teach girls when they cannot fulfil the necessary requirements (or cannot put them to use later as they are constrained by their roles as wives and mothers). The danger of attributing under-achievement to *girls* (rather than to *society*) was evidently not considered by our own Equal Opportunities Commission which mounted an extensive research project on the theme of *Women and Underachievement* (one of the consequences of this will no doubt be numerous statistics to reinforce the belief that girls are not as good an educational investment as boys).

Currently, the educational system contains numerous contradictions. One contradiction is readily revealed by the EOC's reaction to the Holland Report, *Young People and Work* (1977). The EOC maintains that the proposals of the Manpower Services Commission suggest that the policy of training girls for traditional women's job will continue. And, although nearly half of the young unemployed are girls (latest statistics suggest that more than half are girls and that the proportion is growing, Byrne, 1978), the work schemes outlined in this report allowed them far fewer places (*The Times Educational Supplement,* January 1977). Attempts are not being made to compensate for inequalities or to enable girls to move into different occupations for which ability — and self-confidence — in maths and science for example, is often necessary. (Such attempts are being made in the USA and are called affirmative action or positive discrimination.)

The Curriculum in Practice

I am using curriculum to refer to more than a set of subjects with specific content: I am including in my use of the word curriculum the experiences of the students in terms of *who* is teaching them, and *how*. Both the *hidden* and the *manifest* curriculum are encompassed in the use of the term.

Different teachers will interpret materials in varying ways and the students receive numerous messages from the teacher; they can make many assessments about the nature of a subject by virtue of the sex of the teacher. When science is taught almost exclusively by males then messages about sex and science are conveyed to the students. Students are often aware that women teachers are concentrated in certain areas of the curriculum. They note the arts-science dichotomy, especially in

104

the upper half of secondary schools, and some may even feel that men do the more 'complicated subjects'. The subject choices of girls must, to a certain extent, be affected by the models they have before them. If there are no women teaching 'hard' or abstract sciences, like chemistry and physics, or mathematics or technical drawing, then this reinforces other messages that reach the girls concerning the appropriateness or possibility of their succeeding in those areas. On the other hand, cookery and needlework are 'obviously' girls' subjects. The teachers are almost invariably women and in any case these practical skills are part of the home environment of girls (and not boys), unlike science, as it is presented.

The context of the learning and the characteristics of the learning group will affect the quality of the lessons and therefore their potentially sexist or non-sexist nature. Girls behave differently in single-sex schools, as do boys, and the mixed class situation modifies the learning process. The children themselves note that boys tend to make more noise and disturbance and distract the girls. Girls tend to be shyer and quieter and are prepared just to get on, however boring the lessons may be. Boys are often the source both of the fun and laughter but also the confusion. The dynamics of the classroom are radically affected by the presence of boys. I would guess that even seasoned teachers can be 'dictated' to by dominant elements in a class. If there are boys present then the nature of the materials presented and the interpretations that the teacher makes are crucially circumscribed. (For further discussion see 'Talking in Class' and 'Interaction in the Class-room'). In my own classes I have tended to use materials which I think will appeal to the class *as a whole*. (It is possible to adopt this approach in English where the subject matter is flexible: it may not be a choice in some other subjects.) However, the collective character of a class is not determined by the equal influence of each individual within that class. For example, boys are often more rigid and unwilling to take on unattractive or unfamiliar tasks and therefore can determine the nature of the lessons to an unfair extent. The girls, at least in the co-educational situation, are typically more pliable and willing to please. (*Not* necessarily good characteristics from the point of view of their own development, though sometimes a welcome release for a teacher.) Here I am not suggesting that the influence of the boys is consciously felt by most teachers. It usually exerts a more subtle pressure which a teacher may not even be willing to acknowledge or accept.

A related point concerns girls who find themselves in classes which are male dominated: chemistry and metalwork, for example. In doing these subjects they are going against the mainstream of girls within society *and* the school, which entails many problems. But it is their 'minority status' inside the class which can also affect their performance, their self-estimation and their commitment to the subject. All this can be compounded by an insensitive teacher who is anyway likely to be male. A teacher may emphasise their minority, deviant, or invisible status in a derogatory way; he may differentiate between the sexes in the manner in which he relates to them, and he may have reduced expectations of the girls. Research indicates that girls achieve more in traditional boys' subjects in single-sex schools where sex-stereotyping in subject choice and appropriateness is diminished and maths and science teachers are more likely to be women.[10] (This, of course, raises the difficult question of mixed versus single-sex schooling, a question which must be seriously addressed but one which demands caution in answering. See 'The Education of Feminists: The Case for Single Sex Schools'.)

Classroom dynamics — the interactions between teachers and pupils — teaching styles and attitudes are a significant part of the curriculum.[11] In any communication there is the overt message, but implicit assumptions, incidental and unintended messages are also conveyed. The power relation between teachers, pupils and knowledge carries with it many assumptions intuited and felt by all concerned. Other messages reaching the children concern the relative importance of men and women in society, and what is appropriate or possible for pupil or teacher, male or female, to say, I think, feel or do. Lessons are learned by pupils about status and worth and it is not necessary that such things be referred to explicitly. More specifically, it is important to consider the implications for girls of the overall domination of teacher time and attention by boisterous (and quiet) boys in class (see Clarricoates, 1978, for further discussion). Girls so frequently seem to accept that boys are a natural focus of attention, or source of amusement, or objects of a teacher's concern, as well as being more likely to contribute spontaneously to organised class discussion. Girls are learning and accepting something about the relative value of male and female in that situation and this is surely reinforced by the domination by men of the status posts in most secondary schools.

Apart from the reinforcement and production of sexist ideology which can result from classroom interactions, there is also a bias in subject choice. Generally girls still do more arts subjects than sciences and take practical subjects like office practice, childcare, needlework or art rather than woodwork, metalwork or technical drawing. The only science which is at all popular with girls is biology or, rather, human biology. I would argue that as long as courses such as childcare and development, food and nutrition, office practice and so on are set up within schools as examination subjects, the tendency will be for girls to take up these 'natural' choices. Advice and explicit encouragement to take such subjects is unnecessary. They select them voluntarily and opt out of the traditional boys' subjects. Most girls, especially working-class girls, will conform to the prevalent image of women and refuse to be different by choosing options from the traditional boys' sector, physics or metalwork for example, even if the subjects are open to them. In many schools subjects like technical drawing, metalwork and engineering are linked early in secondary school, which means that girls are less likely to qualify to do the subjects by internal school criteria, let alone want to do them (Deem, 1978). When girls are engaged in office practice or childcare their activities are seen as entirely appropriate and relevant to their future lives. That the skills which girls are learning are different from those which boys are learning in their practical subjects remains implicit. These courses rarely provide girls with really marketable skills and so their economic dependence is being fostered. While it is true that greater emphasis is now being placed on teaching boys basic domestic skills (in effect, it is mainly working-class boys) the relative importance of the courses in the educational experience and future lives of boys is weighted very differently. Some practical skills that boys are encouraged to develop can, theoretically at least, lead to skilled and therefore relatively high-status work. Furthermore, courses for boys like 'Man about the House' are not intended to provide them with skills central to their economic survival. Nor is such provision part of a system of sex-oppression, though where such courses are mainly for working-class boys it may be part of the ideology of a class society.

A course for girls such as 'Mother and Child' is expected to have a close connection to every aspect of those girls' futures. Even the titles of these two courses are revealing. A boy can look forward to being a 'man' about the house and it is left open to him to be an individual as well as a brother, son or a husband. Contrast this with the choice offered to the girl: one role, mother. Some girls recognise this limitation and argue that it is wrongly named because boys too need to learn to look after children. Others decry the whole need for such a course as, they claim, such skills are learnt at home anyway.

Having chosen her options, whatever they are, what will a secondary pupil, reaching the examination courses, learn within each subject area of the curriculum? Actually identifying what might be called 'sexist' in any discipline or lesson is not straightforward. Overtly sexist and biased material can be used to demonstrate the very sexism which informs it and this can often provide a valuable starting point for discussion. But deliberately non-sexist material, which seeks to destroy myths or point out inequalities, or set the record straight, need not necessarily have a long-lasting effect on attitudes and abilities, whether it is taught by feminist teachers or otherwise.[12]

Setting aside teaching styles, commitment and enthusiasm, I examined numerous texts (English, social studies, history, geography, maths and science) which were used mostly with the fourteen-plus age group to locate some of the sexist trends in curriculum materials. (I am not looking closely at English literature here because this topic has been covered and there is a bibliography on Sexism and Books in the Appendix. Furthermore, research on the text books of subjects such as biology, health and first aid and economics, to name but a few, is essential and would no doubt reveal assumptions and attitudes related to those discussed here.)

Social studies teachers and departments have been placed in the vanguard of progressive teaching, ostensibly because social studies is seen as a context in which individuals can develop their consciousness and understanding of society. Their curriculum materials, however, stand in sharp contrast to this rationale, and their texts are no less open to criticism than those of other subjects. There are some issues within social studies itself which are interesting. There is a continual debate as to whether the role of the social studies curriculum is to *describe* things as they are (in this case, to show a sexist world without necessarily singling out that sexism for comment or criticism) or whether it should adopt a critical perspective. To my mind the answer is simple: when a critical approach is accepted as a legitimate element of social studies teaching (and surely a critical approach is not one which is to be avoided) then textbooks will be obliged to present *alternatives*, rather than just describing the sexist norm and failing to evaluate it. Social studies texts (or sections of them) fall into three categories which are crudely sexist:

1 *The derogation of women*
   In these texts women are relegated to a subordinate role or else portrayed through grotesque cartoons. They also present women serving primarily a 'decorative' function.

2 *The invisible woman*
   These books do not focus on women at all.

3 *The insignificance of women*
   These books treat women inadequately and are the most common genre.

108

It should be stressed that since the subject of social studies is society, and particularly individuals and social groups within society, it is difficult to accept that women as a group can be of little concern to its practitioners. Surprisingly perhaps, while blatantly sexist material in the form of caricatures is not common, and usually used with critical intention, it is fair to say that many social studies texts produced for examination classes frequently neglected women, though there were some exceptions.[13] (There are, it must be said, changes taking place at the level of examination syllabuses and question papers where the role of women appears with increasing frequency.)

In both general texts and volumes dealing with special topics, I found that women were often invisible. Books about leisure, crime, courtship, education, advertising, general introductions to social studies and sociology, all showed weaknesses here. The Longman Series 2 was particularly adept at ignoring women or failing to see that women could be a distinctive category for study within these areas.[14] Where books were inadequate it was usually a result of their sketchy approach to a subject. Many books deal with women at work, perhaps focusing briefly on their dual role at work and home, or looking at housework, but not exploring *the extent* to which women work and contribute to the work process (Selfe, 1975; 149-72; North, 1973; 122-46). I am not arguing that the lack of feminist analysis makes the accounts unsatisfactory, but rather that indisputable facts are actually *withheld* and half of society is virtually ignored.

I need to emphasise two points here: firstly, most textbooks represent a misleading view of reality in which women are neglected or treated in a cursory manner and this is their ideological function (see 'Education or Indoctrination'). Secondly (and this is a more subtle and complex point), I would suggest that while some writers may believe that they are presenting reality, they are, in effect, reinforcing stereotypes and patriarchal relations. While we know that more men at present work in certain jobs, as engineers, in factories and so on, we still need to see and read that *women can also do these jobs*. As with so many books, social studies texts are often more reactionary and stereotyped than life itself. Textbook writers have a problem if, for example, they want to discuss cleaners. Most people assume that cleaners are women (though I am not sure whether this is statistically true) and so to present, in the text or in an illustration, a man in such a job could be to misrepresent the general worker in such a field. However, my point is that it is *not* always a woman who is a cleaner and surely one aim of social studies should be to break down gender stereotyping in occupational choice.

A parallel case is the example of a boy suffering from anorexia nervosa (Thompson, 1978; 74). I commend the approach which aims to show that both sexes can suffer from this problem but regret that this section did not discuss the fact that today it is girls who most often suffer, for many complex socio-psychological reasons related to being female. Such a discussion could help to break down sex specific divisions. In order to be fair we currently need to be *biased*. So much of the curriculum is weighted in favour of males, and if such inequality is to be redressed, then curriculum materials must move towards 'positive discrimination' in favour of women.

A related problem concerns the impact of presenting what, to a feminist or even a critical sociologist, are controversial ideas in a textbook where these support and reinforce accepted but stereotyped norms. I found an extract from Dr Spock in a book on courtship[15] which argued that a girl should 'put off' boys who were making sexual advances beyond the acceptable by *apologising* for this rejection. The advice went on to suggest that it was natural and correct for a girl to 'save herself' for 'Mr Right'. It is in a case like this that explicit criticism of such a viewpoint is needed, in the text itself or from the teacher using the book, to redress the balance at least. While most teachers (and perhaps textbook writers) would probably agree in theory that the development of a critical perspective in students was one of the ideal aims of teaching, they seem to depart considerably from it in practice. If textbooks are any guide then it seems that little attempt is made to provide students with evidence or arguments to help them to question – and develop a counter position to – the sexist norms and expectations of society. The predominant tendency in most social studies books is to present the norm and expect discussion without offering any alternatives on which criticism can be based.

Ultimately the logical conclusion of these arguments is the demand for a feminist perspective within each text or from the teacher. Only a feminist perspective will see the distortions and implications of a book which deals with crime and punishment without examining the issue of why girls and women are less involved in crime and also looking at those areas of crime that they are involved in and which are under-reported or treated as 'illness', for example, shoplifting, see Roshier, 1976. Only a feminist framework would look further into a case of female drug taking to see if anything specific to the situation of being female is relevant (Hanson, 1976). Furthermore, such an approach would, in this context, examine the high rate of alcoholism and pre-scribed drug taking in Britain by women, without automatically resorting to simple answers of their personal inadequacy. A feminist analysis would not allow an argument on courtship attitudes to claim that boys seem to look for more responsibility in preparation for marriage while girls tend to become more motherly as they look towards marriage. Avoided too would be the simplistic argument that we cannot say if this is 'natural' or 'cultural' (Hanson, 1973; 7-8). No feminist sociologist could discuss teenage romance magazines without placing them in the broader context of the ideology of femininity and domesticity. Nor would feminists deal with advertising or the mass media without examining the particular way in which women are treated (Nobbs, 1976; 86-100). A feminist argument on abortion could not take place in a discussion on morality, thereby omitting any consideration of a woman's right to autonomy over her own body (O'Donnell, 1975; 29-38). This is a contemporary social issue of considerable importance and one which is the legitimate subject of social studies.

Geography, as a subject, tends to concern itself with what is done, in what manner and where, especially when it looks at industry and resources. Its focus is not so much on the individuals who work and produce as on the production process, and this rather impersonal and abstract approach makes it difficult or even unnecessary to look for any exclusion of women, although this occurs. For example, a text which adopts a general, objective style can often create the wrong impression through its use of the pseudo-generic 'man' (see Marchington, 1974; Morey, 1975). Although the written text may be very general and refrain from referring either to men or women, the illustrations make a definite point for the majority contain male figures (Poxon and Poxon, 1975). Where women are illustrated the results are often less than desirable for they frequently seem to be included for their decorative or 'selling' power.

Among the geography texts I examined there were two particular sexist tendencies. The first was in terms of the invisibility of women, who were ignored, or under-represented. For example, in Third World countries women play a crucial role in farming but this was certainly not the impression which would be gained from the books.[16] The second tendency was the desire to simplify (or avoid) any analysis (a rather ironical position) which of course makes distortion almost unavoidable. Examples of this were discussions of population growth which made no mention of birth control (Crisp, 1975; 20) and figures on the distribution of the sexes through occupations which were offered without explanation or analysis (Bealt, 1977; 67 passim). It must be noted, however, that feminist analysis in this area is only in the initial stages. One factor which does deserve attention and investigation is the degree of popularity of geography among students as it is a relatively popular subject among girls but it is taken by fewer girls than boys.

History textbooks also provide interesting documentation, for even among highly qualified history scholars the centrality of women in history is not yet accepted. Since school texts so frequently seem to depend upon the received knowledge of at least one intellectual generation before them, children will be condemned for some time to reading about the exploits of men. History as an intellectual discipline now includes social history which looks at how people actually lived within the limitations of the economic and political events. Labour history too has developed into a recognisable historical research area and women's history is following suit. These approaches have a pre-occupation with the activities of ordinary people rather than with important figures and are concerned with providing an alternative perspective on our past. Women's history has yet to take root within our universities and so must wait even longer before it makes an impact in the classroom despite the availability of many histories of women produced in the last decade or so, which could provide starting points for a better balanced approach to history.

More social history is being taught but examination syllabuses still focus on political and economic history which conventionally excludes women. I looked at several texts directed at the upper half of secondary schools and roughly the same categories emerged as for social studies. Typical was a view of the past which left women invisible. A book on the first world war made no mention of women's contribution to the war effort at home or abroad (Hoare, 1973). A book on Britain since 1700 ignored the nineteenth-century feminists and the birth control movement (Cootes, 1968); books on political and economic history were almost exclusively about men (Arnold, 1973; Wilson, 1971). There was even a chapter in one book entitled 'The Home' in which the focus was on the man, portrayed relaxing after some 'Do-it-Yourself' work (Hobley, 1977; 28-9). There are modern history books which ostensibly focus on periods of great social change but the reader could be forgiven for reaching the conclusion that there have been no social changes which have involved/affected women (Monti, 1976; Case and Hall, 1976).

There are, of course, history books, or rather sections and chapters in books, which do focus on women. Generally these are inadequate, non-analytical and sometimes almost caricatured. Historians' treatments of the suffrage movement are a case in point: the coverage is frequently brief and uninformative (Case and Hall, 1976; 90; Hardman, 1975; 55-7; Cootes, 1968;246). Sometimes discussion which starts well descends into trivia, such as a discussion of women's part in the labour market in the twentieth century which ends in an uninspired discussion of fashion (Robson, 1973; 174-6). I also noticed a tendency to assume that by the twentieth century women had overcome most of the problems of inequality. Mention is made of the Equal Pay and Sex Discrimination Acts but there is no attempt to question their ultimate effectiveness. One book included a comment that Hitler had a 'mystical appeal' to women, but fails to discuss why or how, and suggests that Hitler's views on the home as woman's place seem old-fashioned to us today, something unfortunately far from the case (Hardman, 1978; 44). Another book claimed that by the end of the first world war much of the old prejudice against women having an equal place with men in society had gone (Case and Hall, 1976; 100). I found, too, an assertion that fashion today is a sign that women's emancipation is well underway – a claim that cannot go unchallenged (Hill, 1977; 235). The lack of feminist perspective is emphasised by statements such as: 'There can be no doubt that women and girls have failed to make full use of the opportunity now open to them' (Hardman, 1975; 57), which implies an ideologically and materially unfettered equality of opportunity. Another historian notes that women have not come to rival men, despite the equality established through legislation (!), but needs to add a critique of such legislation and society if he is to understand its failures (Jones, 1971; 178-9).

What is required in history, if girls are to have equal opportunity with boys in school, is both a full investigation and exposure of women's past – recorded and documented in special women's history books – *plus* an integration of women and their contribution to history within existing accounts. This means studying the women who were great and important ('heroine history') as well as the ordinary women.[17] The two sexes are not experiencing equal educational opportunity while the only version of the past they are presented with looks almost exclusively at males and has been recorded almost exclusively by males.

Science and mathematics, because of their subject matter, necessitate the adoption of a different approach. This is not the place to explore arguments which characterise the scientific mode of thought as in some sense masculine (though this may have a vital role to play in our understanding of the science of our culture if it is so: see Kelly A., and Haste, H.W., 1979). I intend to analyse the sexism in such texts on a more immediate, if mundane, level. Questions which can be posed include: what impression do we get of the 'mathematical world' and way of thinking; what does maths connect with; who might it concern; who are these books directed at? (The same questions could also apply to chemistry and physics.) Sensible of the fact that maths is not a popular subject among children in general there is often an attempt to show how the 'everyday' can be viewed mathematically. However, the 'everyday', according to these texts, is a world of football, cricket, men driving cars and traditional boys' hobbies whether the topic is statistics, measurement or velocity (Marshall, 1970, Book I; 1975; SMP Book F; 1970). The world of maths is male and this is reinforced in several books by the number of questions which revolve around men and boys doing things susceptible to mathematical calculation, (Marshall, 1970, Book I, and Smith, 1967). Occasional gestures towards the girls being included in maths are made, typically, via a girl sipping tea or standing decoratively posed in a mini skirt in a phone booth (Marshall, 1975; 11 and Smith, 1967; 23). The School Mathematics Project books are more abstract than many, depending less on pictures. But even in these boys feature more through their visibility in the questions and examples. A supreme example of sexist attitude can be found in the early pages of one SMP volume demonstrating the use of flow diagrams (Book F; 4-5). A flow diagram discriminates between girls and boys, directing the girls to consider a flow chart dealing with a knitting process, while the boys are to examine a flow chart of a cement mixing operation. The two sexes are told exactly what they should be interested in, and all in the name of mathematics. It would be a short-sighted solution to try to remedy this bias by showing mathematics operating in the domestic realm to the same extent as it operates outside it, just to draw girls' interest. The main point is that even when examples could be *non-sex specific*, these books make them *sex specific*. No attempt is made in any of the books I looked at to integrate girls into the world of engineering or technology.

Chemistry and physics books revealed the same patterns. The male predominates in the pictures, examples and the questions (See Mee, Boyd and Ritchie, 1971). One very lively looking book (Davies, Denial, Locke and Reay, 1973) provides typical examples of the features I would criticise: a focus on the history of the science dealing with the main discoverers, who all seem to be men; a use of the pseudo-generic 'man' and 'he' when the reference is to men and women; more pictures of men than women; a series of cartoons in the margins which portray boys more frequently than girls to illustrate some concept or show active participation in scientific experiment. But we should note that the process of deterring girls from science begins well before they enter secondary school. It takes the form partly of encouraging them to relate to the personal and subjective while boys begin to grapple with the impersonal and objective.

Our school textbooks present a biased, distorted and sometimes explicitly sexist view of the world and there is no doubt that they could be improved. Teachers, on the simple grounds of justice and impartiality, should be bound to supply alternative information and arguments. It remains true that, given a feminist awareness, even the textbooks discussed above could afford a non-sexist education resource if they were to be used critically, but I am pessimistic about this happening in all but a few cases. Teaching training institutions do not yet take sexism in education into consideration. It takes time, energy and commitment to change attitudes, especially when so few alternative resources are available, and there is so little support for those who do undertake to provide a more equal and less discriminatory form of curriculum.[18] This is compounded by the general inertia of the teaching profession (due in part to the demands of the job), its conservatism, and its penchant for simplifying any material that is taught.

If it is hard for a feminist teacher to modify expectations and beliefs, and to implement changes, then it is likely that non-feminists will find it even harder. A male teacher, for example (who may be well informed and well intentioned), could still find the whole exercise just too much trouble. If he perceived it as an erosion of his own power he could even find it completely unacceptable, and resist such changes. We must recognise that change will probably only come slowly. My experience suggests that teachers, generally, will tolerate only a mild and moderate form of women's equality or emancipation. Judging by some of the reactions I get, feminist analysis is not something with which they seek closer acquaintance. Consequently they do not recognise either the need or the value of non sexist or anti-sexist teaching materials, feminist critiques or discussions which challenge the sexist status quo. For the feminist teacher who wishes to bring about change many conflicting positions must be accommodated. She must try to make it clear that women are oppressed but must do this in a way which does not heap further denigration on women. In a society where it is common to 'blame the victim' it is self defeating continually to portray women as victims. She must try to balance this oppression with the presentation of positive images of women (and even finding such images is no mean feat: for further discussion see 'Materials in the Classroom'). She must try to show that women's very real abilities have been undervalued in male society while also attempting to convey the message that the *potential* of women has been limited while they have been oppressed.

Although some of my findings indicate that sexism is rampant in education – and that there is a long way to go before any credibility can be attached to the slogan 'equality of opportunity', I remain optimistic. While such sexist practices are being increasingly challenged then sexist ideology is being undermined, at least in its present form. Opposition to, and decline of patriarchy and capitalism grow in part

115

out of a change in consciousness. Surveys of sexism in the curriculum *could* become an obsolete exercise.

Notes

1 See Angela McRobbie, 1978, 'Working-class girls and the culture of femininity' in *Women Take Issue* (Women's Studies Group, 1978), pp 96-108. Also 'It is well known by nature that women are inclined to be rather personal', Charlotte Brundson, same collection, pp 18-34.

2 For example, although both the following texts are concerned with sexism and education the role played by capitalist patriarchy is not discussed: *Undoing Sex Stereotypes: Research and Resources for Educators* (Guttenag & Bray, 1976); *Unlearning the Lie* (Harrison, 1974).

3 See Paul Willis, 1978, *Learning to Labour: How Working-Class Kids Get Working-Class Jobs*; also Young & Whitty (eds), 1977, *Society, State and Schooling*; also Dale, Esland & McDonald (eds), 1976, *Schooling and Capitalism: A Sociological Reader*.

4 See, for example, *Women Take Issue* or the journals *m/f*, *Feminist Review*, *Scarlet Woman* or *Women's Studies International Quarterly*, Vol I, No 2, 1978; also Kuhn & Wolpe (eds), 1978, *Feminism and Materialism*.

5 Women as workers: 49% of married women were economically active in 1976 (provisional figure); estimated to rise to 52% in 1981 and 56% in 1991. 41.6% of unmarried women were economically active in 1976 (Department of Employment). 41% of women with a job designated it as part-time though the hours could still be quite long. Other points to remember: a relatively high proportion of women are over 60; many women *work* in the home.

6 There is currently a debate about the nature of domestic labour and its part in capitalist production. One aspect of the argument concerns the equivalence of domestic labour with wage labour in Marxist terms. See *Women Take Issue*; also C. Delphy, 1977, *The Main Enemy: a Materialist Analysis of Women's Oppression*, Women's Research & Resources Centre, 190 Upper Street, London N1.

7 Quoted in *Women Take Issue* from an unpublished paper by Mackintosh, Himmelweit & Taylor, p 44.

8 See DES Statistics of Education. The following figures are, at the time of going to press (1980), the most up to date figures available in such detail. In 1974 the following entries and successful passes were recorded and these give an indication of subject preference:

	Boys	*Girls*
Physics	76,074	10,221
Biology	35,261	78,465
Technical Drawing	69,418	860
Metalwork & Woodwork	92,015	553
Domestic subjects	5,524	109,787
Commercial	10,031	50,231
French	37,127	59,492
Maths	152,672	142,801

Source, DES Statistics of Education, 1974, Vol II, School Leavers, Table 33, p 70.

 9 *The Times Educational Supplement*, 13 October 1978, 'What Terry Did' from which Pinney quotes are taken and also the information on the EEC education commissioner.
10 See, for example, J. Shaw, 1976, 'Finishing School — Some Implications of Sex Segregated Education' in Barker & Allen (eds) *Sexual Divisions and Society: Process and Change*, Tavistock, London, pp 133-49; also A. Kelly, 1978, *Girls and Science*, Almguist and Wicksell International; also J. Ernest, et al, 1976, *Mathematics and Sex*.
11 See Rosemary Deem, 1978, *Women and Schooling*, pp 47-52; also Frazier & Sadker, 1973, *Sexism in School and Society*. Both books include references to other literature on the hidden curriculum.
12 Guttenag & Bray, 1976, describe an intervention programme carried out in the USA where a systematic attempt was made to alter sex-stereotyped understandings of the world. They found girls were more open to ideas at all ages studied and could change. Teenage boys' beliefs were often more entrenched and sexist, when exposed to non-sexist curriculum materials.
13 Some relatively good books are J. Thompson, 1978, *Studying Society*, 1978; *It's a matter of People*, both Hutchinson, London; A. Jones, A. Marsh & A.G. Watts, 1974, *Male and Female: Choosing Your Role in Society*, CRAC.
14 I am also critical of J. Nobbs, 1976, *Modern Society: Social Studies for CSE*, Allen & Unwin, London. For the Longman series, please see the textbook bibliography.
15 See W.J. Hanson, 1973, *Courtship*, Longman, pp 12-13. He finally questions what is natural in a cross-cultural perspective on differences but this is at the end of the book and is somewhat half-hearted.
16 See E. Young, 1961, *A Course in World Geography 2*, Arnold; also *Spare Rib*, 70, 1978, Rogers, 'Development — A Man's World'; also *Women's Report*, Vol 2, Issue 6, 1974, 'Women in the Third World:

Tanzania'. The latter two articles deal with women in the Third World today.

17 See L. Gordon, *Towards a Radical Feminist History*, KNOW Inc, PO Box 86031, Pittsburgh, Pa 15221, USA; also Berenice Carroll, 1976, *Liberating Women's History*, University of Illinois Press; also M. Hartman & L. Banner, 1974.

18 Apart from the point about the rigidity of boys in their study, Guttenag & Bray, 1976, report that the enthusiasm of the teacher involved had much to do with the effectiveness of the programme.

REFERENCES: School Text Books

History
ARNOLD, D., 1966, *Britain, Europe and the World 1871-1971*, Arnold
CASE, S.L. and D.J. HALL, 1976, *A Social and Economic History of Britain 1700-1976*, Arnold
COOTES, R.J., 1968, *Britain since 1700*, Longman
DUFFY, M.N., 1967, *The 20th-Century Topic Books: The Emancipation of Women*, Blackwell
HARDMAN, J.K., 1975, *Britain: an economic and social history 1760-1975*. Book 2, 1870-1975, Collins
HARDMAN, 1978, *Britain in the Modern World*, Book 2, 1918-76, Collins
HILL, C.P., 1977, *British Economic and Social History 1700-1975*, Arnold
HOBLEY, L.F., 1977, *Since 1945*, Evans
HOARE, R., 1973, *World War One*, Macdonald
JONES, R.B., 1971, *Economic and Social History of England 1770-1970*, Longman
MONTI, L.A., 1976, *Britain 1945-70*, Bell
ROBSON, W., 1973, *20th-Century Britain*, Oxford University Press
WILSON, D., 1971, *Peoples, Revolutions and Nations, A.D. 700-1970*, Evans

Social Studies
BADLEY, F.S. and J. MCLOUGHLIN, 1973, *Social Studies: a study of government and law and society*, Hulton
DICKINSON, S., 1976, Leisure Series 2, Longman Social Science Studies
GROOMBRIDGE, J., 1971, *Connexions: His and Hers*, Penguin
HAMBLING, C. and P. MATTHEWS, 1974, *Human Society*, Macmillan
HANSON, W.J., 1977, *Aggression and Control*, Longman
HANSON, W.J., 1973, *Courtship*, Longman

HANSON, W.J., 1976, *Drugs: A Factual Report*, Longman
HANSON, W.J., 1977, *Learning*, Longman
HURD, G. (ed), 1973, *Human Society, an Introduction to Sociology*, Routledge & Kegan Paul
JONES, A., et al, 1974, *Male and Female: Choosing Your Role in Society*, CRAC, Hobsons
NOBBS, J., 1976, *Modern Society: Social Studies for CSE*, Allen & Unwin
O'DONNELL, A., 1975, *Education and Society*, Series 2, Longman
O'DONNELL, G., 1975, *The Human Web: an Introduction to O-level Sociology*, Murray
ROSHIER, R., 1976, *Crime and Punishment*, Series 2, Longman
SELFE, P.L., 1975, *Sociology: an introductory course*, Nelson
THOMPSON, J.L., 1978, *It's a matter of people*, Hutchinson
THOMPSON, J.L., 1978, *Studying Society*, Hutchinson
WHITTACKER, D., 1975, *Social Services*, Series 2, Longman
WILKINS, E.J., 1970, *An Introduction to Sociology*, Macdonald & Evans

Geography
BEALT, A., 1977, *Western Europe: A Systematic Geography*, Pitman
BURNETT, T.B., 1973, *General Geography in Diagrams*, Longman
CLARE, R., 1974, *The Third World*, Macdonald Colour Units
CLARE, R., 1977, *Earthquakes, Volcanoes and Mountains*, Macdonald Colour Units
CRISP, T., *People and Places*: 2, 1974, *Towns*; 3, 1975, *Fuel and Power* 4, 1975, *Transport*; 5, 1975, *Industry*; 6, 1975, *Different Worlds*, Nelson
GRAVES, N.J. and J.T. WHITE, 1976, *Geography of the British Isles*, Heinemann
LOWRY, J.H., 1960, *A Course in World Geography*: 4, *The British Isles Physical and Regional*, Arnold
MACLEAN, K., and N. THOMSON (eds), 1977, *Problems of our Planet*, Bartholomew/Holmes McDougall
MARCHINGTON, T., 1974, *Conserving the Earth's Resources*, Macd Macdonald Colour Units
MOREY, D., 1975, *Background to Geography*, University Tutorial
POXON, E.M. and J.D., 1975, Visual Geographies: 6 *North America*, Pergamon
RANDLE, T.W., 1975, *Geographical Studies in Western Europe*, Oliver & Boyd
STEPHENSON, K.B., 1977, *Geography of the British Isles*, Blandford
YOUNG, E., 1961, *A Course in World Geography*: 2 *People round the world*, Arnold

Physics and Chemistry
ABBOTT, A.F., 1973, *Ordinary Level Physics*, Heinemann
ALKINSON, A., 1964, *Certificate Chemistry,* Longman
DAVIES, L., et al, 1973, *Investigating Chemistry*, Heinemann
HASSALL, K.A. and C.H. DOBINSON, 1966, *Essential Chemistry*, Iliffe
LITTLER, W., 1931, *Elementary Chemistry*, Bell
MEE, A.J. et al, 1971, *Science for the 70s*, Book 2, Heinemann
NELKEN, M., 1975, *CSE Physics*, Hart-Davis
SPIERS, A. and D. STEBBENS, 1973, *Chemistry by Concept*, Heinemann

Mathematics
MARSHALL, G., 1970, *World of Mathematics*, Nelson
SMITH, H., 1967, *Common Core Mathematics*, Book 2, Hulton

Anne Lee

'Together we learn to read and write':
Sexism and Literacy

'The ink is black, the page is white,
Together we learn to read and write . . .'
sing a group of children in the music corner. Mandy and Sonny are
building a railway. Darren and Sita are playing in the sand. Fiona,
Jasuinder and Moses are playing in the dressing-up corner. Other groups
of children are painting and drawing, weighing, measuring and
shopping, chatting to each other as they learn, sharing and extending
their ideas and experiences. I'm working with a group of children who
are producing a comic for the class to take home to their family and
friends. At the moment I'm completely lost by the discussion the group
is having, since they are writing one of the stories in the Italian dialect
that their local community speaks. So I look up, and watch the classroom scene for a few moments.

It appears that this kind of classroom, with its hive of activity, tends
to encourage happy, fluent literates.[1] Literacy teaching, or rather
literacy learning, usually flourishes best when the written word is incor-
porated as naturally and meaningfully into the child's environment as
the spoken word has been. Given the numbers of children to be found
in a conventional primary classroom, and the range of linguistic and
cultural experiences that they bring to school, it is difficult in the usual
'teacher/whole class' interactional context for the teacher to find the
time and space to present appropriate learning situations for each
individual child at the 'right' time.[2] The easiest way, therefore, of

providing 'natural and meaningful situations' in which children can apply their 'intentions' of mastering their environment to the process of becoming literate is to utilise the children's own resources. They can frame and test hypotheses about written and semiotic codes in contexts structured to encourage interaction between pupils and which incorporate literacy as an integral part of the whole learning environment.

So, suppose a class of children has the opportunity to participate in a literacy/learning environment, where talking, listening, writing and reading are not separated from the rest of the activities that are going on, where they are encouraged to frame and test hypotheses with each other as well as with the teacher, can we then suppose that they are all being given the same message about literacy skills? 'Together we learn to read and write', sing the children, but are they learning the same things?

We could examine this question from a variety of viewpoints: the possibility of differential treatment being given to children on the basis of culture, class or attractiveness (or a combination of these factors), for instance. Or we could look at the possibility of different expectations about schooling being brought into the classroom by children and their parents, and the effect this has on the learning that takes place in the classroom. I want, however, to pay particular attention to one factor that shapes the expectations, and behaviour, of children, parents and teachers — that of sex.[3] All children are individuals, acquiring different information at different rates, since they are subject to a wide variety of influences. Even so, can we extract some common strands that appear when we look at girls learning to read which are different from those that emerge when we examine boys' early reading?

The Evidence So Far

There is a growing body of evidence that suggests quite marked discrepancies between male and female young readers (St John, 1932; Asher and Gottman, 1973). Blom (1971) notes that of elementary school children referred for remedial reading instruction, between sixty and ninety per cent were male. (There are some questions to be asked here about referral, remedial reading and the position of males in the predominantly female elementary environment). Dykstra and Tinney (1969) note female superiority in reading readiness. Maccoby and Jacklin (1974) maintain that in few other areas can female superiority be established as strongly as it can in reading ability.

The reason for this discrepancy in reading performance between the sexes was, for a long time, put down to maturational factors. However, over the past few years increasing attention has been paid to the effect of motivation on reading performance and it now seems likely that sex differences in reading performance are influenced, in part at least, by the attitudes both children and adults bring to reading. Boys tend to view reading as an activity that is more appropriate for girls (Kagen, 1964; Stein and Smithells, 1969). Neale, Gill and Tismer (1970) have demonstrated that boys tend to have more negative attitudes towards reading than girls do. Where do these attitudes originate, and how does the school confirm them?

Early Influences

The home environment which the children have experienced before they come to school determines, to a large extent, the attitudes they will have about reading, writing, talking and listening during the first few months of school life, although these may be modified later. Belotti (1975, 68) illustrates vividly the kinds of sex-stereotyping that can occur in the child's early life:

> . . . . the parents have fixed in their minds a very precise model to which the children must conform according to sex . . . the whole process of upbringing seems to revolve on this differentiation . . . we intervene if a girl laughs coarsely, but it seems all right for a boy to do so . . . a girl is not expected to shout or talk in a loud voice, but in a boy, it seems natural.

To her extensive account of early sex-stereotyping practices, Belotti could have added initial reading experiences. I have met many girls who come to school able 'to read anything, including the newspaper' according to their parents, usually the mother (and there are many more questions to be asked about parental expectation, schooling and sex, and the effect this has on the performance of children than we have space to look at here), but I have not yet met a boy who is supposed to be able to do this. There seems to be an expectation that girls will go to books more naturally than boys when the children are young. Often girls have little else to do, since they are frequently discouraged from competing in the rough and tumble physical games that encourage boys to move outside the service, domesticity and repetition that are presented to the child in the mother's life-style. They are encouraged, instead, to move to the vicarious experiences presented in print, often through the 'mothering' role they play with younger children which takes the form, on many occasions, of working on early literacy activities such as drawing, painting, tracing, story-telling and so on. Girls' games also have less status than those of boys. It is far less likely that a boy would be asked to stop playing a game to go and set the table than a girl, for instance, and so, as Belotti notes, girls grow up with the idea that their games are somehow less important than those of boys. How does the school respond to this early sex-stereotyping practice?

Early Schooling

'Little girls' come to school with notions that part of their life-style includes performing tasks for others in the dometic arena and also with the knowledge that their games have less status than those of boys. (Sutton-Smith and Rosenberg (1961) note that boys will give up games once they become popular with girls.) When children come to school for the first time they meet a situation that usually resembles their home in some ways. Primary schools are predominantly female environments where a great deal of attention is given to making the surroundings similar to the home, maybe to soften the effect of the enforced confinement of its young inhabitants in this strange place. Carpets, curtains and attractive displays are to be seen. Children are cared for mainly by women. There are even au-pairs (that is, classroom helpers) in some schools who help teachers to carry out those less interesting or dirty jobs that interfere with the smooth running of the classroom. Given the similarity between the home environment and early school experience, it is hardly surprising that the children's play reflects the early sex-stereotyping that has taken place in the home, despite the fact it is now located in a different setting.

However, the early sex-stereotyping learned at home does not only continue in the life of the classroom, but also in the whole organis- ation and structure of the school. Young children meet few men in their early school days, but those they do meet are usually in positions of power and control, such as the head or deputy, or having interesting jobs that take place outside the immediate domestic environment of the classroom. They see praise being given to the (usually male) football team, and hear the telling-off (tinged with excitement) given to the naughtiest boy in the school, and they begin to adopt the 'male as norm' value that school, in its formal and informal, visible and invisible structures and hierarchies presents from the very first day. We can see, therefore, that although the teacher might be trying to present the same opportunities to each child, the message being given by the school is that to receive recognition, and to have a certain amount of control over your own life, you usually have to be male (and white and middle- class). It is hardly surprising, therefore, that girls tend to opt out of the more active and noticeable areas of school life and turn to reading and writing as channels for their energy and creativity.

Yet these two factors — the continuation in school of the sex- stereotyped experience of the home, and the 'male as norm' value offered by the school — do not seem to me to be sufficient to account

124

for the *extent* of the differences between the sexes in reading performance. In order to understand this issue more fully we must look more closely at the organisation of the classroom, and at the teacher's response to the attitudes and behaviour of girls and boys.

Classroom Organisation

At nursery school very young children are usually encouraged to use any apparatus but by the time the child reaches the infant classroom, activities considered appropriate for girls, and those considered suitable for boys, have begun to emerge. Almost unconsciously the teacher reinforces the pattern — Lego for boys, tracing for girls; the playhouse for 'domestic play' (and the reinforcement of sex-stereotyped behaviours), exploring an old radio for the boys. Since girls have been encouraged to respond to authority more easily, they usually accept the teacher's control more readily and are frequently given tasks of a somewhat more repetitive, and quieter nature (such as word/picture jigsaws, phonic games, rhyme cards). These frequently act as very useful pre-reading activities, as opposed to the more lively, varied activities often found for boys who tend to get bored more easily, and who begin to assert their independence against the female authorities (mother and teacher) who have been placed over them. As well as proving themselves to be worthy of entering the adult, male world by participating in rougher games etc., the boys are also likely to reject any activities that seem to be popular with the girls. (See Sutton-Smith and Rosenberg, 1961).

How do teachers respond when boys participate less willingly in learning to read because they perceive it as a girls' activity? From my own experience and observations it seems that teachers work harder on trying to provide examples and experiences that will hold the boys' attention. They might even give the same piece of information twice, first for all the children, and then again especially for the boys. I was once talking about words that began with the letter 'b'. The girls were quite content to listen to the examples that I was giving, but to get the attention of the boys I had to provide a more lively example — in this case, Brainy Batman — to which the girls listened again, and so they were getting the same information twice. When I started to keep track of how often this was happening I found that it was far more frequent than I had supposed. It seems that girls listen far more willingly to teacher information than boys do. This means that they pick up much useful experience in contextual cluing, phonic skills, and anticipatory skills that they can apply to the printed page. It seems possible that girls gain far more information that is useful for reading than boys do. We can see from the organisation of activities in the classroom, and the teachers' response to differing behaviours of girls and boys, how the likelihood of girls performing better in reading is made more concrete.

They're not getting the same message
Boys and girls might learn to read and write together, but it is clear that they pick up very different messages about reading. Girls seem likely to bring more suitable experience to the printed page than boys do in three particular areas:

a   they have had more pre-reading activities
b   they have absorbed more information from the teacher that will help them with reading
c   they have a strong sense of the appropriateness of reading as an activity for them.

We're not offering the same opportunities to the boys – they are missing out! Gross (1978) presents evidence that kibbutz girls and boys show no differences in reading level performances, reading readiness level, or in the perception of reading as an appropriate activity for them to participate in, and this suggests that we must look closely at the way in which sexism influences reading performance. We must evaluate our whole approach to the learning of reading – its organisation within the school and classroom, the pre-reading activities given to the children, the messages conveyed about the appropriateness of reading as an activity for all the children; and I have not even touched on the *content* of the printed page.

What can be done to give boys a fairer chance to succeed at reading and to encourage girls to break out of the narrow confines that encourage them to read about life instead of actually living it? It is not enough to provide new literature that we think goes beyond the stereotypes that exist in society, not only about sex roles, but also about race and class. We must encourage children to be critically conscious of the images they do meet, as well as trying to provide alternatives. We must also look beyond the printed page, at the organisation of the classroom and school and the effect this has on the reading performances of girls and boys. From there we need to look beyond the school environment, at the relationships between men and women in society as a whole, and its effect on the children's perceptions of the reading process. In looking at these areas we will begin to sow the seeds of greater awareness that will eventually allow *all* children not only to have a greater opportunity to succeed at reading but also to have more control over their own lives.

Reading and self-constructs
If this analysis of the causes of sex differences in reading performances

is accurate — even if incomplete — it raises important questions about teaching in general and reading in particular. Margaret Spencer (1976; 15) has commented on the crucial role played by self-perception (or self-constructs) in learning and has suggested that the way students view themselves in a learning situation is extremely important. She asks whether the students see themselves as competent, whether they think their efforts will meet with success, and suggests that any decisions they reach will influence the way they set about performing the task.

We are beginning to become aware of the operation of self-constructs and to realise they are significant in any discussion of sexism and education. When certain skills or activities are designated as the preserve of one sex, then the other sex may feel tentative about approaching them, and this could well influence students and contribute to their performance in school. It could be one explanation both for the under-achievement of girls in maths and science and for boys in reading.

It has been substantiated that girls do better at reading (in the early years) and boys do better at science (in the later years) but it would be a mistake to assume that this is necessarily inherent in being female or male. We need to look no further than the way students are treated differently in the classroom (depending on their sex) to find some of the reasons for these differences. We need to change some of the class-room practices and some of the social attitudes at the root of this differential treatment. While we continue to decree that some human skills are appropriate for girls and others are appropriate for boys, while we continue to divide the world along arbitrary gender lines, we are circumscribing the development of both sexes. We are discouraging both sexes from full and free participation in learning and this can no longer be justified.

Notes

1 By the term 'literates' I mean readers, writers, listeners and talkers who can not only *understand* the vast amount of visual and aural information being pumped out in our highly technological society, but who can also *critically process* the messages they are being given.
2 Boydell (1974) has analysed teacher/pupil interaction in classrooms where teachers were highly committed to individualised learning and teacher/pupil contact, and has noted how little time each teacher was able to spend with each child where both were actively engaged on a learning task.
3 This is not to deny the obvious importance of race and class in shaping the opportunities being given to the child and in influencing her perception of them.

Dale Spender

Gender and Marketable Skills:
Who underachieves at maths and science?

History tells me
That it is not so long since *languages*
Were considered very important.
Anyone who wanted to get on in the world
Needed languages as an entry qualification
For this was how you sorted those who were capable
From those who were not.

Girls, it seems,
Were not.
They were 'naturally'
Not very good at languages
When languages were required
For leaders.

Today
It is maths and the sciences
Which are considered very important
For those who want to get on in a technological world.
Maths and sciences are the entry qualifications
Which sort those who are capable
From those who are not.

Girls, it seems
Are not.
They are 'naturally'
Not very good at maths and science
While these are required
Of leaders.

Of course,
I could resign myself to accept
That girls are inferior
If it were not for one inconsistency.
Today when languages are not needed,
When they are not used to sort those who are capable
From those who are not,
Girls have come to be 'naturally' good at languages.

Have they progressed so far
In such a short time,
I ask myself?
Are they but one century
Behind?
In the twenty-first century,
Will they become
Very good at maths and science?

Possibly.
As long as maths and science
Are not required
As entry qualifications!

It is not that girls have changed so much
In the last 100 years,
It is that the entry qualifications
Have changed.

Tomorrow,
If weaving and cake making
Are considered very important
And those who want to get on in the world
Need them as an entry qualification
Because they sort those who are capable
From those who are not.
Girls, it seems
Will not.
They will be 'naturally'
Not very good at weaving and cake making
When they are required
For leaders.

It's a very convenient arrangement.
It's very clever of those who control the entry qualifications
To be able to control nature as well.

For we can chase our own tails
And spend years
Testing girls for their inadequacies
We will not find them,
For we are looking in the wrong place.
The underachievement lies not in the girls,
But in those who do not wish to accept them,
As equals.

Stevi Jackson

Girls and Sexual Knowledge

Learning about sex in our society is a complex and often difficult process, learning to come to terms with one's own sexuality even more so. It involves not only the acquisition of abstract knowledge, but also requires that we make sense of that knowledge in terms of personal sensations, emotions and relationships. This process of sexual learning may be problematic for either sex but for girls specific problems arise from the ways in which sexual knowledge is organised, so that they experience difficulties not only in managing moral taboos but in gaining access to relevant information.

I am taking it as self-evident that knowledge is socially constructed, that is, it has been created by human beings who have a particular world view which is the product of specific social organisations and historical conditions. What counts as sexual knowledge is not 'a body of objective facts' which pertain to sex, but a set of beliefs which reflect the priorities and the morality of the dominant ideology in the society in which this knowledge is constructed.

It is usual for distinctions to be made between girls and boys regarding what sexual information is appropriate, when, how and from whom it should be acquired, and in what context it should be applied. Furthermore, sexual knowledge is currently organised so that it places a high value on reproductive and masculine perspectives, and reflects the subordinate role of women in contemporary society. It has been argued that '. . . those in a position of power will attempt to define what is taken as knowledge, how accessible to different groups any knowledge is, and what are the accepted relationships between different knowledge areas and between those who have access to them and make them available' (Young, 1975; 32).

When it comes to sexual knowledge it is possible to see some of the assumptions made about it within the dominant ideology and, although it would be naive to see this as a 'conspiracy' of those in power, these assumptions (which are, of course, generally accepted by both sexes) not only reflect the inequality of the sexes, but also help to maintain it.

In this paper I am concerned with the ways in which the social organisation of knowledge influences the sexual learning of girls. It is their *access* to such knowledge which is of interest: when do they gain this sexual knowledge? What sources does it come from? What is learned? What is omitted? What role does school sex education play in this process? My argument is illustrated where possible by comments from adolescent girls on their experience of sexual learning. This article makes use of research conducted in East Kent between 1973 and 1974. I conducted twenty-four tape-recorded interviews with girls aged thirteen to seventeen (weighted towards the older girls) from which the quotes are taken. The first twelve interviews were with girls from a small town youth club. These girls were predominantly working-class, from the town itself, or from nearby villages. The remaining girls in the sample were contacted through two grammar schools and were mostly middle-class, again from small towns or villages.

For Adults Only: The Denial of Sexual Knowledge to Children
One of the most conspicuous features of the organisation of sexual knowledge in our society is that it is denied to children. It is considered inappropriate for them and often even dangerous to them. Sexuality is treated as a special area of life and children as a special category of people, both to be kept separate as far as possible. Children are thus assumed to need 'protecting' from this aspect of adult social reality (so that their presumed 'innocence' is equated with sexual ignorance) and thus they are prevented from learning about sexuality until they are deemed old enough to receive such knowledge. In part this is a consequence of the privatisation of sexual life. In many more 'primitive' societies, and in our own in the past, privacy was neither possible nor desirable and children became aware of sexuality through observing, listening to and interacting with others. But it is not merely the existence of private bedrooms and reasonably soundproof walls that keeps

sex hidden from children, for the withholding of information is quite deliberate.

The anxiety of adults to keep sexual knowledge from children usually means that children receive little or no sexually relevant information but the adult attitude itself implicitly teaches something of the moral meanings of sexuality and the social taboos which surround it. Children are likely to be aware that something is being concealed from them and negative or evasive responses to certain aspects of their behaviour or questioning will tell them that a moral label is being applied. Children are thus: '. . . provided with responses that are a function of adult sexual scripts without providing the scripts' (Gagnon and Simon, 1974, 34). It is probable that, in keeping with adult ideals of femininity, girls are subjected to sexual taboos to a greater extent than boys. Girls are also expected to act in accordance with specifically feminine conventions of modesty long before they are aware of the sexual implications of such behaviour. None of the girls I talked to recalled receiving any directly sexual information from their parents much before puberty, but many remembered being told not to engage in behaviour considered immodest such as sitting cross-legged, sitting with legs apart, doing handstands and wearing only underwear around the house.

Children are allowed only glimpses of adult sexual reality, insufficient to understand the meanings attributed to it. Only as the child becomes an adolescent is she recognised as a potential sexual actor for whom some sexual knowledge may be appropriate. But adolescence is a peculiarly artificial and intermediate stage between childhood and adulthood and the individual's status is ambiguous. The young girl is assumed to require sexual knowledge in preparation for the future but is not considered mature enough to engage in sexual activity. The traditional 'protective' attitude towards girls increases the uneasiness adults feel about approaching sexual maturity and this may result in the continued withholding of information.

Gaining Access: The Acquisition of Sexual Knowledge
The transition from childhood to adolescence is marked by the move from primary to secondary school. All but two of the girls I interviewed learned the 'facts of life' at about this time, many of them citing the change of school as significant. The child's arrival at secondary school brings her into a milieu where sexual information is more widely available and is freely exchanged among friends. Michael Schofield (1965) estimated that sixty-two per cent of boys and forty-four per cent of girls learned about conception from school friends. Most of the girls I

talked with mentioned their peers as an important source of this new knowledge. However, even such a simple fact as the link between sex and reproduction may have to be pieced together from a variety of sources and many indicated that this was the case:

> Some you learn from school, and some you hear from your mates — you're never taught really (fifteen-year-old).

> One of my sisters-in-law told me, and my mum and at school, and in books (seventeen-year-old).

> It was a mixture, you know, from school and friends and the lady I babysit for (fifteen-year-old).

Many also indicated that they had been confused at first, taking some time to 'sort it out'. Parents had contributed to this learning in varying degrees. Often they were resorted to for confirmation of what had been gleaned elsewhere. Although a few parents were informative and supportive, most communicated negative responses, ranging from embarrassment to moral injunctions:

> My Mum used to get embarrassed, my Dad didn't say anything. My Mum used to tell me some things (but) I learned really before she told me (seventeen-year-old).

> Don't do this, and don't do that and get a bad name — that was drummed into me (sixteen-year-old).

> My mother thinks it's dirty — she used to drum it into me from a young age that it was dirty. She said it wasn't very nice, you know, out of marriage . . . I was told never to let a boy touch me (fourteen-year-old).

For most girls, parents continued to be enforcers of taboo rather than sources of information.

The beginnings of conscious sexual learning seem to be fraught with confusion and ambiguity. Because learning does not occur gradually throughout childhood it can come as a shock to many and this, when associated with earlier taboos and the sense of learning something clandestine, may lead to an initially negative reaction:

> I thought it was 'orrible — but you've got to know, haven't you? (thirteen-year-old).

> I thought it was dirty 'cos she (mother) told me it was (fourteen-year-old).

> I thought it was disgusting when I first found out (seventeen-year-old).

I was revolted by the idea (sixteen-year-old).

I was shocked really -- but then fascinated as well (seventeen-year-old).

There may, however, be a more fundamental reason for this attitude. One girl put it like this:

I was a bit confused, I couldn't quite fathom it. It seemed a bit, well, peculiar – a dreadful thing to do. It was always something talked about after marriage – there was never any doubt about that. You get married, then you have sex, then you have a baby and that was how it was done (sixteen-year-old).

Learning about sex in the context of reproduction may itself be related to an initially negative response. It is likely to make children think of it as rather odd and perhaps distasteful, as a necessary mechanical or surgical procedure for those who want to produce a baby. It often also leads to misunderstanding: it is not unusual to find young adolescents who believe that people only do 'it' once each time they wish to conceive. Whatever the source of their knowledge, and whether they learned of it as 'natural' or 'dirty', all the girls I spoke to had discovered the existence of sexual relations in a reproductive context, it was 'where babies come from'. It was only later that they learned of the possibility of sex being pleasurable, a way of relating to another person. The female peer group on the whole seemed to function to lessen negative attitudes, although some degree of ambivalence remained. There are, however, more lasting consequences of the reproductive focus of sexual knowledge.

Boundaries to Knowledge

To learn about sex as reproduction is to equate sex with coition, and there is little doubt that, as far as most of the girls I interviewed were concerned, this was what sex meant. Most of them saw sexual knowledge as finite, consisting of an awareness of the link between sex and reproduction. Many felt that they would like to know more about contraception in order to break this link, and some admitted confusion about the emotional and moral aspects of sexuality, but they did not think that there was anything else to know. The usual response to questions as to whether they thought they knew enough, can be summed up by one girl's answer: 'I know enough not to fall pregnant'. On the subject of their own sexual response girls had acquired very little information, with their ignorance of female sexual organs and orgasm being almost total. Given the focus on intercourse and reproduction in the knowledge available to adolescents, boys cannot help but identify the penis as their chief sexual organ. Most girls, however, did not even know of the existence of the clitoris. The lack of awareness of the clitoris is due to a combination of anatomical and social factors. The penis is a more visible organ and hence boys cannot help but be aware of its presence. Girls, on the other hand, would need to investigate their genitals more thoroughly to discover the existence of the clitoris, and such behaviour is so heavily tabooed that few girls seem to do so.

The usual pattern was to learn of sexual intercourse as the basis of reproduction, to discover that this act is considered pleasurable and to see it as the 'real thing' – after all, even adult sex manuals tend to dismiss all else as 'foreplay'. It is hardly surprising that most girls thought that the vagina was the chief source of female erotic pleasure and had been led to expect the maximum pleasure from intercourse alone. (This was as true for those who admitted sexual 'experience' as those who did not.) On the whole they expected sex, as intercourse, to be pleasurable and unproblematic, as simply 'doing what comes naturally'. Only two girls knew of the existence of the clitoris and of its function. The first had been involved in a relationship with an older man who had explained (and presumably demonstrated) the function of the clitoris. The other was interested in feminism, read *Spare Rib* (Britain's monthly women's liberation magazine) and had found out from there. Both of them had, therefore, gained access to this information through sources not generally available to, or not utilised by, the average teenage girl. The lack of availability of such knowledge is further illustrated by the case of another girl who had heard of the clitoris and knew that it was 'the part of the body' that turns you on but who did not know what or where it was. She had gone to some trouble to find out more, consulting a teacher and a dictionary, but with no success. The rest of the girls, with the exception of one who did not directly respond to my questions, did not know that such knowledge existed and were therefore unaware that they had been deprived of it. More surprising, perhaps, was the girls' ignorance on the subject of the female orgasm. Almost all were confused about the existence of a female orgasm. Most had heard the word, or some colloquial equivalent, but only as applied to men. Some had direct experience of male orgasm but still had no idea that equivalent sensations were possible for women. Again, this seems to be a consequence of learning of sex as reproduction, of which male orgasm is a part, so that orgasm and ejaculation were thought of as synonymous. A similar pattern emerged regarding masturbation: more girls were aware that this was possible for women, though none admitted trying it. The majority, however, thought it was an exclusively male activity and were surprised and in some cases horrified that I should ask them about it. It is not easy for girls to identify and remedy this gap in their knowledge. If they succeed in doing so it is likely to be later in their lives. Such information is certainly extremely unlikely to be forthcoming through school sex education.

The Contribution of School Sex Education

The main contribution of the school to sexual learning derives from informal interaction between the pupils because sex education is more usually about sex, and not sexuality. Formal sex education had not, for most girls, played a significant part in teaching them about sexuality. Most of those I talked to were critical of the sex education they had received. On the whole it told them too little, too late, was technical and unrelated to their feelings or was handled without sensitivity:

> We had a film showing you how you get pregnant and how a baby's born – that was all (thirteen-year-old).

> Only films where you see, you know, sort of a picture of a matchstick man here and a matchstick woman there (fifteen-year-old).

> We haven't had any apart from straight biology. I think they should start with a lot of the emotional sex as well as the straight physical (sixteen-year-old).

> It was a bit off-putting. We had films and this sort of thing, you know . . . I think somebody who didn't know about things like this, as some people I know didn't, this was – you'd get a bit of a shock I think (sixteen-year-old).

> I think it was wrong to stop it when they did stop it. We had it in the third year – we had films and all sorts of things about it. And I think the teachers were a bit embarrassed to go on into the upper school. I knew most of it, because it was in the third year which would make us, what, thirteen. So I knew already (sixteen-year-old).

These comments were echoed throughout the interviews with most girls expressing dissatisfaction with the sex education they were given, many dismissing the subject with such comments as 'not very helpful' and 'boring'. The majority had been offered little more than an outline of reproductive biology and found this inadequate on two grounds. Firstly, it told them little that they did not already know and, secondly, it was unrelated to their own feelings and experiences. I found only two girls who wholeheartedly approved of their school sex education and for both of these one or other of these criticisms did not hold.

The first girl had received no sexual information from any other source before this time and she attended a small secondary modern school that ran a fairly comprehensive sex education programme. She had this to say about it:

> The school told you about that [sex] and about different contraceptives and things like this. It was very good — just sort of about growing up in general, you know, changes in life, and we had films about VD and childbirth and cleanliness (seventeen-year-old).

This school appeared to offer more information than most and this girl was the only one in my sample who had received information on contraception. For her, learning as she did at the age of thirteen was soon enough, but most girls felt that sex education should be given earlier. Most had received it in the third and fourth forms (ages thirteen to fourteen) which, given the limited scope of its content, proved to be of little or no value to them. They felt, on the whole, that sex education should begin in primary school (when they were nine and ten years old) or in the first year of secondary school, to pre-empt the rather tortuous learning process most of them had undergone.

The second positive experience of sex education apparently derived from one teacher's willingness to go beyond biological facts:

> It was really good . . . we had a teacher that would talk about sex, would talk about literally anything with us and it was always mixed. And it made you understand what boys felt about sex — we learned about each other really.

Although this occurred in the fourth form (by which time this girl had known the basic 'facts of life' for some years), she nevertheless found it interesting and useful. Many others would, it seems, have welcomed this type of open discussion since complaints that sex education was not related to emotions and relationships were frequent. None of the other girls had received any help from either parents or teachers which would aid them in linking fact with feeling and they felt that, in this context, friends and older sisters were more useful. Another unsatisfactory feature of school sex education emerging from these interviews was its extremely erratic nature, with girls attending the same school reporting very different experiences. The girl quoted above who reported free discussion of sexual matters had just left secondary modern school where two fifth form girls (ages fifteen to sixteen) had only been offered films diagramatically explaining the mechanics of reproduction. The headmaster of a grammar school told me that he left the subject to the discretion of individual teachers (which he recognised was not the best solution) and the girls here had also had varied experiences, with some of the older girls having been given no sex education at all. Whatever the school, the subject of sexuality seems to have been generally passed over quickly in a biology lesson or through one or two films.

A survey of sex education based on headteachers' responses to questionnaires reveals a similar picture of inconsistency. Most head-teachers revealed that they left responsibility for the subject with individual teachers, usually in the biology or religious education depart-ments. The alternative was to call in 'experts' such as doctors or public health officials (Harris, 1974).

Yet, despite its shortcomings, the girls I interviewed were unanimous in considering sex education in schools to be 'a good thing'. Where they justified this view it was with reference to the lack of coherent infor-mation from elsewhere, especially from parents:

> I think it's a good idea really, because I think some parents, they're a bit embarrassed to tell their children (sixteen-year-old).

> I think it's very stupid if there isn't sex education in schools. I think it's essential because some parents just can't talk to their children and they're not going to tell them, and if they're not told in schools then they'll find out, you know, through trial and error (sixteen-year-old).

It is possible that, in suggesting sex education should begin before they found out about conception in the customary peer group way, these girls are implying they would have liked to learn in the context of the school. This accords with Schofield's findings. Of his sample only twelve per cent of the boys and eighteen per cent of the girls learned about conception from teachers, but when interviewed as young adults sixty-three per cent of the men and fifty per cent of the women said they would have preferred to learn from this source (Schofield, 1965; 1973). Educators themselves would seem to agree that some form of sex education is a necessity, albeit a regrettable one. The family is usually cited as the appropriate place for sexual learning but since so many parents abdicate responsibility, educational authorities consider it incumbent upon them to step into the breach. There is, however, no clear policy on the subject. Government reports have mentioned it, local authorities have issued guidelines, but neither give a clear indic-ation of what the purposes or content of sex education should be. Most official documents refer in rather vague terms to educating young people for marriage and parenthood or making them aware of the feel-ings of the opposite sex along with such moralistic statements as 'Sexual intercourse should never be seen as a transient pleasure but as a joyful consummation of close friendship, love and understanding which in marriage have time to grow and deepen' (Inner London Education Authority guidelines, quoted in Harris, 1974; 70). It is clear from this, and similar statements, that educators see sex education as preparing adolescents for a married heterosexual future, rather than helping them to come to terms with their own sexuality in the present. Its aim would seem to be to dissuade young people from expressing their sexuality, which is in keeping with the middle-class ethic of deferred gratification.

American sex education in the 1950s has been described as being '. . . focused on the necessary and unfortunate aspects of sexuality, treating it as a dangerous force requiring careful control. The concept of sex education classes was that the teacher was imparting safety precautions such as those used in handling highly explosive materials' (Gagnon and Simon, 1974; 113).

These attitudes are reported as being a feature of the past, but there is little evidence of their being eroded in Britain. An indication of the persistence of this emphasis on the dangers of sexual activity is given by the responses of 500 headteachers who completed questionnaires on sex education. Eighty-five per cent of secondary school heads claimed that their pupils were given information on VD, but only ten per cent of schools gave information on contraception and the majority thought that this should not be included in sex education (Harris, 1974). This would seem to indicate a distinct focus on the 'unfortunate aspects of sexuality', with the threat of disease being used to warn against engaging in sexual activity. Sex education is often seen as a way of preventing illegitimacy, but given the lack of contraceptive advice it seems that the means of achieving this is simply to preach abstinence. It is unlikely, given this concept of sex education, that girls will be taught anything about their own sexual response. Means of deriving pleasure are taboo subjects for it is feared that such discussion might 'encourage' young people to be 'promiscuous'. But if one of the reasons for giving sex education is to reduce the risk of unwanted pregnancies it might be useful to inform girls that, since nature has endowed them with separate reproductive and sexual organs, they have a 'natural' means of contraception at their disposal. Suggesting that coition may not be the sole or primary means of gaining sexual pleasure might discourage girls from rushing into unprotected intercourse.

But few schools are prepared to take such an approach. In part this stems from moral attitudes to women, the family and sexuality and the social organisation of knowledge of which these are a part. In addition, the organisation of knowledge as a whole within schools makes the teaching of any but the most restricted form of sex education problematic. The result is school sex education which denies vital knowledge to girls and perpetuates sexist assumptions regarding female and male sexuality. The school maintains the position of being blind to the sexuality of its pupils.

The Context and Content of School Sex Education:
Sources of Sexist Bias

Restrictions on the form and content of school sex education derive in part from the difficulties of incorporating sex education into the curriculum and dealing with it in terms of conventional definitions of educational knowledge. Teaching typically involves the presentation of knowledge to children in the form of academic 'subjects', as a series of 'facts' external to both teachers and pupils. School knowledge is, moreover, differentiated from everyday knowledge: ' . . . one use to which the school puts knowledge is to establish that subjects represent the way in which the world is normally known in an "expert" as opposed to a "commonsense" mode of knowing' (Keddie, 1975; 156).

This conception of school knowledge creates difficulties when the subject to be taught is sex education. Sexuality is part of the present and future everyday lives of the pupils, but discussing it within the formal educational context makes it difficult to link facts and experience. To create such a link teachers would need to abandon many of the conventions of educational knowledge and thus give greater credence to pupils' definitions of what is important and work through, rather than against, subjective experience. It would also undermine the teachers' status as purveyors of 'expert' knowledge, since in the realm of personal relationships they are no more likely to possess expertise than any other member of the adult community. Nor will the quality of rapport necessary for such open discussion easily be established if, as is likely, it is discouraged at other times. This problem is further complicated by certain of our everyday notions about sexuality, in particular ideas about sexual privacy, the innocence of children and of sex as a powerful drive. The general reluctance to talk openly about sexual matters is compounded by the nature of adult/child and teacher/pupil relationships. The debarring of children from sexual discourse creates problems in initiating them into it, especially within the authority structure of the school where both teachers and pupils are vulnerable to sanction. The sexuality of the teacher must be masked and there are numerous instances of teacher dismissal for infringement of this rule. The formation of heterosexual relationships between teacher and student are sufficient to bring the weight of authority down upon any teacher who engages in such activity, but in the case of homosexuality, recognition — or even suspicion of their sexuality — can have disastrous consequences for the teacher. With knowledge organised on the premise that the young must be protected from sexuality, that they must be kept innocent (or ignorant, for it really amounts to the same thing in this instance) the school would be one of the most difficult places for homosexuals to come out. Add to this the popular belief that sex is a powerful urge that needs to be controlled, and the fear that adolescents might go 'too far', and it is not surprising that teachers play safe. Sex education does not, in practice, involve a restructuring of school knowledge. The façade is maintained and sex education is reduced to imparting 'facts' within a de-eroticised instructional repertoire (Gagnon and Simon, 1974; 112).

Further limitations on the scope of sex education arise from the ways in which it is located within the school curriculum. Two alternatives exist: either it can be taught within a pre-existing school subject (such as biology, religious education or physical education), or it can be set apart as a special event outside the normal school routine. If the first option is taken, the likelihood of the content being circumscribed by the boundaries of the subject within which it is taught will be increased. If sex education is subsumed under biology (the most frequent choice), it will be limited to the anatomy and physiology of sexual differentiation, conception and birth. If relegated to the relative backwaters of religious education, physical education or social studies, it is likely to be dealt with in terms of morality, health or family structure. Nowhere is it likely to be related to the *experience* of the pupils. The 'special event' tactic may avoid the limits imposed by subject boundaries, but is apt to create its own difficulties. The very fact that it is taught *outside* the routine curriculum emphasises the slightly risqué nature of the enterprise. It is likely to precipitate much speculation among the pupils and to be regarded as a source of forthcoming entertainment, having been defined for them in advance as something unusual and rather clandestine. This is heightened by the common ritual of sending letters to parents requesting their permission to subject their children to sex education, a practice resulting from the school authorities' anxiety regarding the presentation of sexual knowledge where it cannot be justified as a necessary aspect of 'subject' knowledge.

The same fear of causing offence is likely to ensure that the occasion does not live up to the pupils' expectations and that the information they receive will be very limited. The most conservative of sexual attitudes are usually taken into consideration in deciding on the form that sex education is to take. It often means, yet again, that it is reduced to the common denominator of reproductive biology, perhaps accompanied by some moralising on the virtues of marriage and the risk of disease to those who indulge outside the legalised union.

In effect, wherever sex education is taught, it is assumed to be synonymous with reproductive biology. Much greater emphasis is placed on the functioning of internal processes — the meeting of egg and sperm and the implantation and development of the fertilised egg — than on what is subjectively experienced during the act of coition. The processes of fertilisation, foetal development and birth have their own fascination, but are probably of less immediate interest to adolescents than coming to terms with their own sexuality:

> ... few of the problems young people have with managing their own sexuality ... derive directly from a lack of knowledge of the biological processes involved. The fact that whole societies have survived in ignorance of the technical biological facts ... suggests a different order of priorities in defining the content of sex education (Gagnon and Simon, 1974; 112).

This reproductive bias tends to perpetuate the idea that men are inherently more sexual than women. Even the internal processes are defined in terms of male activity and female passivity: 'The most common imagery is that of the noble sperm heroically swimming up-stream to fulfil its destiny by meeting and fertilising the egg' (Gagnon and Simon, 1974; 112). The egg, of course, can never be heroic: it just waits for the sperm to arrive. The language used to describe such processes often conveys the same idea. Babies, it seems, often just 'come out' of their mother's body, with no mention of the strength and activity of the latter. Coition is usually described as 'penetration' or the 'insertion' of the penis into the vagina. Thus the female body is consistently portrayed as the passive receptacle for the male organ and growing baby.

Female sexual organs and orgasms are excluded from this form of sex education since they are not necessary for reproduction. The clitoris rarely receives a mention and is usually absent from diagrams of 'sexual' organs since what are really illustrated are reproductive organs. One typical textbook for teachers, *A Textbook of Sex Education* by Julia Dawkins, suggests that pubescent girls need to know the correct terms for such organs as the vagina, the uterus and the ovaries; the *author*, however, presumably does not need to know the correct anatomical features for the clitoris is not even mentioned. When it comes to older children Dawkins follows the ostensibly liberal line on masturbation saying that masturbation should always be discussed with boys and this is justified by reference to the avoidance of 'guilt' over a 'natural' process. But masturbation is far less common in girls and need not be discussed. Girls are however entitled to be told that it will do them no harm but only if they ask (Dawkins, 1967; 71). This is a common pattern in more liberal forms of sex education. Male masturbation, since it can be explained in terms of biological imperatives (supposedly the result of a build-up of excess sperm), is thought worthy of mention; female masturbation is not. Male orgasm, too, is usually covered since it is necessary for conception, while the female orgasm is not. Thus the female sexual organ, female orgasm and masturbation are all defined as irrelevant. This approach, stressing masculine activity and reproduction, is not only sexist but heterosexist, because it perpetuates the assumption that lesbian/homosexual relationships are in some way unnatural. Lesbianism/homosexuality is, not surprisingly, rarely discussed and, if it is, is likely to be dismissed as a sickness or as a passing phase of sexual development. This will not help any young people experiencing feelings of attraction to their own sex, nor will it make them any less negative in their attitude towards lesbian and homosexual members of society. The attitudes of the girls I interviewed were, as far as lesbianism is concerned, rather negative. They varied from a liberal acceptance of it to outright revulsion and hostility:

I think it's quite normal for the people themselves — I can't see anything wrong with it (sixteen-year-old).

If a girl wants to be like that she's entitled to be — I don't think anything against it (seventeen-year-old).

It revolts me — but I think it's wrong to condemn someone if they're a lesbian (sixteen-year-old).

I suppose it's because, you know, they go to a school where there's no boys and that their parents haven't let them go out with boys and they're just too frightened to talk to them I suppose (fifteen-year-old).

It's horrible — I wouldn't like to know anybody like that — it's not normal (seventeen-year-old).

It makes me shiver — ugh! (seventeen-year-old).

If sex were learned of as a pleasurable activity, as a way of relating to people rather than as a way of reproducing, lesbianism as well as female sexuality in general could be viewed more positively. If girls were aware of the nature of their own sexual response lesbianism might seem less 'unnatural'. It is interesting that the first two comments quoted above came from the two girls in my sample who were among the most knowledgeable about female sexuality.

Even if sex education is confined to the 'facts' it tends to be sexist in the way such facts are selected and presented and in the assumptions as to what constitutes sexual knowledge. Attempts to go beyond this, to discuss feelings and relationships, may often compound rather than resolve the problem. If teachers seek guidance on how to approach such topics they may well turn to books intended for this purpose, but most of those offering help to teachers overemphasise the differences between the sexes and incorporate many unfounded sexist assumptions.

For example, one such 'expert' stresses the need for boys to understand female sexuality in the following terms: 'It is not always easy for a man . . . to understand her (often unconscious) desire for pregnancy as a result of intercourse when to him the physical relief of tension is the more important aspect'(Schill, 1971; 59).

Another, arguing for beginning sex education before puberty, says: '. . . it is especially important for boys to know the further implications of the woman's role in sex and how it is linked with homemaking and motherhood and her whole emotional life before their own sex drive becomes too persistent' (Lernhoff, 1971; 20).

The latter author recommends a book for adolescents written by Kenneth Barnes and entitled *He and She*. It has the following words of wisdom to offer: '. . . until she is married and deeply roused by all that marriage means, the desire for sexual intercourse is not very strong in a girl' (Barnes, 1958; 115).

It would be possible to provide an almost endless string of similar quotes pontificating on the differences between the sexes and stressing the greater urgency of male sexual desire. If teachers rely on such literature, or if girls themselves refer to it, the misconceptions drawn from the focus on reproductive biology are likely to be strengthened. If it is accepted by both sexes that boys have a greater sexual appetite than girls then a climate is created in which many unfortunate, violent and barbaric acts can occur. If, as is often the case, both in books and in school sex education, sexual feelings are discussed primarily in relation to marriage, the problem will be further compounded by inhibiting any discussion of alternative means of sexual expression. Sex education will thus remain firmly related to the traditional feminine role. It will also help to preclude the possibility of women (and men) discovering their own sexuality.

Part Five: The Classroom

Dale Spender

Talking in Class

Women don't talk as much as men in mixed company and girls don't talk as much as boys in mixed classrooms. These facts, which have been provided by numerous research findings, appear to conflict with a stereotyped image of the female as an excessive talker (Kramer et al, 1978). However, like many other stereotypes, it can be demonstrated that not only does the stereotype bear little resemblance to empirical reality, but it also serves a particular purpose. Before analysing the reasons for female non-participation in verbal activities in the classroom it can be quite enlightening to take a closer look at the 'chattering female' stereotype to see the way it has been constructed and used.

Behind the constantly reiterated assertion that females are the talkative sex an implicit comparison is being made against some standard or norm. It has been generally accepted that females talk more than males but it is only necessary to tape a conversation at a social gathering, a trade union meeting or in a classroom to find that it is males who do the talking. The yardstick against which women's talk is, in fact, measured is that of SILENCE. 'Silence gives the proper grace to women', wrote Sophocles in *Ajax* and his sentiments are still echoed in today's image of the desirable woman. When silence is considered the appropriate behaviour for women then, quite conveniently in a sexist society, almost any talk a woman engages in can be considered too much!

Although we have evidence that men talk more than women we have not found it difficult to continue to believe the myth that women talk too much. This is because we have accepted the deeply entrenched sexist premise that women have few, if any, rights to speak in a patriarchal society. Cora Kaplan (1976) has claimed that there is a taboo against the voice of women in patriarchal society and has some convincing evidence to substantiate her claim. Women do not have the 'authority' to speak and when they do speak, they do so without 'authority'. The stereotype of the female as 'inferior' is subtly woven into sociolinguistic practices and this is clearly illustrated by Joan Roberts:

> The extraordinary idea that women are the talkative sex is a peculiarity of masculist logic . . . If women are in fact more verbally proficient, their continued exclusion from public speech, either spoken or written, seems a flagrant misuse of superior talent. To get out of this illogicality, women's talk is seen as gossip, men's as discourse. When women first publicly broke their angry silence, the shock was not only that they spoke but that they had anything to say. That 'silly chatterboxes' could not only think but also write . . . in a logical manner was a funny joke, an absurdity, barely tolerable and hardly acceptable . . . In historical reality, the female sex is best characterised *not* by talk but by silence born of subjugation (Roberts, 1976; 38).

These are the lessons which students learn before they enter educational establishments. Both sexes bring to the classroom the understanding that it is males who should 'have the floor' and females who should be dutiful and attentive listeners. It would indeed be surprising if these practices were not continued within education, but the ways in which educational institutions actually utilise these understandings, and capitalise on them to reinforce and maximise this double standard, are quite pernicious. Female silence is exploited by educational institutions and contributes to the over-representation of males and the under-representation of females in those who achieve educational success.

Girls do not get the initial message that they shouldn't talk from the school (they get it first at home) but the school certainly reinforces it. Within educational institutions girls are quickly made aware that their talk is evaluated differently from the boys. Girls who take verbal initiative in the classroom, who are verbally 'ostentatious', are likely to find themselves severely reprimanded for being 'loud', 'aggressive' or 'bossy'. Boys who engage in comparable activities are likely to be commended for their verbal facility and praised for demonstrating qualities of leadership. The message delivered in educational institutions is loud and clear; it simply doesn't do for girls to talk like boys. Girls must be more refined, more discreet in their verbal behaviour if they want approval from either the teacher, or the boys, in the classroom.

When Angele Parker (1973) did her research on interaction in the classroom, she not only discovered that the boys talked more but also that both sexes regarded talking in class, particularly in the form of questioning or challenging, as specifically masculine behaviour, and no doubt the same would apply to most teachers as to students. It was perfectly proper that boys should conduct arguments, air their views and query information, but it was not at all proper for girls to do the same thing. The girls, of course, are well aware that there are penalties placed on their talk, particularly if it is serious and marks them as actively intelligent. Not talking in class is a logical form of behaviour. It is also one which is encouraged by the material they are required to talk about.

John Elliot (1974) was disturbed by the lack of female verbal participation in his classroom. He was teaching a topic entitled 'War' and noticed that the girls had very little to say. He tried to remedy this by using his authority as a teacher to provide the girls with the opportunity to talk, but found that there were two (at least) unfortunate effects. If the girls did make a contribution it was quickly ridiculed and put down by the boys. This was 'their' topic, they were the ones who spoke with authority; what could a girl know about war? But Elliot found something else as well. He found that the girls were threatened by being required to talk to boys. Elliot came to the conclusion that he was forcing the girl students to play an 'unfeminine' role when he insisted that they take part in classroom discussion with boys.

> Sometimes I feel like saying that I disagree, that there are other ways of looking at it, but where would that get me? My teacher thinks I'm showing off, and the boys jeer. But if I pretend I don't understand, it's very different. The teacher is sympathetic and the boys are helpful. They really respond if they can show *you* how it is done, but there's nothing but 'aggro' if you give any signs of showing *them* how it is done (Kathy, aged sixteen, Inner London comprehensive).

Matina Horner (1974; 44) has done extensive research on the way in which girls avoid success. Our society, says Horner, has a stereotype of the sexes and a stereotype of intelligence and, in the case of females, the two aren't compatible. We have 'a general inability to reconcile competence, ambition, intellectual accomplishment and success with femininity'. We persist with the image of the female as passive, pliant and polite and we punish any departures from this image. Female students know the way our world works and deliberately set their sights on underachievement because there is less friction that way.

150

According to Horner this is a source of some conflict, particularly at adolescence. Girls are actually faced with the task of deciding whether to opt for reduced achievement, and gain popularity (with, of course, the accompanying reduction in educational attainment, in employment prospects and in financial independence) or whether to opt for maximised achievement and disapproval (and the threat within the prevailing ideology of a lonely and unattractive existence). This is a conflict which is not experienced by male students for whom there is no incompatibility between achievement and popularity. It will not have escaped the attention of either girls or boys that men who do well in the world's terms have little difficulty in finding a partner, whereas women who do well in the same terms are frequently portrayed as partnerless. This single existence is considered uninviting and its origin is frequently attributed to 'female aggression'.

One factor, however, which has never been researched is the possible role that such conflict, in itself, can play in the inhibition of learning. We are all aware that students under pressure, or locked in conflict, cannot function at their best, yet we continue to place these pressures on adolescent girls who are doubly burdened when it comes to educational achievement. Firstly there is the burden which goes with intentionally reducing their performance (and over which they may possess some control) and secondly there is the burden of conflict generated by having to make such a choice (and over which they may have very little control). The girl sitting quietly in class may be nursing valid resentment and frustration and such feelings are hardly advantageous to learning.

Silence can be Golden

However, many girls do perform well in school and there are some teachers who will state that girls are easier to teach because of their docility and diligence. Within the educational system there are often rewards for those who are quiet, conscientious, unquestioning. It has been established that in some educational test situations, girls do better than boys (the outdated eleven-plus, for example). When Katherine Clarricoates (1978; 362) undertook her research in primary schools she found that teacher preference was for 'rigidly conforming girls in order to "facilitate classroom management" ' but she also found that teachers *liked* teaching boys.

> On the whole you can generally say that the boys are far more capable of learning, much nicer to teach.

> Boys are interested in everything and are prepared to take things seriously while girls tend to be more superficial about subjects: they

151

ask the 'right' questions simply because it is expected of them . . .

Although girls tend to be good at most things in the end you find it's the boy who's going to be your most brilliant pupil.

The teachers just quoted were not using the evidence to hand when they made such judgements for they also readily acknowledged that the girls at this age did better in class than the boys. Although the girls indicated their competence and their superiority, teachers were able to dismiss this and classify it as not genuine ability. When boys ask the right questions, it shows that they are bright; when girls ask them it shows they know what is expected of them. These teachers did not perceive these girls as 'positively intelligent', states Clarricoates, their many virtues — which included better behaviour, better conduct, cleaner and neater work — could all be discounted and seen as of little value. This is nothing short of the 'wholesale theft of true intellectual development in favour of boys', declares Clarricoates (p 358), for even where it is patently obvious that the girls are doing extremely well it can be rationalised as 'not counting'.

When classroom management is the over-riding concern of teachers — and there are many who contend that control is the major educational objective in the classroom (Levy, 1974) — the passivity of girls can be seen as a desirable feature. Again, however, it can work against girls for if they are not interested in the curriculum materials they are presented with, they can choose not to participate and their non-participation can take many forms, few of which are disruptive. They rarely seek to impose their dissatisfaction on the whole class but will elect to withdraw in a variety of unostentatious ways. Girls may not want to talk about war, as John Elliot found out, but at least they are less likely to create chaos if required to endure it. However, when 'girls' topics' are introduced to boys, many teachers are in no position to control the outcome (Clarricoates, 1978). Boys could challenge why they had to do such things, and in the process could bring about the cessation of the lesson. Hence the book lists which are geared primarily to boys, the history texts which are directed towards boys' interests, the English topics which range from motorbikes to violence to football. One of the consequences of girls not talking in class is that their interests do not need to be accommodated. This not only applies in schools but continues into higher education where girls can persist in their passive verbal behaviour which permits the operation of further penalties. Joan Roberts (1976) makes reference to the training in 'selective stupidity' provided for girls which leads not only to a reduction of their horizons but also to pronounced feelings of low self-esteem. Girls may begin by 'choosing' to be stupid but may also come to believe in their own stupidity and to accept that they are not worthy of mention in the curriculum. When girls do not receive the same attention as their male peers, when they are not presented with materials that encompass them, their lack of confidence is confirmed. There is a constant implicit message that they 'do not count'. This can in turn reinforce a negative self-image, reduce their level of aspiration and lead to even further withdrawal.

Such a cycle needs to be broken. One of the first steps towards that goal is for females to start talking, for there is yet more evidence which suggests that restrictions on female talk can also be restrictions on female learning. Douglas Barnes (1976) points out repeatedly that learning is an active process and requires talk; new information is not absorbed by some osmotic process but must be 'talked into place'. When there are so many pressures on females not to talk, these could well be pressures which work to inhibit learning.

This raises the question of the desirability of mixed versus single-sex schools, a question to which there is no easy answer. In single-sex schools girls do not experience the same constraints upon talk. In an all-girls classroom, those who talk are girls. A range of verbal roles is available, not just the subordinate ones. This can even apply at university level, as Florence Howe found when she talked with female students at Goucher (a single-sex college). One woman stated that she had chosen a single-sex college specifically because she need not 'worry about what boys would think of her' in the daily life in the classroom (Howe, 1974; 72). In a single-sex environment it is possible for girls to pursue their interests without having to hide the results.

This is not true for all women, however. When I talked to women students who had been to single-sex schools they weren't always whole-heartedly enthusiastic about them:

> It really only postpones having to interact with males and I don't think you are automatically better equipped when you are eighteen. My single-sex school sheltered me and when I came here it was an awful shock. I still don't open my mouth in seminars. I'm still scared, easily put down by men. It seems to me that some of the women who went to mixed schools are much better at dealing with this. They have had practice. They have a lot more confidence than I have (Marian, aged twenty-one, university student).

Eileen Byrne has stated that we now need 'a major national debate specifically on co-education or single-sex education' because co-education, which was adopted 'in the hope that the presence of girls would add a slightly civilising element to the boys and that the presence of the boys would act as a spur and incentive to the girls' hasn't fulfilled its expectations (Byrne, 1978; 133). Byrne takes up the argument that in co-educational schools the girls will see that almost all the responsible jobs are held by men; to that we need to add that boys dominate in classroom interaction. While it does not seem that this is conducive to female learning and development it would be wise to be wary before simply advocating the 'return' to single sex education (see: 'The Education of Feminists: The Case for Single Sex-Schools'). It could be that modifications in the mixed classroom would be preferable to segregated education but these modifications would need to be extensive and would need to be accompanied by changes in society.

It is vitally important for women to start to talk but it is not necessary that we emulate the habits of men. Research has indicated that although men talk more, they exert more control over talk, and that they interrupt more (Zimmerman and West, 1975). Women listen more, are more supportive when they do talk (Hirschman, 1973, 1974) and have greater expertise in terms of sustaining conversations (Fishman, 1975). It is precisely these qualities which have been neither valued nor acknowledged. Rather than women learning to talk like men it would seem to be preferable if men were to learn to listen more and to be more supportive of the conversation of others. This could revolutionise our patterns of talk in society, and a vast range of oppressive images, of both men and women, will be undermined.

To be a silent woman is to be an accomplice in female subordination, to reinforce many of the constraints which keep women 'in their place'. The image of female silence as appropriate is maintained by the technique of castigating women and girls for talking and the one way that this image will be broken is for women and girls actually to begin to talk. Talk is a powerful tool. That is precisely why it has been denied to women in patriarchal society. To assert our right to talk is one way of asserting the equal validity of our experience.

Elizabeth Sarah

Teachers and Students in the Classroom:
An Examination of Classroom Interaction

When feminists turn their attention to the education system
and criticise schools for their sexist practices, there is an unspoken
assumption at work: we live in a *patriarchal* social order, educational
institutions are situated within a wider social structure. Marxist analyses
explore the role taken by the various social institutions in helping to
maintain a capitalist economic system and thereby the hierarchical
divisions and conflictual relations between the classes (Miliband, 1969,
1970; Pounlantzas, 1969). They are very useful when it comes to assess-
ing the relationship between a multitude of institutional arrangements
(for example, the family, schools, the legal system) and a patriarchal
social order. What *is* going on in schools, both materially, in terms of
educational provision for the two sexes, and ideologically, in terms of
the nature of the values which are disseminated? To what extent do
schools *function* to maintain sexual divisions and the domination of
women by men?[1]

To speak of the education system in terms of its *role* in helping to
reproduce patriarchal social order has important implications for the
behaviour of the teacher. What is the extent to which being a 'teacher'
necessarily involves being an 'agent' of the dominant social system? Is
the teacher in a position to teach anything other than what she/he is
supposed to teach? Apart from the constraints of the teacher's role, the
issue also arises that if the school, like all the other institutions of the
wider society, is involved in creating and sustaining sexual divisions,

155

how important is the individual teacher's contribution to this process? On the assumption that children learn about the society in which they live through their contact with a variety of social arrangements, to what extent can responsibility for their socialisation into sex roles be seen to lie with the teacher? On the one hand, the teacher is a crucial link in the socialisation process, working within an institution, the principal, avowed function of which is to 'educate' children. On the other hand, the teacher's message is far from unique and a child who never entered a classroom would hardly miss any crucial lessons regarding appropriate sex-role behaviour.

In my opinion, it is essential that when we take a narrow focus and examine what is going on in the classroom, we remember to place the latter within the context of the school as a whole and also of the wider society. Unless we see the teachers' role in perspective it is almost impossible to evaluate what they are doing. An uncritical reading of many of the studies of classroom interaction that have been undertaken, principally in the United States, might tempt us to accept the misleading conclusion that the teacher is responsible for *determining* the sex-differentiated behaviour of pupils: sex-appropriate educational outcomes being decided by teachers' classroom actions and by the ideas they put across.[2] While it is, of course, important to know what teachers are doing and saying in the classroom, it is also important to understand their behaviour. Is the average teacher primarily engaged in creating or in reinforcing a patriarchal social order? And what about the teachers who try deliberately to teach children that the sexes are equal? What are they doing?

Before I turn to an examination of classroom interaction, I should like to outline briefly the nature of the context in which the classroom is placed: *where* and *what* do children learn, both before entering the classroom (in a chronological sense) and outside the classroom (on the assumption that a social world does exist beyond the classroom door)?

In most maternity hospitals sex-typed comments on the behaviour and appearance of newborns are aired within a few moments of birth. The male baby who has an erection while being weighed is referred to jokingly as 'a dirty little man': the female baby born with curly hair is told she is pretty, and some hospitals keep pink and blue blankets for girls and boys. All these responses mark the beginning of a gender-learning process[3] which is critically important for the child (Oakley, 1972; 173).

As Oakley clearly demonstrates, the world outside the classroom is a very important training ground for the learning of sex-appropriate behaviour. Parents treat female and male children differently, and so does everybody else who comes into contact with them. What would you have to say to, or about, a baby if you didn't know its sex? (See Chetwynd and Hartnett, 1978; Spender, 1978.) By the time they are small children, sex differentiated treatment in terms of physical contact, verbal communication, dress and the toys they are given to play with, have succeeded in producing firm gender identities. Of course, as the 'little girl' and 'little boy' become increasingly acquainted with the outside world, via contact with other children, television and story books, what they have already learned about sex-appropriate behaviour is reinforced (Oakley, 1972; 173-88).

The second major institution, after the family, to play a major part in children's lives is school. What children learn in school is not confined to the curriculum which they are officially taught.[4] The school is a social world which bears a very close resemblance to society at large. While in the primary school most of the teachers are female — and the continuation of a mothering role is unmistakable — the schoolkeeper is male. The dinner ladies are of course female. In secondary schools sex differentiation within the staff hierarchy becomes more distinct. The majority of people in positions of authority are male and on the whole women teachers predominate in subjects such as English and home economics, while the men are in physics, chemistry and technical subjects (Griffiths, 1977; 32; Lobban, 1978; 54). As Jenny Shaw points out, girls are presented with a model in which women do not achieve positions of status (Shaw, 1977; 54; Lobban, 1978; 54). Curriculum materials are another crucial area so far as the learning of sex roles is concerned. Sexist fiction and sexist textbooks combine to reinforce sexual divisions (Lobban, 1978; 54-6; 1974; 1974-5; Fisher, 1974; Federbush, 1974; Trecker, 1974; Frazier and Sadker, 1973; 102-5, 114-23).

In spite of the Sex Discrimination Act (1975), the sex differentiated curriculum is by no means a thing of the past (see 'Teach Her a Lesson'). Girls and boys are still doing different things and even when they have the option to do subjects formerly associated with the opposite sex, they are often either actively encouraged to make traditional choices by their teachers and parents, or their own preferences are for subject areas traditionally associated with their sex (Griffiths, 1977; 30; O'Connor and Bethell, 1977). The situation is no different when it comes to choosing an 'appropriate' career (Sharpe, 1976; 160-1, 170-2; Griffiths, 1977; 32; O'Connor and Bethell, 1977). Even when sexual divisions between subjects are eliminated, gender identities and sex-role expectations, already well formed, influence the way in which pupils *interpret* what they are doing. Here are some comments, for example, from a 'Design and Housecraft' course

(Griffiths, 1977; 31 and 37-9; Wolpe, 1977, 8-9):

> Boy: It might come in handy to know how to cook, in case my wife gets ill.

> Girl: If my husband's out at work and the plug on the iron goes or something, then I'll need to know how to change it.

There are probably differences between mixed and single-sex schools with regard to the images of sex roles which are presented but these can only be a matter of degree. In girls' schools you will find more female teachers of science but, on the other hand, fewer science facilities than in mixed schools (Byrne, 1976). Girls are also more likely to be encouraged to do well academically, while in mixed schools it is harder for girls to view their futures in academic terms 'in the face of, and in the presence of boys' (Shaw, 1977b; 53). In girls' schools, being both clever and attractive is reasonably compatible; in mixed schools, girls find the combination far less viable (Shaw, 1975; 137).

It is not difficult to document the sex differentiated expectations held by teachers based on their assumptions about, and evaluations of, the two sexes. One only has to examine the nature of pupil/teacher interaction in the ordinary classroom (Frazier and Sadker, 1973, Joffe, 1974; Levy, 1974; Lobban, 1976; Sears and Feldman, 1974; Sharpe, 1976; Spaulding, 1963; Torrance, 1962; Wolpe, 1977). However, my present focus is *not* the way in which the teacher's values and assumptions concerning sex roles ensure that the two sexes receive sex differentiated knowledge (Spender, 1978) about the value, meaning and nature of their activity in the classroom (thereby reinforcing what the pupils have already learnt about being a 'girl' and being a 'boy'), but rather the *value system* itself which operates in the classroom. Sex differentiated knowledge in the classroom is not an ad hoc arrangement, dependent solely on the values of the teacher, rather it is the outcome of a number of different forces: the sex composition of the staff (hierarchy and subjects), the actual segregation of the sexes in various ways, the ethos of the school as a whole and, very importantly, the values and practical arrangements that are the features of society and which are *experienced* by both staff and pupils in their daily lives. In the classroom, all these forces come together in the interaction between the pupils (Shaw, 1977; 56-61) and between the teacher and the pupils, to create and sustain an ongoing value system[5] which is, in an important sense, *beyond* the control of individuals in the classroom, notably the teacher. The individual teacher's behaviour in the classroom may help to sustain and reinforce the status quo but the situation is not of the teacher's own making.

This point is important when we consider the teachers who have egalitarian values. If the individual teacher's values and behaviour are crucial for the development of sex differentiation in the classroom, then one might expect that the teacher who considers the two sexes are of equal value might be able to influence segregation patterns in the direction of decreased differentiation. If, on the other hand, the patriarchal value system is an established entity before the teacher arrives on the scene, then the influence of the teacher's values will be minimal.

I should like to start with my own experience as a student teacher. Taking a cue from the first year pupils' interest in the newly-released film 'Star Wars', I decided to do a project with them on Space Travel and Planetary Exploration, combining imaginary elements with references to actual events and issues. I began the project with an examination of 'Life in a Spaceship'. Next I introduced the notion of travelling through space and the dangers that might be encountered — with extracts from 'Out of the Silent Planet', a novel by C.S. Lewis. Realising that space*man* is an accepted synonym for astronaut and that it would not occur to the children that spacetravellers would be other than male, I changed the 'he' in the extracts to 'she' thereby introducing the notion of space*women*:

Boy 1   That's not right. You don't have women in space.
Me   Why not?
Boy 2   They're too busy looking after the family.
Me   Well, I've spoken to this woman astronaut on the phone and she's been on lots of missions. She's not married but her friend, who is, is also an astronaut — and when the children aren't at the nursery or in school, her husband looks after the family.
Boy 3   It's not right — women *must* be mothers.
Girl   There are women astronauts. I read about it.
Boy 4   It's stupid.

Clearly, I was not introducing the idea of spacewomen to young and open minds. The notion of the innocence of children is not well founded (Milner, 1975). Children begin to lose their 'innocence' the minute they emerge from the womb. I was not able to influence the boys' ideas because they weren't equipped to deal with the idea I had presented — where did it fit in with the knowledge they already had about the sexes? The boys' written responses reflected this fact. Not one boy mentioned women: the accounts were all about space*men*.[6] The girls, on the other hand, made use of the idea and wrote readily about space*women*. Obviously, writing about spacewomen was a matter of acknowledging their own worth and potential and the very lively pieces of writing I got from the girls — as full of technical details as those of the boys — was evidence of their active participation in the project. For example:

Mission to the Moon
I was on my way in my module to the moon. We were now getting close and I was getting ready to land. There was a bump and the module had landed. I looked out and saw a dusty ground with lots of craters. After looking round through the window I lowered the ladder and climbed down. It was very difficult to walk about in my thick, shiny suit. In my hand I carried a bag to take some samples back to earth. When I had filled the bag up I went back to the module and got some small stronger bags and a small machine like a stapler. I injected the machine into the ground and when the needle came up it brought some samples from underneath the ground with it. I then put the samples in the small plastic bags . . . (eleven-year-old).

When I introduced the notion of space*women*, I was able to influence the knowledge the girls were receiving about themselves, but not so with the boys, and the binary system[7] was sustained in the classroom as a result of this manifest divergence of interest. I'm sure that eventually, if the message were strong and persistent enough and came from several areas, even the boys would begin to have doubts in time. However, in my experience the big problem is that of behaviour. That girls and boys behave differently in class (both academic and non-academic behaviour)[8] is readily recognised; the behaviour of the teacher tends to be determined by this different behaviour of the students. The teacher with egalitarian values may enter the classroom with the *intention* of treating the sexes in the same way but it is the students themselves who make this difficult, or even impossible, because they have learned their different socially sanctioned roles and their classroom behaviour makes different demands upon the teacher. This problem is probably most acute for student teachers (who are generally more concerned with issues of control). I found that I spent a lot of my time focusing attention on the boys who were misbehaving and practically ignored all the girls who were getting on with their work.[9] When, after much coaxing, a boy wrote a few lines I often responded with praise or encouragement (my rationalisation — 'well, the girls didn't need encouragement'). A number of writers have pointed out that the result of constantly reprimanding boys for misbehaviour is, in effect, to reinforce their assertiveness (Levy, 1974; 144).

There is very little material available on the subject of the teacher's experiences of sex-differentiated behaviour in the classroom and the effect it has on what the teacher 'teaches'. However there is a very interesting article describing a teacher's experience working with a mixed ability group of fourth year girls and boys on a 'War and Society' project, which reveals the way in which 'students' own conceptions of their sexual/social identities . . . prevented them from contributing to and participating in the discussion as individuals with a personal point of view' (Elliot, 1974; 12). Elliot found the majority of girls would not become involved in the project and resisted very strongly being encouraged 'to participate on an equal basis to, and as actively as, the boys – particularly when the subject matter was viewed as the territorial preserve of the boys' (p15). At the same time, the small number of girls who did contribute to the discussions felt isolated, and, by protecting their 'rights' to talk, Elliot only succeeded in reinforcing their uneasiness about behaving in an 'unfeminine' manner (p15).

It is not surprising that very few teachers choose to ignore the 'separate social worlds for boys and girls' (Shaw, 1977; 56) which co-exist uneasily within the classroom. If they don't actively reinforce sexual divisions with messages that, indeed, the sexes *are* significantly different, at least they help to sustain a binary system by simply recognising that it exists and so they allow their experience of what girls and boys will and won't do to determine what they try to teach them. For example, when teachers justify reading a boys' book to the class on the grounds that 'the girls will read anything so I always choose something to interest the boys',[10] they are reinforcing sex differentiation as much as if they told the pupils directly that boys are 'naturally' forceful and aggressive while girls are 'naturally' gentle and passive. 'Can I have two strong lads to help me?' Teachers are extremely sensitive to the fact that boys won't have anything to do with things they consider 'sissy' (Griffiths, 1977; 33; Shaw, 1977; 57; Spender, 1978). However, when teachers choose boys' books as class readers they are not so much imposing their own values on the class as responding to the manifest behaviour of the pupils: the girls *will* read a book about boys, the boys *won't* read a book about girls. Obviously, the sex-differentiated behaviour of the pupils is a product of a system of sexist values but not necessarily those of the individual teacher in the classroom.

I have stressed the problems associated with attempting to undermine sexual divisions in the classroom but not because I believe that it is impossible for teachers to confront the patriarchal value system. The growing resources of teaching materials designed to combat sexist ideas and the work of an increasing number of feminist teachers (see 'Feminist Practices in the Classroom') is evidence that teachers are not simply passive agents of the system. However, teachers at work in their individual classrooooms are up against a lot, not least the risk of losing their job if 'standards' are not being maintained. The most that individual teachers can hope for is that the few pupils they come in contact with will come to regard sex roles as *man-made*, rather than biologically *given*. Of course to instil such an awareness would be a considerable achievement but it would not amount to combatting sexual divisions. For sexism in education to be effectively challenged the attack must be on all fronts. Sex differentiation is not the fault of the teacher, or the curriculum, or the composition of the staff hierarchy (and staff distribution) or the ethos of the school, or the home, or wider society: it arises as a result of the fusion of all these elements. If sexism in education is to be eliminated, the whole patriarchal social order and the ideology which legitimates it must be confronted.

Notes

1 'The use of sex as a basis for organisational and curricular decisions is irrational in educational terms, for children usually have no prior experience of the subjects to which they are assigned. It makes sense only in the wider perspective of schools as agencies maintaining and reproducing accepted social divisions.' (J. Shaw, 'Finishing School: Some Implications of Sex-Segregated Education', in *Sexual Divisions and Society: Process and Change*, D. Leonard Barker and Sheila Allen (eds).)

2 *And Jill Came Tumbling After: Sexism in American Education* — edited and introduced by Stacey et al — is an excellent collection of articles describing sexism in education (many of which refer to studies of classroom interaction). However, the articles fail to consider the problem of the *significance* of their findings — what are the teachers *doing* in the classroom and how important are their contributions to the socialisation process? The articles I am chiefly referring to are: Joffe, 'As the Twig is Bent', Levy, 'Do Schools Sell Girls Short?' and Sears and Feldman, 'Teacher Interactions with Boys and with Girls'.

3 Oakley distinguishes between 'sex' as a biological term and 'gender' as a psychological and cultural term referring to the social roles which distinguish the sexes.

4 The 'Hidden Curriculum' is the name given to the multitude of things which pupils learn in schools which are not deliberately taught as part of the official curriculum: 'because of the operation of the pervasive hidden curriculum-interaction patterns, a seductive reward system, unbalanced staffing and curricular materials — sex stereotypes introduced in the home are reinforced and refined in school' — (*Sexism in School and Society*, Frazier et al). Also *The Hidden*

Curriculum, Curriculum Development Centre, 1975.

5 A study of 'Age and Sex Differences in Children's Opinions Concerning Sex Differences', Stevenson Smith, *Journal of Genetic Psychology*, 1939, Vol 54, 17-25, reveals that children have very definite ideas concerning the characteristics which differentiate the two sexes, indicating that children are introduced to the patriarchal value system at a very young age. One hundred girls and 100 boys in each year of age between eight and fifteen years voted as to whether girls or boys possess a greater degree each of nineteen desirable and fourteen undesirable characteristics: 'The pooled opinion of both sexes and all ages is overwhelmingly that girls, rather than boys, are bright in school, cry when hurt, and cannot endure pain, are easily frightened, especially in the dark and by strangers, are kind to animals and small chldren, are not given to teasing or destructiveness, tire easily, move slowly and do not stick to a hard job, are truthful, honest, not likely to cheat and will do the right thing even when not watched. The boys in comparison to the girls show a complete reverse of this picture.'

6 The fact that the boys' accounts were about space*men* only may be due partly to the fact that children tend to be egocentric in their writing and to write directly about matters as they are affected by them, James Britton, *Language and Learning*.

7 Shaw refers to the 'binary system' in her article 'Sexual Divisions in the classroom', in Teaching Girls to be Women Conference, Essex, April, 1977, introduced by J. Barnet and J. Cown (unpublished). She argues that two separate social worlds exist in the classroom, one for girls and one for boys (p 56) and distancing techniques operate to separate and segregate girls from boys (p 59). Girls and boys actively reinforce sexual divisions as a result of their knowledge of sex roles (p 60).

8 In 'Do Schools Sell Girls Short' in *And Jill Came Tumbling After: Sexism in American Education*, Levy puts forward an interesting explanation for the 'acting out' behaviour of boys (143-4): 'For boys, school is a contradictory experience; as males they are supposed to be assertive and dominant, as pupils — obedient and docile; whereas for girls there is continuity; school reinforces the social expectations of passivity and conformity. There is no conflict between "feminine identity" and the school experience of being a "passive pupil".'

9 Griffiths points out in her article 'Sex Roles in the Secondary School' in Teaching Girls to be Women Conference (see above) that in her experience more notice is taken of boys who are louder, while the girls are often ignored because they are quiet (p 33).

10 A comparison of Elliot's findings with the typical experience of most teachers, concerning 'acceptable' class readers, suggests that girls are prepared to read boys' books because they like reading anyway — it is a 'passive' activity. However, girls resist intruding into traditionally male subject areas when participation involves *competing* with the boys verbally — 'talking' in class (as opposed to 'reading') being a mainly 'male' activity — (see 'Talking in Class'). Of course another point is that on the whole girls are not very interested in boys' subjects (although a few less passive girls may prefer to identify with male characters in books than female characters) and so while they don't mind reading a boys' book because reading requires little effort on their part, they are often basically too indifferent to want to become actively involved by talking about issues traditionally associated with boys (see 'Sexism and Literacy' for a discussion of the sex differentiation in reading ability: boys are expected to have more difficulties with reading and they do seem to have difficulty in perceiving reading as an appropriate activity for them to be engaged in).

Dale Spender

Disappearing Tricks

> MAN: 'Human being, *especially* an adult male human being', *Webster's Collegiate Dictionary*

Words are symbols. They stand for, or represent, an object. In the last decade there has been a debate about the symbol *man* (and its pronoun, *he*) for there is ambiguity about what these symbols represent. On the one hand, the prescriptive grammarians of the past not only ruled that *man* and *he* represented the male of the species; they also ruled that *man* and *he* represented the species as well, and therefore included women. Many people have taken the prescriptive grammarians at their word and accepted their ruling without always being familiar with their reasons. There are, however, individuals, many of them feminists, who have declared that this was a rather ridiculous rule partly because it has led to ambiguity and confusion, and partly because the reasons for the rule were blatantly sexist. While some may still be content to accept that the use of *man* and *he* which we have been taught is legitimate and inoffensive, and that its sexist overtones of rendering women invisible are nothing but a mere linguistic *accident*, there are others of us who regard this rule as most unacceptable and who wish to change it. There was nothing accidental about the way in which the rule was introduced and there is nothing accidental about the consequences which ensue. Because it was a rule which was intended to promote the primacy of *man* at the expense of *woman*, we are committed to its elimination and

165

to the introduction of more equitable linguistic forms which favour neither sex.

The rationalisation that *man embraces woman* is a relatively recent one in the history of our language. Using *man* and *he* to encompass *woman* is a practice that was unknown in the fifteenth century. In 1553 we have the record of a certain Mr Wilson who argued that it was more 'natural' to place the man before the woman (as, for example, in male and female, husband and wife, brother and sister) and as he was writing for an almost exclusively male population of educated people who were interested in the art of rhetoric, there were few women in a position to protest against the so-called 'natural order'. By 1646, however, the argument had taken a different turn. Not only was it by then considered natural that the male should take precedence, it was also, according to one Mr Poole, that the male gender was the *worthier* gender and therefore deserved priority. Claims for the superiority of man over woman increased and were strengthened when, in 1746, Mr Kirkby invented his *Eighty-Eight Grammatical Rules*; Rule Twenty-One stated that the male gender was more *comprehensive* than the female. This marks an interesting shift in the argument. The Oxford English Dictionary defines *comprehensive* as *including much*, so Mr Kirkby was claiming that the male gender included much more than the female. This is of course a personal opinion which Mr Kirkby and his colleagues were entitled to hold, but it is not a linguistic opinion and these are not grounds for making linguistic judgements and for formulating rules to be imposed on all users of the language. Again, however, it seems that there were few protests about Rule Twenty-One; certainly Mr Kirkby had no women colleagues who could have objected to the rule and pointed to the flaws in his reasoning. And so the grammatical rule that *man embraces woman,* because *man* is more important, came into being and has been imposed upon the speakers of the language.

Mr Kirkby's rule however, was not always taken up with enthusiasm. Many people were unaware of it (and could therefore be labelled as ignorant) and some ignored it. People persisted in using *man* to mean male and *woman* to mean female, and *they* to refer to a person whose sex was unknown (as for example in 'Anyone can say what *they* like' or 'Everyone has *their* rights'). But the male grammarians were upset by this flagrant disregard of their rules and began to insist on *correctness* – meaning conformity to their rules – as a necessary characteristic of 'an educated man'. Their efforts were successful; being correct became important and so that there could be no doubt about what was correct or incorrect in the case of *man* and *he*, an Act of Parliament was passed in 1850 in which *man* was legally made to stand for *woman* (Bodine,

1975). There were of course no women members of parliament who could have cast opposing votes.

There can be no mistake about the reasons for the introduction of this rule and the consequent Act of Parliament. They were to give prominence and primacy to the male sex, and to give linguistic substance to the sexist bias of influential men. There is little likelihood that this usage would have evolved of its own accord; it required considerable intervention on the part of grammarians to introduce it and to insist on its use.

The current moves, then, by feminists to take out what the male grammarians put in, cannot be referred to as 'tampering' with the language. We are not trying to change something which is pure and unadulterated. On the contrary, we are trying to remove an artificial linguistic rule which should never have been given credence and which has never been justified on linguistic grounds. However, although the efforts of the male grammarians were not justified, they were, nonetheless, successful. We have in the past accepted their rule but if we continue to operate it we will help to support a practice of making man visible at the expense of woman. We will also be influenced by this practice for it has been found that one of the results of using the term *man* has been that the image of the male sex becomes foremost in our thoughts; while *man* is the favoured linguistic term, it is the male sex which is the favoured image in our consciousness.

There is evidence that people think of the male when they use the term *man*. Alleen Pace Nilsen (1973) found that young children thought that *man* meant male in sentences such as 'man needs food'; Linda Harrison (1975) found that science students thought of male people when talking of the evolution of *man*; J.Schneider and Sally Hacker (1972) found that college students thought of males when confronted with titles such as *Political Man* and *Urban Man*. And both Linda Harrison and Wendy Martyna (1978) found that men used the term *man* much more frequently than women. When Wendy Martyna asked the people in her sample what they thought of when they used the word *man,* the men said they thought of themselves. Women, however, said that they used the term *man* because they had been taught that it was grammatically correct. In Martyna's sample, at least, the women, who ranged from kindergarten to college students, recognised that they were not encompassed in the term *man*; they could not think of themselves when they used the word. If *man* was truly an encompassing word, a generic term, then women, as well as men, should be able to see their own image within it. That men think of themselves and not of women when they use the term *man* is an hypothesis which can readily be put to the test. Muriel Schulz (1978) examined the writings of many leading sociologists (past and present) and found that although they may have used terms like 'men of ideas' and 'the nature of man', supposedly to include *all* members of the species, they in fact meant only males. Alma Graham also found that many men revealed that although they may claim vehemently that *man* includes *woman*, their usage indicates otherwise:

> In practice, the sexist assumption that man is a species of male becomes the fact. Erich Fromm certainly seemed to think so when he wrote that man's 'vital interests' were 'life, food, access to females etc.'. Loren Eisley implied it when he wrote of man that 'his back aches, he ruptures easily, his women have difficulties in childbirth. . .'. If these writers had been using *man* in the sense of the human species rather than male, they would have written that man's vital interests are life, food, and access to the opposite sex, and that man suffers backaches, ruptures easily, and has difficulties in giving birth (Graham, 1975; 62).

With examples like this it is difficult to maintain the argument that *man* includes *woman* as the grammarians of old absurdly (but conveniently) claimed. For these are not just examples of occasional slips, they are the logical outcome of the grammarians' law that the world is to be considered male unless proven otherwise. There are yet more illustrations of the way in which the word *man* is used by us to mean just *men*. We can say that *man makes wars*, that *man plays football*, and that *he is an aggressive animal* without suggesting that we are mistaken or that we are being funny, even though we realise that these statements apply to only half the population. When women are left out of the activities that are being described, it seems that there is something wrong. But what happens when men are left out? The human species does a great deal more than make wars and play football but there is a problem when we use the word *man* to refer to other, equally human, but not necessarily male activities. Can we say *man devotes about forty hours a week to housework* without sounding as though we have made a mistake? Can we say *man lives an isolated life when engaged in childrearing*, or that *man is usually hospitalised for birth in our society* without saying something that sounds absurd? *Are menopause and menstruation significant events in the life of man*? When we think about it, it becomes increasingly clear that in our language, *man* means male. It is an example of the way in which the world is male unless proved otherwise; and housework, childcare and menstruation and menopause are otherwise. They are not classified with men and we therefore cannot use *man*, which means men, to refer to them!

One may be saddened but not surprised at the statement 'man is the only primate that commits rape'. Although, as commonly understood, it can apply to only half the human population, it is nevertheless semantically acceptable. But 'man, being a mammal breastfeeds his young' is taken as a joke. (Miller and Swift, 1976; 25-6).

If we could say *man has been engaged in a constant search for the means to control his fertility*, we would have very different meanings embedded in our language; we would have a very different consciousness. We would be starting to make women with their problems and their pleasures visible and real.

While *woman* has been forced out of the language in many contexts, and the invisibility of women has been reinforced, our present society, which is predicated on the principle of male supremacy (and the accompanying male visibility) has not seen fit to protest because the issue has not been regarded as a problem. Women are socially devalued so it is not inconsistent to devalue them linguistically. Mainly as a reponse to feminist efforts, however, this issue is beginning to be seen as a problem and already there are changes underway. Many government agencies in America have tried to dismantle the mechanisms which maintain asymmetry between the sexes. When the evidence that *man* made *woman* invisible was put to certain government agencies, many were persuaded of its validity. The argument was enough to convince the United States Department of Labour to issue a revision of occupational titles in order to provide more equal employment opportunities. The old job titles were considered to be discriminatory towards women because they excluded women and suggested that their entry into such jobs was inappropriate.

Three thousand five hundred job titles were revised to eliminate reference to age and sex so that *policeman* became *police officer*, for example, and *salesman* became *sales agent*. Of course, the Manpower Administration had to begin with itself, changing its own title to that of The Employment and Training Administration and renaming its publication *Worklife*, recognising that the old name, *Manpower*, excluded the sizeable workforce of women:

> Since children learn about society from language it is an easy lesson for girls to learn that many situations described by male identified words do not include them. Implicit in the omission is the understanding that a large part of the world is inappropriate to them. (Berger & Kachuk, 1977; 3).

Of course, boys may learn the same things from language, but the words which exclude males are much less frequent, and of much lower status. Boys might not feel so offended by exclusion. Being left out of housework (*housewife*), or out of child care (*governess, au pair girl*), may not be as hard to take as being left out of politics (*congressman, chairman*), religion (*clergyman, priest*), work (*businessman, foreman, craftsman* and, of course, the verb *to man*) or society (*gentleman*).

The use of *man* to include *woman,* however, reveals not only sexist prejudice but also linguistic ignorance. It contradicts another grammatical rule, which is that English has *natural* gender. When a language has natural gender objects are supposed to be labelled on the basis of sex so that the world is divided into masculine, feminine and neuter according to its sexual attributes (or lack of them). English is *supposed* to have natural gender and this is *supposed* to make it superior to languages which have grammatical gender, such as French and German for example. Grammatical gender is not based on sex, but on arbitary decisions (which are considered to be confusing) so that in German, for example, a tree is masculine, a tomcat is feminine and a wife neuter. English did once have grammatical gender (Anglo-Saxon was similar to modern German in this respect) and it is often claimed that the move to natural gender was a big improvement. The reason given for this is that natural gender is so much less confusing; people are classified according to their sex. In English, sex and gender are supposed to correspond and are therefore called *natural*.

But in describing the language in this way, one significant factor has been overlooked. English is only natural and unproblematic *if one is male*. There is nothing natural about women being referred to as *man* and *he;* they are not being classified on the basis of sex, and they do constitute half the population. The claim for natural gender in English is a claim based purely on the male experience of language and while *they* may not feel that there is any confusion, women may not share their assessment. It is confusing for women; it can be even more confusing than is the case with languages that have grammatical gender. At least if one is learning French or German one does not expect a correlation between sex and gender and one can become accustomed to being a woman and referred to as male or neutral. But in English we are specifically taught that sex and gender do correspond linguistically, and that it is wrong to refer to a tomcat as she, a tree as he, or a wife as it. But it is all right to refer to women as *men* or *he*.

So, there is inconsistency in the claims of the grammarians. If English does have natural gender then it is wrong to refer to women as *he/man*. And if *man* does include *woman* then it is wrong to claim that English has natural gender. One could ask why the male grammarians have not noticed this inconsistency?

In my work with secondary school students in a London mixed comprehensive I decided to investigate whether they felt excluded when they were excluded from the language. I wanted to find out how they felt about the use of *man* and *he* to encompass *woman*, so I tried to overcome any difficulties by presenting the concepts in a simple and concrete way. I began with a discussion of magic and that favourite conjuring trick of making things disappear. We talked about whether or not it was possible to make people invisible and I held out the carefully baited hook that it probably was possible and that, in fact, it wasn't even unusual as we were all magicians, making people invisible every day. The bait was taken and I began to focus upon language. I had some pictures of men and women which had captions using the so-called generic *he* and *man*. Illustrations of males and females reading were subtitled with 'Each student needs individual attention if *he* is to master reading'. Pictures of the Football Association Cup Final were accompanied with statements such as 'Everyone wants to grow up to be a football hero'. Newspaper photographs which prominently displayed Ms Thatcher in her proverbial hat were followed by 'Politicians remove their hats in the presence of the Queen'. I do not think it would be biased on my part to state that the girls caught on to the idea more quickly than the boys. They took no more than three to four minutes to formulate the rule and the following is an extract from some of the comments made by one of the young women:

> Can't you see you just pretend. . . You pretend you're talking about everybody, but you don't, you're not. It's only men. . . Look at this, no, look D, Come one. He says 'Everybody', but he doesn't mean that, you don't think the means *me* do you? That *I* want to be a football hero? He doesn't, course not! *Men's* everybody. . . and that's the trick.

At this stage their involvement was in the 'game' and although they were able to use the rule (adequately summed up by this student as 'Men's everybody') there was no comment about the injustice of the rule in that it made only women disappear. The boys were very eager to play, we made a lot of magic and many women disappeared:

> Australians are beer-drinking surfies.
> All Americans play baseball.
> Teenagers have to become members of gangs if they want to be accepted.

These were some of the 'tricks' which were performed, but after having spent about twenty minutes making women disappear, I changed the focus. I reminded the students that only half the magic trick had been performed by making people invisible. There wouldn't be many magicians making a living if they could not complete the magic and bring people back again. I did not know what the students would do with this information. I envisaged that they would put women back into the picture in some way, but I neither predicted nor determined what that way should be. There was some discussion about bringing people back again and then C. began to alter some of the captions. She did so by simply applying the principle of reversal. Among some of her 'magic' was the following:

> Adolescents think only of marriage and make-up.
> Australians look good in bikinis.

She certainly made the female 'visible' by this process and was both pleased and amused by her efforts. Although I tried to indicate that she had made females visible at the expense of males, her only comment was 'About time' and with the other girls in the group she proceeded to give new captions to many of the pictures and to provide captions for those pictures which were without them and which included women and men.

It would be an understatement to say that the girls were thoroughly enjoying themselves. The boys, however, did not share their enthusiasm and passed from discomfort to hostility. They declared the whole thing 'stupid' and one of them withdrew from the group. I could only surmise that the feeling of exclusion which they experienced made them feel extremely uncomfortable and caused them to protest. Perhaps not being accustomed to 'not counting' and being made invisible, made it more difficult for them. My assumption about the reason for their behaviour was reinforced by an event described by Casey Miller and Kate Swift in which a group of males, who were being 'left out', also protested. Although the boys in my group had less sophisticated rationales for their behaviour, I suspect that their reaction might well have been the same.

> Men who work in fields where women have traditionally pre-dominated — as nurses, secretaries and primary school teachers for example — know exactly how. . . (the). . . proposed generic pronoun. . . (she). . . would affect them; they've tried it and they don't like it. Until a few years ago most publications, writers and speakers on the subject of primary and secondary education used *she* in referring to teachers. As the proportion of men in the profession increased, so did their annoyance with the generic use of feminine pronouns. By the mid 1960's, according to the journal of the National Education Association, some of the angry young men in teaching were complaining that references to the teacher as 'she'

were responsible in part for their poor image and consequently, in part, for their low salaries. One man, speaking on the floor of the National Education Association Representative Assembly, said 'The incorrect and improper use of the English language is a vestige of the nineteenth-century image of the teacher and conflicts sharply with the vital image we attempt to set forth today. The interests of neither the women nor of the men in our profession are served by grammatical usage which conjures up an anachronistic image of the nineteenth-century school marm.'

Here is the male as norm argument in a nutshell. Although the custom of referring to elementary and secondary school teachers as 'she' arose because most of them were women, it becomes grammatically 'incorrect and improper' as soon as men enter the field in more than token numbers . . . Women teachers are still in the majority but the speaker feels that it is neither incorrect not improper to exclude them linguistically (Miller and Swift, 1976: 33-4).

Irene Payne & Dale Spender

Feminist Practices in the Classroom

Throughout these articles we have argued that one manifestation of sexism in schools is the negative presentation of women in the curriculum. We must not make the mistake of thinking that these negative images comprise sexism and that all will be well when they are transformed, for sexism will persist, almost unchallenged, unless practices as well as images are changed. Being a feminist teacher in a classroom is not just a matter of introducing positive images of women whenever possible, nor of devoting a three week period in a year to a discussion of sexism in society . . . in any subject. It is a matter of constantly questioning the way teachers and students make sense of a patriarchal world. When there are such enormous prejudices about sex and gender in our society a fundamental task of education is to look at those prejudices and the selection of evidence that we make in the light of them. It can't be just for thirty minutes on Thursday afternoon, but every lesson, every day.

Some colleagues might be threatened by our 'political' stance but so might the kids. No genuine debate can take place within any classroom unless there is a climate of trust and openness and the teachers as well as the kids are included in this. As a feminist teacher in the classroom I (Irene) think one of the first conditions for the development of a continuous debate on sexism is that the kids have some sort of relationship with me which will survive some of the strains that can be placed on it when deeply entrenched beliefs are challenged. That's why I think it important to be honest with the kids I teach (and not hide behind the convenient mask that teachers are provided with, that often allows them to be non-human beings) and take 'risks' in terms of exposing my personal experience. After all, that is what they are being asked to do. Only if we as teachers offer our own experience and ideas will they be prepared to do the same. I don't pretend that the dialogue will be equal but we should aim to make it so, giving space for all kids to make their contribution.

One way I have found helpful in 'opening up the personal' was to write my own experiences of being a girl in my family. The kids all had copies of my 'story' and not only did it help them to see me, their teacher, as a person, it helped them to see that there are lots of common problems in families. My story served as a focus for a lot of talk and many mutual complaints. The disadvantage, of course, was that the boys were not at all comfortable and many of them expressed their feelings in an aggressively sexist way – and this is hardly a desirable outcome. But I do think it can be an *initial* reaction, and that it can change, and the fact that the boys did not like it was not a reason for not doing it. In order to face the issue of sexism boys may initially have to do quite a few things they don't like and this is a sensitive area and needs to be carefully handled.

What did emerge from my story (which was a source of support for the girls) was that the girls began to see themselves as a group, to assert their collective identity and from that position of strength they were able to take on what the boys were saying and to argue against it. In principle I am against the teacher having to insist that the girls and their opinions be taken seriously (there will be no one to take on this role for them outside the classroom) and so it was most satisfactory when there was no need for my intervention. By putting their own case in terms that could not be dismissed, they became a source of positive images of women in the classroom – for themselves as well as the boys – and from my point of view this is much more profitable than bringing in 'outside' material to convince both sexes that the partiarchal images of women are inaccurate and inadequate.

When sexism is a classroom issue the girls have a much greater opportunity to talk than they do on most issues that are the usual substance of classroom debate. Also they can talk with *authority* (another rare opportunity). If the girls see it as important and necessary to support one another this can be a vital classroom experience for them. Of course it wasn't entirely comfortable for me after I gave them my story for I was forced to argue, defend and modify my position with the kids. This seems to be an important way of breaking down the whole teacher/taught relationship. The issues of sexism evoke strong personal responses which students can be encouraged to articulate. I think the teacher needs to be prepared to say 'this is how I see things as a person' (and not as some expert, dehumanised, neutral creature) or else the process is in danger of turning into a feminist *lecture* and students are very good at switching off when it comes to lectures, whatever the subject.

The personal dimension is essential but the children also need to appreciate why it is we hold particular sets of ideas, why we 'explain' society the way we do. Both sexes need space for analysis where they can be detached and unthreatened, where they can talk about sexism without necessarily being implicated. If, for example, they can discover that they all learned roughly the same things about what a family is (or should be), what girls and boys are (or should be), then the emphasis can move to the way these values have been acquired.

The bulk of traditional material in the school curriculum is of little value for the type of work I want to undertake in the classroom except as a source of evidence for the nature and extent of sexism. I feel a constant pressure to find and introduce alternative sources. I would like a book on women's history, for example, to demonstrate the discrepancy between history as it has been selected and presented, and history as it might have been written; and a book which provided a cross cultural perspective in terms that the kids could understand. (Ann Oakley's *Sex, Gender and Society* (1972) can be useful for extracts but it is a bit too much to take on in complete form with some of the younger kids.) So, in the absence of such alternative material I have often asked the kids to make their own and have given them projects which send them into relatively unexplored and challenging territory. Here are some examples.

1 We produced a booklet on women's history (particularly the history of the East End of London, the working-class area where I teach). The role that women played in the two world wars and their past struggles were explored and a booklet was compiled. The questions soon extended beyond women. The whole question of how history comes to be written becomes just as crucial as the documentation of the positive images of women. There was considerable demand from other schools for the booklet and we had to reprint it.

2 I keep a bulletin board of 'history in the making' on which I try to make visible the contemporary struggles of women, like the Asian women's strike at the Grunwick factory, for example. This has helped to produce many discussions about selective processes in the media (why are women and other oppressed groups given so little coverage?). Similarly, there are many other areas where the

invisibility of women can become an issue which may initiate individual/group/class projects. How many women scientists are acknowledged? How many male/female authors are studied? How are women shown in the media? In all these areas how can we account for the lack of recognition of women's contribution?

3 Making women's cultural contribution visible is another task I have taken on. I have made sure that there are women's calendars, posters and other art work on the classroom walls. There are book reviews of women's books (and catalogues from feminist publishers), announcements of seminars, discussions, conferences and campaigns. There are theatre groups (and reviews from those who go to see them), pamphlets, newsletters, lists of women's studies courses, women's art shows, all of which provide dramatic examples of the work that women are doing. The Hackney Flashers have produced an exhibition (available for hire, please see 'Materials for the Classroom') and a slide pack which we have used in the classroom and there are other exhibitions available as well. Magazines like *Spare Rib* in Britain, *Hecate, Vashti, Rouge* and *Refractory Girl* in Australia, *Chrysalis* and *Heresies* in the US, *Broadsheet* in New Zealand are invaluable sources for news on women's creative work.

4 We decided to look at the school itself to see what we were learning there about sex roles. We began with a discussion of all the differences we'd noticed in the treatment of girls and boys in the school then checked our lists against the one I had taken from *The Gender Trap* (Adams and Laurikietis, 1976) which showed kids that our observations were not confined to our own school. We then broadened out from the way in which kids were treated to examine the way the school was organised in general. I used a pictorial hierarchy to get the kids to work out the distribution of women and men in the school structure. A clear pattern of power and status emerged. The low status and low paid jobs in the school —cleaners, office staff, dinner ladies — were women's jobs. The pictorial diagram — with men at the top and women at the bottom — provoked further discussion on the gender stereotyping in all work situations.

5 We undertook a project about who does the talking in class. It is relatively easy to keep a record over a week or so. When the girls realise that it is the boys who do most of the talking, interrupting, as well as frequently choosing the topic, they are likely to tackle the boys about it and promote change. This can be a class or a group project.

6 We decided to investigate decision makers. This can be an

opportunity to study a range of organisations from the school to local government, the business and legal worlds and so on. This will no doubt reveal that men are generally the decision makers. This can raise many questions for there are some students who will be sure that this is evidence that women aren't suitable for responsible positions, while to others it will suggest discrimination. (The Sex Discrimination Act and positive discrimination can be discussed in this context.) Other ways of exploring the same area is to ask the question, what would be different if women were in charge? Have a look at everything from supermarkets to transport systems, from house design to child care and so on. There are numerous activities here. Not only can they assume consciousness-raising dimensions when the kids begin to realise that women would not design an Underground system with escalators on which push chairs could not be taken, it may also encourage the girls to construct a world in which their own needs are given proper expression.

7   A Preview of the World of Work and Employment prospects. What avenues are open for girls and what for boys? (The discussion can become heated if and when girls realise, for example, that they are virtually excluded from apprenticeships and day release courses.) What sort of advice are they getting about jobs? And what about unemployment? What are the figures for male and female school-leavers? Statistical evidence can raise crucial questions about the kids' expecations of, and attitudes to, work.
b   Wages are another fruitful area for discussion. What are the statistics on men's and women's pay? Why do the majority of women earn less than men? What effects has the Equal Pay Act had? What about women's unpaid work in the home? We also conducted a survey within the class to find out how many mothers worked outside the home, as well as in it. We discovered that the over-whelming majority of mums did both. These findings were followed up by working out, together, all the jobs which needed doing in the house and who did them. The injustice of the distribution of the jobs was clear, even to the most sexist boys. We then had the problem of sorting out the reasons for this and of explaining why women put up with it. The kids indicated that they had a very good understanding of the hold which custom and tradition have over us. There were also quite a few declarations that they wouldn't have the same hold in the future.

8   A Look at Love and Romance. What is love and do we need it? A history of love (it hasn't always meant what it means to us today) or a cross cultural comparison of love can be a good starting point.

178

That love is an oppressive ideology can be another way of beginning a heated discussion. Love comics and love stories, when looked at critically, can become extremely funny. (I once provided the kids with the pages of a comic but without the dialogue and asked them to fill it in; we then had to discuss why they all had virtually the same story. Some of them said that 'love comics' were ruined for them by this exercise.).

9 Looking at what we learn. Having the kids do their own analysis of the curriculum materials and classroom practices can help them to become more aware of the nature and extent of sexism in their daily school lives. To have a student challenging a science teacher, for example, over his practice of getting the boys to do the experiment and the girls to clean up, is more effective than a teacher (who was not present) challenging him.

One of the questions which must be asked is how effective all this is. The kids are caught in the contradictions of a sexist society and we cannot assume that by presenting them with some 'contrary' information, we will automatically change them. But at least they are aware that there is more than one way of organising and viewing society. For many of them this will represent their only contact with an 'alternative' view on sexism.

There are some signs that the information I have helped them to put together actually does make an impact. For example, one group of girls took up a sexist issue with a male head of year. They objected to the way he addressed them as 'love' and put his arm round them. They drew his attention to this and made their views quite clear to him. This is only one incident, and a small one, but it is an example of how classroom learning can begin to impinge on and challenge the everyday world. Recently another group of kids, after a discussion of sex differences in school, drew my attention to the fact that I had just ignored two girls talking but had told off some boys for the same 'offence'! It is these observations and challenges that we have to open ourselves up to. Of course there will not be instant success; neither society not the school will change fast. But we can give the kids some sense that change is possible and desirable and goes beyond just an individual analysis. One of the important tasks of a teacher seems to be to give the kids a sense of themselves as part of a social group with power to change society.

Part Six: Racial and Sexual Oppression

Grace Evans

Those Loud Black Girls

I worked as a teacher in several Inner London secondary comprehensive schools between 1976 and 1984. Social Studies was my subject specialism when training but I went on to teach children with special needs, English, and English as a second language. Unlike most of my colleagues I was a Black woman teacher and had a political background which included a commitment to feminism and the exploration of race as a personal and political reality.

In staffrooms a common cry to be heard from white teachers – usually women, for male teachers seldom revealed that everything for them was not firmly under control – was, 'Oh, those loud Black girls!' This exclamation was usually followed by the slamming of a pile of folders on to a table and the speaker collapsing into a chair or storming off to get a cup of coffee. The words were usually uttered in response to a confrontation in which the teacher's sense of authority had been threatened by an attitude of defiance on the part of a group of Black girls in a classroom or corridor. The girls' use of patois and their stubborn refusal to confirm to standards of 'good behaviour', without actually entering the realm of 'bad behaviour' by breaking any school rules, was exasperating for many teachers. The behaviour of the girls could be located in the outer limits of tolerable behaviour, and they patrolled this territory with much skill, sending out a distinct message of being in and for themselves.

The behaviour of the girls I knew well, not only because from time to time, much to my chagrin, I had been confronted by it in the classroom, but because I had been a Black student once (though in a north-eastern

183

American city where white children were in the majority) and there had been 'loud Black girls' then, too.

I was not a loud Black girl myself; I was one of the quiet, almost to the point of silent, Black or 'coloured' girls who did her homework, worked hard, seldom spoke unless spoken to and was usually to be found standing on the margin of activities. I demanded no attention and got none. In the early years of my schooling I was considered by most of my teachers to be at best an average or just above average student, certainly not a particularly promising one. If it had not been for an elder brother whose academic excellence was noted at an early age I probably would have remained ignored by teachers, but word got around in the schools I attended that I was his sister, and teachers began to expect more from me. Looking back, I believe that my silence stemmed from two things: a perception on my part of minority status and a very deliberate priming for the professions that my parents began when I was very young.

From the vantage point of my adult professional state, sitting in the staffroom hearing colleagues complain of 'those loud Black girls', I was never sure of how to respond. I was aware of the teacher's remark as being an expression of defeat, anger and racism, but it was not always in my power to take the speaker through the process of coming to understand the dynamics of the situation and the nature of their response to it. Through my body language I refused to collude with the speaker's racism. I straightened my back, raised my eyebrows and drew my lips together tightly in an expression of silent knowing and disapproval. I often thought I detected a plea for empathy, as if the distraught teacher were asking, 'Aren't they the same with you?' My agreement would have absolved them from guilt and responsibility, and so it was withheld.

As one of the few Black teachers I was aware of being expected to fulfil a number of roles. I identify these roles as keeping order, legitimising the system and acting as a 'cultural representative' from one of Britain's minority ethnic communities.

The active recruitment of Black teachers into inner city schools was at least in part a response to the crisis in British schools created by the resistance of Black pupils to the racism they encountered. Black teachers were thought to provide good role models and to be better able to handle Black pupils. There is, however, a gulf which separates Black teachers from Black pupils in the state school system, a gulf which is best explained by a brief outline of the legacy of education in the West Indies.

Educational institutions were established in the West Indies in the nineteenth century, before emancipation, to transmit the culture of Britain to a largely African population. Its aim was firmly to establish the enslaved group's allegiance to the European motherland. In the period preceding independence in the twentieth century the education system took on a new role, the creation of a buffer class of professionals and white-collar workers to fulfil the administrative posts of the departing British colonial administration.

For the people, the education system provided the only means of escape from a life of material hardship. The possession of a good education ensured entry to the professions or a white-collar job, and both represented movement upwards on the ladder of social mobility. The fact that education was and is the only way out of poverty for the majority of people cannot be overstressed. A beautiful and moving portrayal of the struggle for education coming from Martinique is Euzhan Palcy's film *Rue Cases Nègres* or *Black Shack Alley*, made in 1983 and based on the novel by Joseph Zobel, published in 1950.

The prize of a good education was attained at the cost of great sacrifice on the part of one's parents, sometimes the entire family. Aside from this cost, another price is paid by the recipient of an education, and this is the personal cost of the process of de-culturalisation, or de-Africanisation, whereby all personal expressions of one's original African culture are eliminated and European codes established instead. The mastery of standard English to replace West Indian patois is only one aspect of this transformation. It includes training the body to adopt European body language and gesture, and the voice to adopt European tones of speech and non-verbal expression. Loudness is discouraged, as it reflects field life and rural peasant status.

The price of a good education, a European education, in short, was, and still is, the denial of one's Black cultural identity. This is the price of entry to the middle class. It is this legacy of education as a double-edged sword that creates a similar suspicion towards Black teachers on the part of Black students as exists on the part of the Black community towards Black members of the police force. The presence of Black faces does not change the essential nature of an institution, nor does it alter its ethos.

The role of what I have termed 'cultural representative', which I found myself to be playing as a Black teacher, was one common to teachers from Britain's minority ethnic communities at the time I entered the profession. Crude interpretations of multicultural education held that bad race relations were caused simply by misunderstandings between people, and that fostering understanding of cultural traditions of various minority ethnic groups in Britain offered one way of eliminating prejudice and discrimination. This approach put racialism, or attitudes and prejudices towards Black people held by white people, at the centre of the issue of race relations while ignoring the economic and power relations which generate and perpetuate racial inequality. In keeping with this notion of multiculturalism, Black teachers were called upon – and, indeed, many saw it as their duty – to talk to white teachers and to students about their cultural traditions and identity. This work, of trying to educate white people out of their racism, was emotionally exhausting and at the expense of the Black participants entirely. I, personally, do not believe that it worked. After talking of the dimension of race in my life, I was often left with the sense of having parted with something precious and having been offered nothing in return. A teacher in the staffroom would be able the next day to return to her or his classroom and treat Black children with the same distant contempt or patronising attitude they had used before, while priding her or himself on having had such an open and frank conversation with me.

I found it difficult to be a Black woman teacher in an institution where the ethos was both racist and sexist. I often felt caught in crossfire, as once, when seeking support from a senior white male colleague in dealing with an incident of verbal racist abuse directed at me. The abuse came from a white, male fourteen-year-old. He had called me a Black bitch, amongst other things, and had made other references to my colour. I suspect that if he had omitted the references to race the boy would actually have been dealt with more severely. As it happened, the senior teacher failed to acknowledge the racist nature of the boy's verbal assault on me. The approach which the teacher adopted suggested that he clearly thought aggression and indiscipline were natural responses of white people faced with a Black person in a position of authority. The senior teacher lectured the boy in front of me about how more respect should be accorded a woman teacher. He pleaded with the boy to sympathise with me (as a woman or as a Black?) and to be aware of 'how difficult it is for Ms Evans to control a large classful of students'. He did not indicate whether my difficulties stemmed from the inadequacies of my gender or my race.

Alongside the personal bigotry and racism of individual teachers and other staff, there was, in schools where I taught as in schools at present, institutionalised racism. The near total absence of images of Black people in visual displays on the walls of the classrooms and corridors amounts to an assault on Black identity, giving the impression to anyone entering the school building that it is a white institution, run for and by white people. Where Black images are to be found, in textbooks and learning materials, images are not often positive – rather they portray us as lacking in civilised ways and in need of 'development' along European lines. Black civilisations are either ignored or appropriated, as in the presentation of ancient Egypt as a European civilisation and Egyptian people as white. Black literature appears in the English syllabus rarely, and seldom are books by Black writers available in school libraries. Omission and distortion are the features which mark the treatment of Black experience, achievement and history in schools.

The hidden curriculum contained in the social hierarchy of school as a place of work carries a message of Black inferiority. In school Black women workers are to be found doing the least well paid jobs as cooks, cleaners and ancillary workers. Looking at the subject hierarchy of the secondary school, it is a small intellectual leap to make from identifying the subjects with the least status – home economics, needlework, child development – to observing that it is in these spheres of work that Black women are to be found in the outside world.

While I may have had my power as a teacher undermined by the behaviour of individual colleagues and by the institutionalised inequalities of the school, I was not entirely without power. I occupied a place in the hierarchy by virtue of my position as a teacher. I was an adult, and this fact alone gave me power where students had none. I was not going through the rite of passage from adolescence to adulthood which spans the years of secondary education. If I found it so hard, so full of conflict and contradictions, being a teacher, what was it like to be a Black schoolgirl?

Feminist research has put forward convincing demonstrations of the ways that girls are systematically disadvantaged within education. Are Black and white girls disadvantaged in the same way? From a Black Afro-Caribbean perspective, it is difficult to prioritise girls when looking at under-achievement as the performance of girls far surpasses that of boys (Chigwada, 1987). But to look at the issue solely in terms of the objective measure of achievement of examination results allows us only a narrow glimpse of the development of persons from childhood to adulthood, which is the process of education in its widest sense.

The authors of *The Heart of the Race*, the first book by Black Afro-Caribbean women in Britain to offer an analysis of contemporary Black women's lives, state the following about women and education:

Black women cannot afford to look at our experience of Britain's education system merely from our perspective as women: this would be to over-simplify the realities we face in the classroom. For Black schoolgirls sexism has, it is true, played an insidious role in our lives. It has influenced our already limited career choices and has scarred our already tarnished self-image. But it is racism which has determined the schools we can attend and the quality of the education we receive in them. Consequently, this has been the most significant influence on our experience of school and society (Bryan, Dadzie and Scafe, 1985; 58).

If the notion of the dual oppression of Black women has any meaning in the context of education, it lies in the double message that schools transmit of Black inferiority and female inferiority. But in answer to the question of whether the message of gender inferiority is the same for

Black girls as it is for white girls, I think not. Black womanhood has a historical legacy which distinguishes it from white womanhood. Black women's femininity in the West has been defined as deviating from the norms of white femininity (Carby, 1982). The ideology of Black women's sexuality and femininity has been constructed within a racist framework and this ideology has as its historical basis the exploitation of Black women under colonialism and slavery. Stereotypes of Black women include the mammy, the Aunt Jemima figure, the masculinised beast of burden and the sexually licentious, exotic nightclub singer/dancer/prostitute. It is impossible not to connect the encouragement given to Black girls at school to excel in sports, music and dance with the existing stereotypes of Black femininity.

In effect, there is a double standard of femininity which has operated for white and Black women. Sojourner Truth spoke of this in her well-known speech to an audience comprising those activists in the uneasy alliance between nineteenth-century abolitionists and feminists.

> That man over there says women need to be helped into carriages and lifted over ditches and to have the best place everywhere. Nobody ever helps me into carriages or over mud puddles, or gives me any best place! And ain't I a woman? Look at me! Look at my arm! I have ploughed, and planted and gathered into barns and no man could head me! And ain't I a woman? I could work as much and eat as much as a man – when I could get it – and bear the lash as well! And ain't I a woman? (Loewenberg and Bogin, 1978)

Angela Davis has pointed to some of the historical influences on Black womanhood. She has identified a legacy of Black women under slavery 'of hard work, perseverance and self-reliance, a legacy of tenacity, resistance and insistence on sexual equality – in short, a legacy spelling out standards for a new womanhood' (Davis, 1981; 29).

While not seeking to deny the ways that the family has been a source of oppression to Black women, Angela Davis points out the ways that the Black slave family was the site of woman's empowerment, as it was the only sphere in which her activities could be directed to a self-chosen end.

> It is true that domestic life took on an exaggerated importance in the social lives of slaves, for it did indeed provide them with the only space where they could truly experience themselves as human beings. Black women, for this reason – and also because they were workers just like their men – were not debased by their domestic functions in the way that white women came to be. Unlike their white counterparts, they could never be treated as mere 'housewives'. (Davis, 1981; 16–17)

Clearly, Black girls draw on an experience of defining womanhood which differs from that of their white counterparts. How does this mediate their experience of receiving messages of women's inferiority in the overt and hidden curriculum at school?

While the challenge to sexism in the field of education is growing, it is not clear whether the meeting point of gender and race oppression is ever clearly identified. Too often our attempts to understand and challenge inequalities run along their separate tracks.

I suspect that much of what passes for women's studies in schools is actually more deserving of the name 'white women's studies'. Gender construction is not universal. Some of the ways girls come to an understanding of womanhood are culturally specific. There are differences between the experiences and historical legacies of Afro-Caribbean, Asian and African women. We do share traditions of strong female support networks in our communities. We also share the experience of racism in this society. But the ways in which we are affected differ, as do the experiences we bring to our daily interaction with white institutions such as school. I have specifically focused on the experience of Afro-Caribbean women and I have used the term 'Black' to refer to Afro-Caribbean people and people of the African diaspora.

If we look to the points where educators seek to alter the message of inferiority regarding gender or encourage understanding in pupils of issues of sexism, do we do so with an awareness of the various constructions of femininity that lie behind the experience of womanhood of the students before us? Are we speaking to the Black girls in the classroom? There is a danger that the movement to counter sexism in schools will carry into the field of education some of the errors of the Women's Movement regarding race. We need to examine the ways that the Women's Movement has perpetrated a type of cultural imperialism that takes the oppression of white women as its norm and develops its theory from the experience of a small minority of women in global terms.

When we finally get the issue of abortion on to the history or social studies syllabus, we must ensure that it is not presented only in terms of abortion rights but that there is recognition of the ways that Black women have had to fight to preserve their fertility against the threat of enforced abortions, sterilisation and dangerous contraceptive drugs such as Depo Provera. Similarly, our understanding of the traditions of struggle of Third World women must be deepened. Our teaching about gender inequality must be informed by an awareness that the type of practices we are quick to condemn – arranged marriages, circumcision, dowries, all the hallmarks of Third World women's oppression in the eyes of many white feminists – have been part of all our histories.

The Combahee River Collective Statement of Black Feminism includes this point made by Angela Davis about Black women's lives: 'Black women have always embodied, if only in their physical manifestation, an adversary stance to white male rule and have actively resisted its inroads upon them and their communities in both dramatic and subtle ways.' (Combahee River Collective, 1983; 273)

Returning to 'those loud Black girls' in schools, I wonder how many women teachers have a sense of the resistance they offer to the forces that seek to make them silent receptacles of a world view that obliterates their past and present reality and would relegate them to the menial labour of their foremothers?

From time to time, on a bus or out shopping in the area where I used to teach, I come across some of 'those loud Black girls' who were my pupils, and it gladdens me to see that, despite the attempts to silence them, they are growing into loud, proud Black women.

Part Seven: Sexism and Heterosexism

Lorraine Trenchard

Young Lesbians at School

> *Heterosexism*: 'The assumption that everyone is heterosexual, combined with the belief that heterosexuality is the only natural and valid form of sexuality.'

Heterosexism – the oppression of and discrimination against lesbians and gay men – exists within educational institutions, as well as outside them, and plays a role in reinforcing sexism. Homophobia – the fear of lesbians, gay men and of homosexuality, and also the fear of those feelings in oneself – is one of the mechanisms of heterosexism. Heterosexism regulates how people of the same sex interrelate, and it bolsters sex-role stereotyping by defining and contrasting acceptable opposite-sex/same-sex patterns of behaviour. Heterosexism has the power to inhibit close bonding between women for fear of being presumed to be lesbian. Heterosexism is a force which affects everyone.

'Heterosexism' is a fairly new word for a well-established oppression. It operates, like racism and sexism, on both the personal and the institutional level, and may, like the other oppressions, be simplified to its component elements – prejudice and power. Also like racism and sexism, heterosexism is reliant upon the perpetuation of myths and stereotypes to reinforce its body of misinformation. The result is to alienate and distance, to build up a sense of 'other' or 'different' in a negative, destructive and disempowering way. Any effort to challenge oppression should include challenging all forms of discrimination, for example on the grounds of race, gender, disability and class.

Living in a society which is dominated and designed by men is difficult for any woman. Sex-role stereotyping puts pressure on young women to conform to the wife/mother image, to get married and have children. A woman's value is often measured in terms of these roles. For many a young woman these sexist assumptions will undermine her independence, her confidence and her feelings of value as an individual with her own choice before her. For a young lesbian they will also be denying an integral part of her identity.

British educational institutions have traditionally ignored women and made them invisible in the curriculum, the language, the classroom and the power structure. Among the women made invisible in this way are lesbians. The symbiotic nature of sexism and heterosexism means that women are not seen as having a positive and independent sexuality. Women's sexuality is seen only in relation to men, and lesbians, in refusing these relationships, are seen to exist in a sort of sexual vacuum. Historically, lesbians have not been recognised or given credence – as in the story about Queen Victoria blocking anti-lesbian legislation because she refused to believe that such women existed.

Even under the umbrella term 'homosexual', lesbians are often forgotten or ignored. Sexism thus actually works to give gay men more power. Gay men are often given more attention, the issues which concern gay men are deemed to concern 'all homosexuals', and the term 'homosexual' is often used without qualification, to refer to gay men. Not only do these attitudes reinforce the lack of visibility of lesbians in society, but the term 'homosexual' does not reflect the difference and separate experiences of lesbians compared to those of their gay male counterparts. It does not make clear that young lesbians face the double oppression of sexism and heterosexism.

School years are ideally about learning and growing, and about fulfilling individual potential. This process takes place through formal channels – the curriculum, the classroom and lessons – and through informal, interpersonal channels – relationships with teachers and peers.

Some people have argued that school is not the appropriate place for discussions about homosexuality or lesbianism. I would argue that discussions would provide a necessary balance to playground perceptions of these issues, couched mostly in terms of abuse. Heterosexism and homophobia are present in schools; what is lacking is any structured discussion and positive information on homosexuality and lesbianism. Mark Baker, a Post-Graduate Certificate of Education student at the University of London Institute of Education, writes in his thesis paper, 'Gays in Education' (1984):

It soon became clear to me that the pupils of [a South London

Comprehensive] School (especially, but not exclusively, the boys) use the usual terms of abuse associated with gays regularly. Gay abuse is to be found from the first year upward. Not in a specifically sexual sense, although that meaning comes into the abuse as the pupils become more sexually aware, but in a generally negative sense.

The spheres of classroom and playground are not mutually exclusive: attitudes will cross from one to another, and indeed there will be influences inside school from outside, for example parental attitudes. However, a first step forward is to acknowledge that schools help to create social values and mores, they don't merely reflect them. Given this, it follows that schools can also educate against ignorance and prejudice, and that they should be addressing the issue of heterosexism and homophobia not only to futher the ideal of a non-oppressive society, but because there are young lesbians in every school whose needs are not being met, whose existence is denied, whose experience is often trivialised by comments such as 'it's just a phase', and whose life is not being acknowledged or reflected in the classroom or curriculum.

In 1983 the London Gay Group Research Project (Trenchard and Warren, 1984) examined the experiences of young lesbians and gay men (under 21) living in London. Of the respondents, 136 were young women. Their ages ranged from 15 years to 20 years; they were from all racial groups (in our survey, mainly white) and had a range of religions and beliefs from Muslim to Pantheist (of those who had a religion, most were C of E); and they came from all social classes (in our survey about half the young women said they were working class). Four of the young lesbians had been married (one was still married, two were separated and one was divorced). Six had some sort of disability. About half of the young women had always lived in London; and of those who moved to London, one third had moved because they were lesbian. It is from this research that the following quotes and figures are drawn.

In terms of the formal channels of information, 60 per cent of the young women reported that neither homosexuality nor lesbianism was mentioned in lessons. Of those who said that the topic had been mentioned, only one in five said that this was in a way which was helpful to them. Only one in forty said that homosexuality was mentioned in sex education:

I do not remember homosexuality/lesbianism coming up at all in sex education (in my school in the first year) or in discussions on relationships/world issues. (Age 17)

If people were taught more about the subject it might help them to understand, and possibly help their friends cope if they need to talk about being gay. Also, it is still classed as a 'hush hush' subject and therefore people build up barriers and feel they are different or wrong. (Age 18)

At my school homosexuality was *never* discussed in human biology lessons, and therefore, not surprisingly, all sorts of myths about it arose, e.g. all lesbians like little girls. (Age 19)

Homosexuality was mentioned once – in parentcraft. (Age 18)

At school they mentioned it in the sixth form, in sociology. It was mentioned under deviancy. You know, lumped between murders and the insane. (Age 18)

Another of the formal channels of information is the school library. However, here too the young lesbians had little success in finding positive information. Only about 10 per cent of the young women said that their school library stocked books which mentioned lesbians; less than half of these said that the books were helpful:

The only book it was mentioned in was the Bible. (Age 19)

With little support and information, the young women faced a difficult time, either because they were questioning their sexuality or because they had acknowledged their lesbianism and were facing prejudice and harassment. Isolation was one of the most common of the problems:

I always felt alienated at school. I just locked myself in my bedroom like a hermit for about six years, and I just wouldn't come out . . . I just felt like I didn't belong. Not ever. You really kind of withdraw into yourself 'cos you can't ever communicate. (Age 18)

I didn't realise, or admit to myself, that I was gay at school . . . I didn't know what I was feeling. In my final year I was a bit of a wreck, cried a lot . . . even missed classes because I was crying. It affected my work and teachers used to ask what was the matter. It was terrible. (Age 19)

At school I was mixed up. I was unable to cope with the fact that I felt/saw things differently from everyone else. (Age 20)

If a young woman was open about her lesbianism, then she faced another set of problems and pressures. These ranged from being ostracised to verbal and physical abuse:

No one talked to me for about a year, I nearly got beaten up and all the girls thought I'd jump them. (Age 17)

My so-called friends didn't believe me, then acted as if I had a nasty illness. (Age 16)

[I had problems at school as a lesbian because] I wasn't interested in the social life. I was considered boring because I didn't want to go to parties. I wasn't able to talk about girlfriends. (Age 17)

[My problems at school included] teasing, harassment, threats of violence, having my bicycle tampered with, having food thrown at me etc. (Age 20)

There seemed to be little evidence of teachers challenging anti-lesbian remarks or attempting to provide a positive or supportive atmosphere. Many young lesbians felt that the complexity and reality of human relationships were as distorted by what was presented in school as they are in the media:

[You should be taught] you're not a freak to be gay. It's hard to think you're normal, especially when everything in the media, television, adverts etc., portrays the happy man and woman image. Treat everyone as an individual, with different feelings, try when teaching not to generalise. It's the media and the way you're taught to think that makes you feel abnormal. (Age 19)

There was evidence that these factors sometimes led to anxiety and stress which affected academic performance:

I had difficulty concentrating on school matters because I didn't understand myself. There needs to be an acknowledgement that teenagers can make decisions about their sexuality at an early age. (Age 20)

This unsupportive atmosphere may lead to truancy, or beyond that to the young woman feeling so depressed or desperate that she attempts suicide. One in five of the young women who answered the research questionnaire said that they had attempted suicide because they were lesbian:

I never realised I was a lesbian until I was almost 17. I was madly in love with my best friend at school. She didn't speak to me, decided she'd had enough of me. I sat with a gun pointed at my head . . . (Age 18)

When teachers or the school authorities did intervene it was sometimes in a negative and inappropriate way:

> My school was a church school. My lover was head girl. We were very open, and they expelled me. (Age 20)

> School referred me to a psychologist or psychiatrist on the pretext of 'being worried about my work'. They mentioned EEG, then ECT, then I ran away from home. (Age 17)

> Attitudes amongst staff and parents need to be changed drastically. I was treated as a pervert and a threat to the other girls. I was thrown out. (Age 20)

Despite the rather hostile environment at school, over half of the young women said that they had friends at school who knew that they were lesbian. About one in four said that a teacher knew that she was lesbian. More than half of them knew other lesbians (pupils and teachers) at their schools.

The young lesbians in British schools are experiencing sexism and heterosexism, often racism, 'ablebodism', etc. as well. What they all have in common is a lack of power because they are young. Yet despite the fact that the educational system does not cater for them, they have made decisions about their lives and educated themselves beyond the myths and stereotypes to feel positively about their lesbianism. They also made constructive criticisms about schools:

> I think that other forms of sexuality as well as heterosexuality should be taught and discussed. At my school homosexuality was never mentioned unless it was in a joke. I think that if non-gays were made more aware of gays they'd come to accept us more and they might even realise that we don't go around screwing everything in a ten-mile radius and that love does actually come into it too. (Age 16)

> If teachers could be openly gay and under no threat, not only could they give a positive image of homosexuality, but important support and information. Freedom to discuss sexuality in lesson time is very important and teachers should initiate this. Prejudiced views against homosexuals should be viewed [in the same way] as are racist remarks, in that discrimination is factually unfounded and that it is the people making prejudiced generalisations who are ignorant or evil, not those on the butt end. Obviously schools should stock books about homosexuals, or with gay characters positively portrayed, as well as factual information about gay groups etc. But not just written info.

Books are a great turn-off to some people. There should be videos shown to classes and fact sheets available without asking, and not just from the library. (Age 19)

More should be taught about the value of feelings and the scope of relationships available to people, and less should be taught about the mechanics of heterosexual sex (i.e. the emphasis on the idea that sex *is* heterosexual intercourse). Teachers and pastoral staff should be made to realise that the attitudes of anti-gay pupils/teachers are responsible for the 'problems' concerning being gay/lesbian and that being gay/lesbian is not a problem. (Age 20)

The young lesbians I have met have shown themselves to be aware and worthy of admiration. They have had to think through and question their sexuality, often against prevailing attitudes and ignorance. They have a mature attitude to life, and have questioned the values and assumptions of society with clarity and understanding. They have not merely criticised society, but have made constructive suggestions for changing it, to make things better not only for themselves, but for everyone.

I think what impressed me most about the young women I worked with on the research project was the way they had coped with what often seemed intolerable situations. They survived through crises few older people would without the support of society. They faced rejection by parents, coped with being institutionalised, dealt with alienation, harassment, relationship break-ups and, not least, death – without having a shoulder to cry on, without people to talk to, without the support of family, the understanding of teachers. They faced all these things and yet still emerged feeling positive about their lesbianism. It is not lesbianism that is a problem, but other people's reaction to it. These young women have suffered because of society's heterosexism, yet survived as strong individuals.

What strategies are practical in schools to ensure that young lesbians at present within the system do not face similar problems, and that all young people are educated against prejudice? Many of the strategies we could look at are in fact similar to those we use in fighting against sexism and racism. They involve formal channels as well as informal channels, and a basic need is the commitment to stop colluding with or reinforcing heterosexism and to start challenging and informing.

Teachers are in a position to begin to challenge heterosexism, on both a collective and an individual level. It is important not only to examine the curriculum, learning resources etc., for instances of heterosexism; it is also important to be seen to challenge anti-lesbian or gay remarks.

Ideally, each school should have an equal opportunities policy statement, to include homosexuality and lesbianism. The process by which schools reach this stage is important too. Putting the issue on the agenda and discussing the implications for implementation is in itself a challenge to many people.

Within the classroom situation it is important not to presume that all the pupils are heterosexual. Using gender-neutral terms like 'partner' or, better still, positively acknowledging that some of the pupils will have or already have same-sex partners, helps to create a more supportive accepting and non-discriminating atmosphere. On the same note, if challenging abuse is positive, challenging assumptions is even better, in terms of making the young people think about their own heterosexism. Whether the topic is historical, literary or contemporary, raising questions about a particular individual's sexuality can challenge stereotypes and help to bring the issue into the classroom in a very real way.

One of the areas the young lesbians particularly identified as important was that of information. Ensuring that there are positive books, leaflets and posters in the library, or arranging discussion groups, or speakers from lesbian groups, is another way of supporting young lesbians whilst also challenging heterosexism.

It is important also to use the wider power structures to combat heterosexism. School governors will be playing an ever-increasing role in determining the content of the curriculum, and specifically the approach to sex education. Local Education Authorities and trades unions will need to be lobbied, pressurised and monitored about policies and directions. Young people need to start making demands from within the classroom.

There are many ways to begin to challenge heterosexism, one of which is to follow up the references at the end of this book. The important step is to start taking heterosexism and its influence seriously. Sometimes it is quite literally a matter of life and death for young women in our schools.

Appendix

Jill Lavigueur

Co-education and the Tradition of Separate Needs[1]

The school curriculum in all its aspects, both explicit and implicit, is based on expectations and beliefs which derive not only from contemporary society but also from the historical influences which have helped to mould the traditions of the various types of school. In particular, co-educational and single-sex schools draw upon quite different traditions which made radically different assumptions about the educational needs of the two sexes.

It is customary to claim that segregated education embodies an outmoded view that the two sexes have differing educational needs, whereas co-education makes for similarity of treatment. This is the view put forward in support of co-education by the National Union of Teachers in a policy statement issued in 1975:

The Union recognises that the origins of separate education for boys and girls lie in the history and evolution of education. Schools traditionally educated boys and girls in ways which were intended to prepare them for quite separate and distinct roles in society as men and women; roles which were so different that the teaching methods and curricula were incompatible. Society has changed radically, however, and the pressures to give full equality to men and women in their work, their places in society and the responsibilities and commitments they face should be reflected in and catered for by the schools. To educate children in groups, segregated on the basis of difference of sex, is to effect an artificial separation which bears

little or no relation to life at home or to society in general . . .
A pattern of education based on such separation and founded on
concepts of allegedly distinguishable and incompatible needs of boys
and girls no longer serves the interests either of society or of children
(NUT Statement, 1975 'Co-education and single sex schools: the
Union's views').

While this historical view has a measure of truth in it, it ignores aspects
of the history both of girls' education and of co-education which imply
a very different view of sex roles from the one outlined here. I think
that a more accurate understanding of the way that the two types of
education developed helps to make it clear why co-education per se has
not so far led to equal treatment for the two sexes.

The founding of a proper education system for girls is, of course,
associated with the names of Miss Buss and Miss Beale. They are so
frequently mentioned in tandem that it is perhaps forgotten that their
respective philosophies of education were different and that they
founded two distinct traditions in girls' education. Dorothea Beale, who
became headmistress of Cheltenham Ladies' College in 1858, and
developed the school in a manner which became the pattern for all girls'
public schools, sought to provide an education which was worthy of
comparison with the boys' public schools but which was specifically
for girls. She did not seek to deviate from the Victorian feminine ideal,
only to enhance it. As Cheltenham catered for the daughters of gentle-
men, the school practised the social conventions and held the religious
persuasion accepted by that social class: that is, it was an upper-class,
Anglican-school, with no reason to pursue any kind of nonconformity.
Its pupils could look forward to a leisured future and did not need to
equip themselves for independence. Hence the curriculum did not
neglect feminine accomplishments and academic work and, though of a
far more serious nature than schools had engaged in hitherto, was of a
kind thought particularly appropriate to girls. Accordingly, Miss Beale
did not subscribe to the campaign, initiated by Emily Davies, to open
the Cambridge Local examination to girls. She observed: '. . . the
subjects seem to me in many respects unsuited for girls and such an
examination as the one proposed is likely to further a spirit of rivalry
most undesirable' (Kamm, 1965; 195).

Thus the girls' public school tradition which Miss Beale initiated,
firmly rooted in the values of a conservative leisured class, did indeed
embody a view of girls' education as based upon strict needs. In any
case, the heavily classical curriculum and spartan, sometimes brutal
regimes of the boys' public schools did not really offer a pattern that
could be assimilated.

However, the educational tradition founded by Miss Buss was quite different, and does not at all conform to the picture of single-sex education sketched out in the NUT statement. Its social context was looser and more a sphere of change, and the class of girl it catered for was likely to be forced by financial necessity into making an independent living, as Miss Buss herself had been.

The mid-nineteenth century saw a very great excess of women over men in the population, partly as a result of high levels of infant mortality to which boys were more vulnerable, and of the considerable emigration of adult men to the rapidly developing colonies. A large proportion of women could therefore expect to remain single, and those who lacked a private income were ill-equipped to earn a living as they were without adequate education or training. They tended to be restricted to the poorly paid and usually uncongenial occupations of needlewoman or governess. In order to improve the position of the latter group, the Governess's Benevolent Institution (later Queen's College) was founded in 1846 by the Christian Socialist F.D.Maurice. It was from this beginning that female teachers began to be properly educated and to establish themselves as a profession. Dorothea Beale and Frances Buss both attended lectures at this college which served an important social need at a time when independence was a necessity rather than an ideal for so many women. Miss Buss, for example, was an evening student as she had to earn her living during the day. Queen's College helped to equip her to pursue a substantial career and this was a major function of education for many other young women in her position who were to follow her lead.

The style of girls' public day school established by Miss Buss helped to fit its pupils for such a life of independence. The traditional structure of society outside the school was *not* allowed to determine the world within the school, which was firmly set to follow new directions. Social and religious distinctions were abandoned to a degree quite unusual for the age: in Miss Buss's famous phrase, 'All pupils who enter are considered as upon the same equality'. At a time when nearly all schools, whether public schools or board schools, were under direct church patronage, Miss Buss insisted upon religious freedom and accepted pupils of any faith, including Jewish girls. The social classes were also mixed to an extent unique among schools of that period. In these ways the school showed greater flexibility and vision than did society at large, thus providing a basis for the pupils to initiate a new role for themselves in society and not remain bound by previously accepted conventions.

The two schools founded by Frances Buss, the North London Collegiate School and the Camden Girls' School, established a pattern which was followed by the many girls' day schools founded during the following decades and which continued in the girls' grammar schools set up after the Education Act of 1902. Academic values were put first, while women's traditional social role was to some degree neglected (for example, domestic subjects were never accorded much importance in these schools). Miss Buss set much store by the ability of her pupils to prove themselves in public examinations in open competition with boys — she gave Emily Davies great support by supplying candidates when the Cambridge Local was first opened to girls — and to pursue a rigorous, academic curriculum which made no concessions to femininity. In evidence to the Taunton Commission in 1865 she stated that she believed girls to be quite capable of studying the same subjects as boys, a view given substantial confirmation by her pupils' successes in public examinations.

The two philosophies of education represented by Miss Buss and Miss Beale were paralleled in the movement for the higher education of women by the views of Emily Davies and Anne Clough respectively. Miss Davies battled for the admission of girls, first to public examinations and, later, to university courses, and was the founder of Hitchin (later to become Girton) College. Miss Clough, on the other hand, supported the idea of special examinations for women and of a separately devised curriculum, and pursued this policy as head of the newly-founded Newnham College.

As secondary and higher education were gradually opened up to women, it was the Buss/Davies tradition which predominated, both in girls' grammar schools and in colleges and universities. Miss Beale's philosophy survived to some degree in girls' public and private schools, but insofar as these aimed at higher education for their pupils, preparation for public examinations was necessary and an academic curriculum was followed which was the same in content for both sexes, although there were some differences in subject choices then as now.

The academic tradition in girls' schools was thus based upon a strong belief in *similarity* of intellectual needs between boys and girls, a point which advocates of co-education have consistently ignored during the past decade. It is the philosophy still held in academic girls' schools, as indicated by the statement issuing from Bolton Girls' School:

> The mind is neither male nor female. There is no such thing as feminine geometry. The only sound *intellectual* education is education as a human being, not separately as a man or woman, and without this basic human education, either sex grows up unbalanced (Bolton School Old Girls' Association, 1960; 31).

The emphasis falls strongly upon the life of the mind and although this viewpoint overlooks the extent to which most subjects *are* susceptible to masculine or feminine bias, it represents a concept of education which stresses academic and spiritual values and minimises the importance of sexual differentiation.

The social organisation of girls' grammar schools reflects this attitude. Intellectual accomplishments are valued above practical ones, and there is little attempt to prepare the pupils in any direct way for the role of wife and mother. Naturally, the single-sex environment places women and girls in a position to exercise initiative, leadership and authority, with no pressure to adopt a secondary role, and enables 'masculine' subjects to be studied without the constraints of belonging to a minority group. It leaves girls free to make more adventurous intellectual choices at a time when they may be feeling their way rather cautiously in their relations with the opposite sex. Many of these schools do, however, maintain a certain insistence upon restrained ladylike social (not academic) behaviour, and have an excessive devotion to rules, features which have been inherited from Miss Buss's time when the school had to retain the confidence of Victorian parents. This aspect of girls' schools has become notorious and has fostered the belief that their main concern is to produce refined young ladies; and so the far more basic belief in common intellectual needs has become obscured, not only from the public mind, but even from the rest of the teaching profession, as indicated by the NUT statement quoted earlier.

Only a minority of girls, however, have had access to an academic education of this kind, with its concentration upon the intellect rather than the social or vocational activities traditional to women. Most girls have received their education in the context of the much more practical tradition which has passed from the board schools to the elementary schools, then to the secondary modern schools, and finally formed a major element within the amalgamated traditions inherited by the comprehensive schools.

This majority tradition has been mainly co-educational, not (until recently) because of any belief in the benefits of mixed schooling, but because resources were rarely sufficient to provide segregated schools. When popular education was established in the mid-nineteenth century, schools were divided on a religious basis, the National schools being under the auspices of the Church of England while the British schools were nonconformist, and it could hardly be expected that more than one school of each type would be established in each district. It is misleading, therefore, for the NUT to imply that single-sex education was an accident of history while co-education is a deliberately adopted philosophy, since the mainstream tradition of co-education has purely practical origins. Within these mixed schools, the two sexes were segregated as much as possible: the separate entrances marked 'Boys' and 'Girls' leading on to separate playgrounds can still be seen today on most Victorian school buildings. When the schools later became sufficiently large, the boys and girls were educated in separate sections so that effectively two schools existed within a common building. Thus within the state system, the education of boys and girls together, whenever it occurred, was purely a matter of expedience and did *not* imply any belief in similarity of needs.

Much later, when universal secondary education was developed, single-sex schools were usually built whenever resources permitted, but there was little difference in philosophy or curriculum between mixed and segregated secondary modern schools: *both* expected to prepare boys and girls to fill distinctly different places in society. As these schools in their turn have been amalgamated into comprehensives — forming, of course, the majority element within them — co-education has usually been adopted as the practical solution to school mergers, but the belief in separate needs belonging to the main tradition of popular education has remained without substantial change.

The emphasis in this tradition was upon the teaching of skills: first of all basic literacy, and then practical and vocational skills which would make the pupil a useful member of society. This inevitably involves a closer link between the attitudes within the school and those of society in general than occurs in a highly academic type of school. Moreover, unlike the girls' schools which deliberately sought to improve the position of women in society, the early working-class schools were not founded in order to change the lot of their pupils, but to preserve the existence of an orderly and God-fearing populace at a time when the revolutionary effects of industrialisation, urbanisation and a rapidly expanding population, posed a threat to the established social order. As the Newcastle Commission of 1861 stated, the object of educating the people was to teach them 'a source of morality, enjoyment and comfort in the station in life in which the great mass of them are destined to remain'. This conservative philosophy was not conducive to any unorthodox ideas about the intellectual potential or social role of women, and the board schools merely aimed to make their girls into better and more devout wives, mothers and workers. In accordance with this, girls' duties in the home were allowed to override school attendance when necessary, a practice which still survives in tacit form (see Sue Sharp, 1976; 124; Jenny Shaw, 1977).

It was only after the first world war, when women had, of necessity, taken over many of the hitherto masculine occupations, that the respective educational needs of the two sexes became a matter for proper consideration. In 1923 the Board of Education Consultative Committee reported on *The Differentiation of the Curriculum for Boys and Girls Respectively in Secondary Schools* and recommended that both sexes needed a wider and more humane curriculum than then existed but that little differentiation in content was required, merely some allowance for the physical and social needs of girls, particularly at the time of puberty. It did not propose that the curriculum should be *determined* by these assumed needs, unlike those Victorians who opposed Emily Davies's campaign in the belief that 'to compel girls to attempt both mathematics and classics even to the moderate amount required . . . [for the Cambridge Previous examination] . . . would be seriously injurious to their minds' (Kamm, 1965; 255). This report applied to secondary schools, however, and the elementary schools were unlikely to be influenced by its findings. Their curriculum remained fairly basic, and unlikely to extend the ambitions of either sex.

Fresh thought began to be given to the curriculum when the secondary modern schools were established following the Education Act of 1944. In particular, there came a much more deliberate consideration of the needs of the great majority of girls who did not attend grammar schools and had not benefited from the advances made by the girls in the middle class. This new approach to girls' education was initiated by John Newsom, who expounded his views in a book entitled *The Education of Girls*, published in 1948. Ironically, however, his new approach simply offered a livelier and more humane version of the old assumption of innately differing needs. Indeed, the stress on sexual differences was to be heightened as the school would cater far more deliberately for the future social and domestic roles of their girls. Newsome proposed a syllabus, designed to take into account the 'biological and social function' of girls, which would consist of four main subject areas: English, social studies, a broadly-based physical education, and the acquisition of a practical skill. Claiming that woman's supreme role is to run a home and rear a family, he specifically rejects the educational tradition founded by Miss Buss in which , he states, '. . . equality of educational opportunity became synonymous with imitation and this has persisted, despite a good deal of responsible criticism, to the present day' (Newsom, 1948: 69).

He looks upon Miss Beale's philosophy with greater favour, as she did not neglect feminine accomplishments or seek to imitate a masculine curriculum. He feels that schools should cherish and develop the quality of womanliness and not try to emulate masculine abilities: ambitious women being 'normally deficient in the quality of woman-liness and the particular physical and mental attributes of their sex' (Newsom, 1948; 109).

Extreme though this position may seem to readers now, Newsom's ideas were widely implemented in secondary modern schools (both girls' and mixed) as they tallied extremely well with the philosophy of 'relevance' in the curriculum and with the attempt to make school more acceptable and enjoyable to the older pupils who were now obliged to stay until the age of fifteen. In 1973 the school-leaving age was raised to sixteen and this, together with the more rapid physical maturing of girls, has meant that secondary modern schools must now cater for virtual adults; and so the tendency to link school work to their expected social requirements after leaving school has become even stronger. Hence the course 'packages' on Child Care, Education for Living, Commerce, and so on.

Over the past century, then, and up to the present day, the education of the majority of girls has been intended to equip them for their expected place in society, and to the extent that women have had a different social role from men, so girls' schooling has been based on an assumption of separate needs. This assumption has persisted in a system which has moved from co-education to segregation and back again, but has not greatly changed its philosophy regarding the two sexes. Mixed schooling, in this tradition which catered for the mass of the people, *never implied equality of opportunity for both sexes in the sense in which it is now understood.* The Newsom philosophy, however, claimed parity of esteem for girls' particular educational needs: it was, so to speak, a revival of the philosophy of Miss Beale and Miss Clough.

It therefore seems strange that co-education is associated nowadays with progress and enlightenment, particularly in relation to sexual equality. The reason, I think, is that among the more academic and more middle-class schools, co-education was fairly rare and, where it existed, had often been adopted as a deliberate ideal. The first educationalists to express the case for co-education were the leaders of the Progressive School movement. For example, J.H. Badley, the founding headmaster of Bedales, saw co-education as an integral part of the school's basic belief in balance and wholeness, with emotional and physical health being fostered as well as intellectual vigour:

The principle was adopted here, and later in several of the 'New Schools'. . . as the natural and logical outcome of the view of education as a training for the whole of life by means of the fullest possible range of experience, and not, therefore, to be limited to one sex any more than to one nationality or creed (Badley, 1923;52).

As an educational pioneer, he sought to initiate and adapt to change by means of the education he offered:

Not only has a new world to be shaped out of the ruins of the old that the war has left, but, even apart from this, vast changes, hastened or retarded by war, are visibly in progress. In the relations of nation with nation, of the sexes with each other, all is yet to make (Badley, 1923; 65).

The school, therefore, did not simply reflect or serve the immediate demands of society, but (as was the case with Miss Buss, who was also a pioneer) was in advance of the accepted customs and attitudes prevailing around it. Badley's view of the educational needs of boys and girls still seems enlightened today: the aim of co-education, he says, is 'not to make them alike, but, amongst other things, to see that neither sex is debarred from the fullest individual development by merely conventional differences of treatment' (Badley, 1923; 54). Even he, however, speaks of the need to avoid overstrain to girls during:

> . . . the all-important years in which no excessive demands ought to be made on the physical energy then being stored to meet the future demands of motherhood. To encourage any kind of competition between the sexes, during these years above all, would be criminal folly (Badley, 1923; 63).

One may recall that Miss Buss and Miss Davies had to fight against the belief that girls would collapse under the strain of public examinations, and reflect that benevolent paternalism can be just as much of an obstacle to equality for women as more aggressive discrimination. This protective attitude to girls was also held by other heads of Progressive Schools: for example, L.B. Pekin (the pseudonym of one such headmaster) quotes with approval the view of a former head of King Alfred's, Joseph Wicksteed, that:

> . . . far more than is recognised, the higher education of women, notwithstanding its inestimable social and psychological value, has been responsible for physical and nervous damage scarcely less cruel than the premature sex life, or the relentlessly frequent motherhood, of savage and barbarous peoples (Pekin, 1939; 158).

Pekin certainly did not wish girls to be treated in the same way as boys. He saw the needs of the two sexes as complementary, rejecting the notion of an 'androgynous amalgam' (Pekin, 1939; 55). Again one can only recall the arguments advanced against the policies of Miss Davies and Miss Buss. At the meeting of the Social Science Association in 1864, the Archbishop of York declared that,

> . . . the highest civilisation would err if it produced mannish women. The cultivation of a woman's mind cannot be trained too high; but it must be cultivation proper to her constitution, mental gifts, and work in the world. . .

while Cannon J.P.Norris also opposed the plan to allow girls to sit the same examinations as boys on the grounds that the two sexes were 'marvellously, beautifully and distinctly supplemental one to the other', and that each should pursue its own separate strengths and develop its own 'congenital excellence' (Kamm, 1975: 192-3).

A fairly stereotyped view of girls' natural abilities and potential thus survived in the midst of the Progressive philosophy. And although co-education, in this idealistic tradition, was intended to develop the individual potential of girls as well as boys and not merely to prepare them to fit a purely conventional mould, the attitude towards girls was somewhat tender-minded and protective, and not conducive to the ambitious standards of the more tough-minded pioneers of girls' education.

A belief in the complementary needs of the two sexes is central to the argument in favour of co-education put forward in the course of extensive research on the subject by R.R.Dale. Like all others who have held this view, including Newsom, he sees women as complementing the qualities of men rather than vice versa, the feminine role being the more passive and subordinate one. This assumption can be detected through-out the three volumes of *Mixed or Single-Sex School*? (1969, 1971, 1974). One example is his statement that women teachers should have greater authority in mixed schools: the senior mistress should be designated headmistress yet be second (not third, as is often the case) in seniority, with a man in overall charge.

His views on sex-roles are made most explicit, however, in a more recent article in which he cites psychological evidence to the effect that man is innately aggressive and woman submissive and applies these findings to the school performance of the two sexes:

> The *average* aggressive-submissive apposition has far-reaching consequences. Theorising, one might see aggressiveness in the male leading to physical pursuits, physical crimes, the desire for dominance, creativity, and urge to exploration. In education it may play a part in male untidiness, carelessness, truancy, rebelliousness, failure to do homework — yet also in the drive needed for success. The comparative submissiveness and shyness of the girl may be a factor in her more retiring and less physically active life, less desire for dominance, less inclination to accept posts of high responsibility — and the desire to have as husband a 'manly man' to whom she can look up. The less 'aggressive' behaviour could be partly responsible, indirectly, for the greater neatness and conscientiousness of the schoolgirl's written work (Dale, 1975; 8).

He feels that socialisation is not the major cause of these differences, and that feminists should not 'confuse equality with similarity', since the differences are natural: 'Maybe nature intended man to be the leader and women to provide the stability.' Although he concedes that there is a considerable overlap in the psychological attributes of the two sexes, and that some women are suited to positions of leadership, his general attitude is one of benevolent paternalism, similar to that of Pekin, Wicksteed and Badley.

Dale's philosophy also resembles the Progressive one in that intellectual development is not considered the cornerstone of education but is secondary to moral and psychological development. He prefaces his findings on attainment with the statement that: '. . . high academic attainment is not the most important aim of a school. We are all agreed that good character, right attitudes and healthy emotional development are of far more value' (Dale, 1975; 3).

Certainly Pekin would agree, as he claims that the 'central purpose' of co-education 'is to ensure a right relationship between the sexes' (Pekin, 1939; 11). This kind of priority enables Dale to de-emphasise the fact that his findings on attainment, particularly that of girls, form the weakest element in his wide-ranging research on co-education. He is able to show fairly convincingly certain social and emotional benefits of mixed schools, but in the case of girls he cannot show that they benefit in terms of attainment.

Overall then, it may be seen that neither the idealistic philosophy of co-education nor the more workaday tradition inherited from the nineteenth-century board schools embraced the view that girls should aspire towards similar kinds and levels of attainment as boys. Only the girls' day schools in the Frances Buss tradition have ever pursued such a policy. Within the state system of education, this tradition has now been virtually eliminated as girls' grammar schools have been merged into larger mixed comprehensives. It is hardly surprising, therefore, that the present philosophy and organisation of co-educational secondary schools has so far done little to advance equal opportunities for girls.

The failure to grasp this historical pattern has led to an unduly complacent belief that the almost universal change to co-education which has recently occurred would in itself form a major extension of opportunities for girls. Only a new pioneering spirit, a determination to carry the ideals of genuine choice and equal standards of expectation to girls of all social classes and levels of ability can develop co-education towards policies and practices which assume truly equal partnership between the sexes.

Notes

1 This article is chapter four of Jill Lavigueur's M.Ed dissertation 'Equality of Educational Opportunity for Girls and its Relation to Co-education', 1977, unpublished, University of Sheffield.

Bibliographies

The bibliographies that follow include:

a References in the text – articles, papers and books cited by the authors

b Further reading
i.   Books, papers and articles on issues of gender and education. Although not exhaustive, this section covers a large amount of material, mostly written after the first edition of *Learning to Lose*
ii.   A very small selection of books on feminism, gender issues and women's studies. The catalogues of publishers – especially The Women's Press, Virago, Sheba and Pandora – should be used for information on current books (see p 244–6). The lists of resources (see p 247) are useful, too, to give a broader range and up-to-date information.
iii. Materials for the classroom. This section lists just a few publications, some designed especially for student use. It does not include fiction. Again, publishers' catalogues and lists of resources should be used.
iv.   Journals

c Further information
i.   Publishers
ii.   Resource lists
iii. Organisations.

All the information listed in the 'Bibliographies' section relates to English-language publications only. Most of the material is British.

References in the text

Adams, C. and Laurikietis, R., 1976, *The Gender Trap: A Closer Look at Sex Roles* (Book 1: *Education and Work*; Book 2: *Sex and Marriage*; Book 3: *Messages and Images*), Virago

Ahlum, C. and Fralley, J., 1976, *High School Feminist Studies*, The Feminist Press, Old Westbury, New York

Althusser, L., 1971, *Lenin and Philosophy and other essays*, New Left Books

Ardener, S., 1975, Perceiving women, Malaby

Asher, S.R. and Gottman, J.M., 1973, 'Sex of Teacher and Student Reading Achievement', *Journal of Educational Psychology*, no.65

Backhouse, C. and Cohen, L., 1978, *The Secret Oppression: Sexual Harassment of Working Women*, Macmillan, Toronto

Badley, J.H., 1923, *Bedales: A Pioneer School*, Methuen

Barnes, D., 1976, *From Communication To Curriculum*, Penguin, Harmondsworth

Barnes, K., 1958, *He and She*, Darwin Finlayson

Belotti, E.G., 1975, *Little Girls: Social Conditioning and its Effects on the*

Stereotyped Role of Women during Infancy, Writers and Readers.

Benton, T., 1974, 'Education and Politics' in Holly, D. (ed), *Education or Domination? A Critical Look at Educational Problems Today*, Arrow Books

Berger, G. and Kachuk, B., 1977, *Sexism, Language and Social Change*, US Dept. of Health, Education and Welfare, National Institute of Education

Bernard, J., 1975, *Women, Wives, Mothers: Values and Options*, Aldine, Chicago

Blom, G.E., 1971, *Sex Differences in Reading Disability*, quoted in Zimet, S.G., 1976, *Print and Prejudice*, Hodder and Stoughton.

Board of Education, 1923, *Differentiation of the Curriculum for Boys and Girls Respectively in Secondary Schools*, HMSO

Bodine, A., 1975, 'Androcentrism in Prescriptive Grammar: Singular "they", Sex Indefinite "he" and "he" and "she"', *Language in Society*, Vol.4, no.2

Bolton School Old Girls' Association, 1960, *Learning and Living: a Feminine Viewpoint*, The Association

Boydell, D., 1974, 'Teacher-pupil Contact in Junior Classrooms', *British Journal of Educational Psychology*, Vol.44, Nov., pp 313–318

Braverman, H., 1974, *Labor and Monopoly Capital: The Degradation of Work in the 20th Century*, Monthly Review Press

Britton, J., 1975, *Language and Learning*, Penguin

Brundson, C., 1978, 'It is well known by nature that women are inclined to be rather personal', in Women's Studies Group Centre for Contemporary Studies, *Women take Issue: Aspects of Women's Subordination*, Hutchinson

Bryan, B., Dadzie, S., and Scafe, S., 1985, *The Heart of the Race*, Virago

The Bullock Report, 1975, *A Language for Life*, HMSO

Byrne, E., 1978a, *Women and Education*, Tavistock

Byrne, E., 1978b, *Equality of Education and Training for Girls (10–18 years)*, Commission of European Communities, Brussels

Carby, H., 1982, 'White Woman Listen! Black Feminism and the Boundaries of Sisterhood', in *The Empire Strikes Back*, Hutchinson

Chetwynd, J. and Hartnett, O., (eds), 1978, *The Sex Role System: Psychological and Sociological Perspectives*, Routledge and Kegan Paul

Chigwada, R., 1987, 'Not Victims, not Superwomen', *Spare Rib*, no. 183

Children's Rights Workshop, 1976, *Sexism in Children's Books: Facts, Figures and Guidelines,* Writers and Readers Co-operative

Clarricoates, K., 1978, 'Dinosaurs in the Classroom: A Reexamination of Some Aspects of the Hidden Curriculum in Primary Schools', *Women's Studies International Quarterly*, Vol.1, no.4

Combahee River Collective, 1983, 'Combahee River Collective Statement', in *Home Girls: A Black Feminist Anthology*, Kitchen Table Women of Colour Press, New York

Comer, L., 1974, *Wedlocked Women*, Feminist Books, Leeds

The Crowther Report, 1959, Report of the Central Advisory Council for Education, 15–18, Ministry of Education, Vol.1, HMSO

Curriculum Development Centre, 1975, The Hidden Curriculum: working paper no.6, International Women's Year Conference no.1, 'Guidelines for the avoidance of sex bias in educational materials and media', Melbourne, 13–15 August

Dale, R.R., 1969–1974, *Mixed or Single-sex Schools?*, 3 vols, Routledge and Kegan Paul

Dale, R., Esland, G. and McDonald, M. (eds), 1976, *Schooling and Capitalism: a Sociological Reader*, Routledge and Kegan Paul in assoc. with Open University

Daly, M., 1973, *Beyond God the Father: A Philosophy of Women's Liberation,* Beacon Press, Boston

Davis, A., 1981, 'Standards for a New Womanhood', in *Women, Race and Class*, The Women's Press

Dawkins, J., 1967, *A Textbook of Sex Education*, Blackwell and Mott

Deem, R., 1978, *Women and Schooling*, Routledge and Kegan Paul

Delamont, S. and Duffin, L. (eds), 1978, *The Nineteenth-century Woman: Her Cultural and Physical World*, Croom Helm

Department of Education and Science, 1975, *Curriculum Differences for Boys and Girls*, Education Survey, 21, HMSO

Department of Health, Education and Welfare, 1975, *Non-discrimination on the Basis of Sex*, Federal Register, Vol.40, no.108, pt.2: 4 June, US Government Printing Office, Washington DC

Devon Education Department, 1978, 'A discussion paper on sex equality in education', *Curriculum in the Primary School*, Devon Education Department, Exeter

Dixon, B., 1977, *Catching them Young: Sex, Race and Class in Children's Fiction*, Pluto

Dyhouse, C., 1978, 'Towards a "Feminine" Curriculum for English Schoolgirls: The Demands of Ideology, 1870–1963', *Women's Studies International Quarterly*, Vol.1, no.4

Dykstra, R. and Tinney, R., 1969, 'Sex Differences in Reading Readiness: First Grade Achievement and Second Grade Achievement' in Figurel, J.A. (ed), *Reading and Realism*, International Reading Association

Eichler, M., 1979, *The Double Standard: A Feminist Critique of Feminist Social Science*, Croom Helm

Elliot, J., 1974, 'Sex Role Constraints on Freedom of Discussion: A Neglected Reality of the Classroom', *The New Era*, Vol.55, no.6. Reprinted 'Sex roles and silence in the classroom', *Spare Rib*, no.27

Engels, F., 1974, *Correspondence*, Vol.2: Letter to J. Bloch, Sept 1890, Progress Publications, Moscow

Farley, L., 1978, *Sexual Shakedown: The Sexual Harassment of Women on the Job*, McGraw Hill, New York

Federbush, M., 1974, 'The Sex Problems of School Maths Books', in Stacey, J., et al (eds), *And Jill Came Tumbling After: Sexism in American Education*, Dell, New York

Fennema, E., 1976, 'Women and Girls in Public Schools: Defeat or Liberation?' in Roberts J. (ed), *Beyond Intellectual Sexism: A New Reality*, David McKay, New York

Fennema, E., 1980, 'Success in Maths', paper presented at 'Sex Differentiation and Schooling' conference, Churchill College, Cambridge, 2–5 Jan

Fisher, E., 1974, 'Children's Books: The Second Sex, Junior Division', in Stacey, J. et al (eds), *And Jill Came Tumbling After: Sexism in American Education,* Dell, New York

Fishman, P., 1975, 'Interaction: The Work Women Do', paper presented at American Sociological Association meeting, San Francisco, August

Frazier, N. and Sadker, M., 1973, *Sexism in Schools and Society*, Harper & Row, New York

Freeman, J., 1975, *The Politics of Women's Liberation*, McKay, New York

Freire, P., 1972, *Cultural Action for Freedom*, Penguin

Freire, P., 1973, *Pedagogy of the Oppressed*, Penguin

Gagnon, J. and Simon. W., 1974, *Sexual Conduct*, Hutchinson

Gilroy, B., 1976, *Black Teacher*, Cassell

Graham, A., 1975, 'The Making of a Nonsexist Dictionary', in Thorne, B. and Henley, N. (eds), *Language and Sex: Difference and Dominance*, Newbury House, Rowley, Mass.

Griffiths, J., 1977, 'Sex Roles in the Secondary School: The Problem of Implementing Change', paper presented at 'Teaching Girls to be Women' conference, Essex, April

Gross, A.D. 1978, 'Sex-role Standards and Reading Achievement: A Study of an Israeli Kibbutz System, *The Reading Teacher*, November

Guttentag, M. and Bray, H., 1976, *Undoing Sex Stereotypes: Research and Resources for Educators*, McGraw Hill, New York

Hackney Flashers, Slide Pack, Society for education in film and television

Harman, H., 1978, *Sex Discrimination in School: How to Fight it*, National Council for Civil Liberties

Harris, A., 1974, 'Sex Education in Schools', in Rogers, R. (ed), *Sex Education: Rationale and Reaction*, Cambridge University Press

Harrison, L., 1975, 'Cro-Magnon Woman – in Eclipse', *The Science Teacher*, April

Hartman, M., and Banner, L. (eds), 1974, *Clio's Consciousness Raised: New Perspectives on the History of Women*, Harper & Row

Hirschman, L., 1973, 'Female-male Differences in Conversational Interaction', paper presented to Linguistic Society of America

Hirschman, L., 1974, 'Analysis of Supportive and Assertive Behaviour in Conversation', paper presented to Linguistic Society of America

Hochschild, A.R., 1975, 'Inside the Clockwork of Male Careers', in Howe, F. (ed), *Women and the Power to Change*, McGraw Hill, New York

Hochschild, A.R., 1975a, 'The Sociology of Feeling and Emotion: Selected Possibilities', in Millman, M. and Kanter, R.M. (eds), *Another Voice: Feminist Perspectives on Social Life and Social Science*, Anchor Books, New York

The Holland Report, 1977, *Young People and Work*, Manpower Services Commission

Horner, M., 1974, 'Towards an Understanding of Achievement-related

Conflicts in Women', in Stacey, J. et al (eds), *And Jill Came Tumbling After: Sexism in American Education*, Dell, New York

Howe, F., 1974, 'The Education of Women', also, 'Equal Opportunities for Women', in Stacey, J. et al (eds), *And Jill Came Tumbling After: Sexism in American Education*, Dell, New York

Howe, F., 1977, 'Seven Years Later: Women's Studies Programmes in 1976', report of the National Advisory Council on Women's Educational Programmes

Husband, C., 1974, 'Education Race and Society', in Holly, D. (ed), *Education or Domination? A Critical Look at Educational Problems Today*, Arrow

Illich, I., 1971, *Celebration of Awareness*, Penguin

Illich, I., 1973, *Deschooling Society*, Penguin

Jackson, S., 1978, 'How to Make Babies: Sexism in Sex Education', *Women's Studies International Quarterly*, Vol.1, no.4

Joffe, C., 1974, 'As the Twig is Bent', in Stacey, J. et al (eds), *And Jill Came Tumbling After: Sexism in American Education*, Dell, New York

Joll, C., 1976, 'Teachers' Pay', *Women and Education*, Manchester, no.10

Kagen. J., 1964, 'Acquisition and Significance of Sex Typing and Sex Role Identity', in Hoffman, J.L. and Russell, L.W. (eds), *Review of Child Development Research*, Sage, Beverly Hills, CA.

Kamm, J., 1965, *Hope Deferred*, Methuen

Kaplan, C., 1976, 'Language and Gender', in *Papers on Patriarchy*, Women's Publishing Collective

Keddie. N., 1975, 'Classroom Knowledge', in Young, M.F.D. (ed), *Knowledge and Control: New Directions for the Sociology of Education*, Collier Macmillan

Kelly, A., 1978, *Girls and Science*, Almqvist and Wicksell, Stockholm

Kelly, A., and Weinreich-Haste, H., 1979, 'Science is for Girls?', *Women's Studies International Quarterly*, Vol.11, no.3

Kelly-Gadol, J., 1976, 'The Social Relation of the Sexes: Methodological Implications of Women's History, *Signs: Journal of Women in Culture and Society*, Vol.1, no.4

Kirkby, J., 1746, *A New English Grammar*, Scholar Press Facsimile, Menston

Kramer, C., Thorne, B. and Henley, N., 1978, 'Perspectives on Language and Communications', *Signs: Journal of Women in Culture and Society*, Vol.3, no.3

Kuhn, A. and Wolpe, A-M. (eds), 1978, *Feminism and Materialism*, Routledge and Kegan Paul

Lavigueur, J., 1977, 'Equality of Educational Opportunity for Girls and its Relation to Co-education', unpublished M.Ed. dissertation, University of Sheffield

Leonard, D.B., 1977, 'Opportunities and Choice in the Curriculum', in 'Teaching Girls to be Women' conference, Essex, April

Leonard, D.B., 1979, 'Is Feminism more Complex than the WLM Realises?' paper prepared for the Radical Feminist Day Workshop, White Lion Free School, 8 April, in *Feminist Practice 10 Years on*

216

Leonard, D.B., and Allen, S. (eds), 1976, *Sexual Divisions and Society: Process and Change*, Tavistock

Lernhoff, F.G., 1971, 'In the Classroom', in *Honesty to Children*, Shotton Hall, Shrewsbury

Lever, J., 1976, 'Sex Differences in the Games Children Play', *Social Problems*, Vol.23, no.4

Levy, B., 1974, 'Do Schools Sell Girls Short?' in Stacey, J. et al (eds), *And Jill Came Tumbling After: Sexism in American Education*, Dell, New York

Lobban, G., 1976, 'Sex-roles in Reading Schemes', in *Sexism in Children's Books: Facts, Figures and Guidelines*, Writers and Readers Co-operative

Lobban, G., 1977, 'Sexist Bias in Reading Schemes', in Hoyles, M. (ed), *The Politics of Literacy*, Writers and Readers Co-operative

Lobban, G., 1978, The Influence of the School on Sex-role Stereotyping', in Chetwynd J. and Harnett, O. (eds), *The Sex Role System: Psychological and Sociological Perspectives*, Routledge and Kegan Paul

Loewenberg, J., and Bogin, R. (eds), 1978, *Black Women in Nineteenth-century American Life*, Pennsylvania State University Press

Mack, J., 1974, 'Women's Studies in Cambridge', *The New Era*, Vol.55, no.6

McRobbie, A., 1978, 'Working-class Girls and the Culture of Femininity', in Women's Studies Group, Centre for Contemporary Cultural Studies, *Women take Issue: Aspects of Women's Subordination*, Hutchinson

McRobbie, A. and Garber, J., 1975, 'Girls and Subcultures', in Hall, S. and Jefferson, T. (eds), *Resistance through Rituals: Youth Subcultures in Postwar Britain*, Hutchinson

McWilliams-Tullberg, R., 1975, *Women at Cambridge: A Men's University – though of a Mixed Type*, Gollancz

Maccia, E. et al (eds), 1975, *Women and Education*, Thomas Springfield, Illinois

Maccoby, E. and Jacklin, C., 1974, *The Psychology of Sex Differences*, Stanford University Press

Mackie, L. and Patullo, P., 1977, *Women at Work*, Tavistock

Marx, K., 1859, 1904, *Contribution to the Critique of Political Economy*, translated by N.I. Stone from the 2nd German edition, Kerr, Chicago

Mead, M., 1971, *Male and Female*, Penguin

Mepham, J., 1974, 'The Theory of Ideology in Capital', *Cultural studies*, no.6, Birmingham Centre for Cultural Studies

Miliband, R., 1969, *The State in Capitalist Society*, Weidenfeld and Nicolson

Miliband, R., 1970, 'The Capitalist State: Reply to Nicolas Poulantzas', *New Left Review*, no.59

Miller, C. and Swift, K., 1976, *Words and Women: New Language in New Times*, Penguin

Miller, J.B., 1976, *Towards a New Psychology of Women*, Penguin

Milner, D., 1975, *Children and Race*, Penguin

Neale, D.C., Gill, N. and Tismer, W., 1970, 'Relationship between Attitudes towards School Subjects and School Achievement', *Journal of Educational Psychology*, no.63

Newsom, J., 1948, *The Education of Girls*, Faber

The Newsom Report, 1963, *Half Our Future*, report of the Central Advisory Council for Education (England), HMSO

Nightingale, C., 1974, 'Boys will be Boys, but what will Girls be?' in Hoyles, M. (ed), *The Politics of Literacy*, Writers and Readers Publishing Co-operative

Nightingale, C., 1977, 'Sex Roles in Children's Literature', in Allen, S., Sanders, L. and Wallis, J., (eds), *Conditions of Illusion*, Feminist Press, Leeds

Nilsen, A.P., 1973, 'Grammatical Gender and its Relationship to the Equal Treatment of Males and Females in Children's Books', unpublished Ph.D thesis, University of Iowa

Nilsen, A.P., 1975, 'Women in Children's Literature', Maccia, E. et al (eds), *Women and Education*, Thomas, Springfield, Illinois

The Norwood Report, 1943, *Curriculum and Examinations in Secondary Schools,* report of the Committee of the Secondary School Examination Council, HMSO

Oakley, A., 1972, *Sex, Gender and Society*, Temple Smith

Oakley, A., 1974, *The Sociology of Housework*, Martin Robertson, Oxford

O'Connor, M. and Bethell, A., 1978, 'Pick 'n' Choose', *Teaching London Kids*, no.10

Parker, A., 1973, 'Sex Differences in Classroom Intellectual Argumentation', unpublished M.Sc thesis, Pennsylvania State University

Partington, G., 1977, 'Women Teachers in the Twentieth Century', NFER

Pekin, L.B., 1939, *Co-education*, Hogarth Press

The Plowden Report, 1967, *Children and Their Primary School*, HMSO

Poole, J., 1646, *The English Accidence*, Scholar Press Facsimile, Menston

Poulantzas, N., 1969, 'The Problems of the Capitalist State', *New Left Review*, no.58

Power, E., 1975, *Medieval Women*, Cambridge University Press

Reich, A., 1974, 'Teaching is a Good Profession . . . for a Woman', in Stacey J. et al (eds), *And Jill Came Tumbling After: Sexism in American Education*, Dell, New York

Reubens, E., 1978, 'In Defiance of the Evidence: Notes on Feminist Scholarship', *Women's Studies International Quarterly*, Vol.1, no.3

The Robbins Report, 1936, *Higher Education*, Committee on Higher Education, HMSO

Roberts, J. (ed), 1976, *Beyond Intellectual Sexism: A New Woman, a New Reality*, McKay, New York

Rowbotham, S., 1973, *Hidden from History: 300 Years of Women's Oppression and the Fight Against it*, Pluto

Schill, E., 1971, 'Looking towards Marriage', in Lernoff, F.G. (ed), *Honesty to Children*, Shotton Hall, Shrewsbury

Schneider, J. and Hacker, S., 1972, 'Sex role Imagery and the Use of the Generic "man" in Introductory Texts: A Case in the Sociology of Sociology', paper presented at Sociology of Sex Roles, American Sociological Association, New Orleans, August

Schofield, M., 1965, *The Sexual Behaviour of Young People*, Longman

218

Schofield, M., 1973 *The Sexual Behaviour of Young Adults*, Allen Lane

Schulz, M., 1978, 'Man (Embracing Woman): The Generic in Sociological Writing', paper presented at Sociolinguistics: Language and Sex, Ninth World Congress on Sociology, Uppsala, 14–20 August

Searle, C., 1973, *White Words and Black People*, Penguin

Sears, P. and Feldman, D.H., 1974, 'Teacher Interactions with Boys and Girls', in Stacey, J. et al (eds), *And Jill Came Tumbling After: Sexism in American Education*, Dell, New York

Sharpe, S., 1976, *Just Like a Girl*, Penguin

Shaw, J., 1976, 'Finishing School: Some Implications of Sex Segregated Education' in Leonard, D.B. and Allen, S., (eds), *Sexual Divisions and Society : Process and Change*, Tavistock

Shaw, J., 1977a, 'Sexual Divisions in the Classroom', paper presented at 'Teaching Girls to be Women' conference Essex, April

Shaw, J., 1977b, 'School Attendance - some notes on a further feature of sexual division', paper presented at British Sociological Association's Sexual Divisions and Society Study Group, June

Showalter, E., 1974, 'Women and the Literary Curriculum', in Stacey, J. et al (eds), *And Jill Came Tumbling After: Sexism in American Education*, Dell, New York

Smith, D., 1978, 'A Peculiar Eclipsing: Women's Exclusion from Man's Culture', *Women's Studies International Quarterly*, Vol.1, no.4

Spaulding, R., 1963, 'Achieving, Creativity and Self-concept Correlates of Teacher-pupil Transactions in Elementary Schools', in Co-operative Research Project no.1352, US Dept. of Health, Education and Welfare, Office of Education, Washington DC

Spencer, M., 1976, 'Learning to Read and the Reading Process', *Language and Literacy*, University of London Institute of Education

Spender, D., 1978, 'Collaborative Learning: Woman Talk', Feminist Research Group papers presented at 'Language-linked Problems of Inner-city Schools', University of London Institute of Education

Stacey, J., Bereaud, S. and Daniels, J. (eds), 1974, *And Jill Came Tumbling After: Sexism in American Education*, Dell, New York

Stein, A.H. and Smithells, J., 1969, 'Age and Sex Differences in Children's Sex role Standards about Achievement', *Developmental Psychology*, no.1

Stinton, J. (ed) 1979, *Racism and Sexism in Children's Books*, Writers and Readers Publishing Co-operative

St. John, C., 1932, 'The Maladjustment of Boys in Certain Elementary Grades', *Educational Administration and Supervision*, no.18

Sutton Smith, B., and Rosenberg, R., 1961, 'Sixty Years of Historical Change in the Game Preference of American School Children', *Journal of American Folklore*, 74

Tobias, S., 1978, *Overcoming Math Anxiety*, Norton, New York

Torrance, E.P., 1962, *Guiding Creative Talent*, Prentice Hall, Englewood Cliff, New Jersey

Trecker, J., 1974, 'Women in US History High School Textbooks', in Stacey, J. et al (eds), *And Jill Came Tumbling After: Sexism in American*

Education, Dell, New York

Trenchard, L., and Warren H., 1984, *Something to Tell You*, The London Gay Teenage Group

Walters, A., 1978, 'Women Writers and Prescribed Texts', 'Waste papers' presented at National Association for the Teaching of English Annual Conference, York, March

Whitty, G. and Young, M. (eds), 1976, *Explorations in the Politics of School Knowledge*, Studies in Education, Nafferton, Driffield

Williams, R., 1975, *The Long Revolution*, Penguin

Willis, P., 1977, *Learning to Labour: How Working-class Kids get Working-class Jobs*, Saxon House

Wilson, T., 1553, 1962, *Arte & Rhetorique*, Scholars Facsimiles and Reprints, Gainsville

Wolff, J., 1977, 'Women's Studies and Sociology', *Sociology*, Vol.2, no.1

Wolpe, A-M., 1974, 'The Official Ideology of Education for Girls', in Flude, M. and Ahier, J. (eds), *Educability, Schools and Ideology*, Croom Helm

Wolpe, A-M., 1977, *Some Processes in Sexist Education*, Women's Research and Resources Centre Publications

Women and Education, 1978, 'Girls' Schools Remembered', *Women and Education*, Manchester, no.13

Women's Studies Group, 1978, *Women Take Issue: Aspects of Women's Subordination*, Hutchinson

Woolf, V., 1929a, *A Room of One's Own*, reprinted 1977, Panther

Woolf, V., 1929b, 'Women and Fiction' reprinted in Barrett, M. (ed), 1979, *Women and Writing*, The Women's Press

Young, M.F.D., 1975, 'An Approach to the Study of Curricula as Socially Organized Knowledge', in Young, M.F.D. (ed), *Knowledge and Control: New Directions for the Sociology of Knowledge*, Collier Macmillan

Young, M. and Whitty, G. (eds), 1977, *Society, State and Schooling*, Falmer, Lewes

Zimmerman, D. and West, C., 1975, 'Sex Roles, Interruptions and Silences in Conversation', in Thorne, B. and Henley, N. (eds), *Language and Sex: Difference and Dominance*, Newbury House, Rowley, Mass.

Further Reading

Sexism and education: articles and books

Acker, S., 1980, 'Feminist Perspectives and the British Sociology of Education', paper presented at the British Sociological Association Annual Conference, Lancaster, 8 April

Acker, S., 1981a, 'No-woman's Land: British Sociology of Education 1960–79', *Sociological Review*, Vol.29, no.1, pp 77–104

Acker, S., 1981b, 'Sex Discrimination in Education: A Reply to Shaw',

Journal of Philosophy of Education, Vol.15, no.1, pp 107–118 (qv. Shaw, B., 1979)

Acker, S. et al (eds), 1984, 'Women and Education' in *World Yearbook of Education*, Routledge and Kegan Paul

Acker, S. and Warren Piper, D. (eds), 1984, *Is Higher Education Fair to Women?*, SRHE and FRER Nelson, Slough

Adams, C., 1984, 'The Significance of Gender in Teacher Attitudes towards Sex Equality', a case study of an in-service course, unpublished MA dissertation, Univerisity of London

Adams, C. and Arnot, M. (comps), 1986, *Investigating Gender in Secondary Schools*, a series of in-service workshops for ILEA teachers, ILEA

Adams, C. and Walkerdine, V. (comps), 1986, *Investigating Gender in the Primary School*, activity-based INSET materials for primary teachers, ILEA

Advisory Centre for Education (ACE), 1982, 'Girls can do anything!', *Where*, no.174, Jan, pp 7–10

Advisory Centre for Education (ACE), 1981, 'Sexism in Schools', *Where*, no.165, Feb, pp 11–14.

Advisory Centre for Education (ACE), 1985, *Sex Discrimination in Education: A Guide to the Law, to Identifying and Avoiding Discrimination and to Making Complaints*, ACE.

Archer, J. and Westeman, K., 1981, 'Sex Differences in the Aggressive Behaviour of Schoolchildren', *British Journal of Sociology & Psychology*, Vol.20, pt.1, Feb, pp 31–36

Arnot, M. (ed), 1985, *Race and Gender: Equal Opportunities Policies in Education*, Pergamon, Oxford

Arnot, M., 1986, 'State Education Policy and Girls' Educational Experiences in Beechey, V. and Whitelegg, E., *Women in Britain Today*, Open University Press, Milton Keynes

Arnot M, and Weiner, G. (eds), 1987, *Gender and the Politics of Schooling*, Hutchinson

Barton, L. and Walker, S. (eds), 1983, *Race, Class and Education*, Croom Helm

Bayley, S. Morris, J. and Sheppard, J., 1983, 'Sexism in Schools', *Association of Educational Psychologists*, Vol.6, no.2, Autumn, pp 12–17

Bloomfield, J., 1984, 'Option Scheme Management of Equal Opportunity', paper presented at Girl-Friendly Schooling Conference, Manchester Polytechnic, 11–13 Sept

Bone, A., 1983, *Girls and Girls-only Schools: A Review of the Evidence*, EOC, Manchester

Bossert, S.T., 1987, 'Understanding Sex Differences in Children's Classroom Experience', in Doyle, W. (ed), *Focus on Teaching*, Chicago University Press

Bowles, G. (ed), 1983, 'Strategies for Women's Studies in the 1980's', *Women's Studies International Forum*, Vol.7, no.3, special issue

Bradbury, R. and Newbould, C., 1983, 'Sexist Microcosm', *Teaching History*, no. 36, June, pp 9–11

Braithwaite J., 1981, 'Sex Differences in the School-related Achievement of Disadvantaged Preschool Children', *Early Child Development and Care*, Vol.7, no.1, pp 83–97

Breathnach, E., 1987, *Storming the Campus*, Arlen, Dublin

Brixton Black Women's Group, 1980, 'Disruptive Units', *Speak out*, 1980

Broadfoot, P. and Sutherland, M.B. (eds), 1987, 'Sex Differences in Education', *Comparative Education*, Vol.23, special issue

Brown, K., 1983, *Futura Girls*, Shropshire LEA

Browne, N. and France, P. (eds), 1986, *Untying the Apron Strings: Anti-sexist Provision of Under-fives*, Open University Press, Milton Keynes

Brush, L.R., 1979, *Why Women Avoid the Study of Mathematics: A Longitudinal Study*, ABGT Associates, Cambridge, Mass.

Bryan, B., Dadzie, S. and Scafe, S., 1985, 'Learning to Resist: Black Women and Education', in *The Heart of the Race: Black Women's Lives in Britain*, Virago

Bryant, M., 1979, *The Unexpected Revolution: A Study in the History of the Education of Women and Girls in the Nineteenth Century*, University of London Institute of Education

Buckley, A., 1979, *Sex Discrimination in Secondary Education*, a case study of the subject choice of boys and girls in two mixed comprehensive schools, City of London Polytechnic, MA dissertation

Bunch, C. and Pollack, S. (eds), 1983, *Learning our Way: Essays in Feminist Education*, Crossing Press, Trumansburg, NY

Burstyn, J.N., 1980, *Victorian Education and the Ideal of Womanhood*, Croom Helm

Burton, L. (ed), 1986, *Girls into Maths Can Go*, Holt, Rinehart & Winston

Campbell, A., 1984, *The Girls in the Gang: A Report from New York City*, Blackwell, Oxford

Cannon, M., 1985, *Education of Women during the Renaissance*, reprint of 1916 edition, Hyperion, Conn.

Catton, J., 1986, *Ways and Means: The CDT Education of Girls*, Longman

Ceccini, F.G., 1981, *Research on Sex Stereotyping: Why Focus on the School?* Council of Europe, Strasbourg

Chandler, E.M., 1980, *Educating Adolescent Girls*, Allen & Unwin

Chapman, A., (ed), 1986, *Feminist Resources for Schools and Colleges: A Guide to Curriculum Materials*, third edition, Feminist Press, Old Westbury, New York

Chipman, S.F., Brush, L.R. and Wilson, D.M., 1985, *Women and Mathematics: Balancing the Equation*, Lawrence Erlbaum Assoc.

Chisholm, L.A. and Holland, J., 1986, 'Girls and Occupational Choice: Anti-sexism in Action in a Curriculum Development Project', *British Journal of Sociology of Education*, Vol.7, no.4

Chivers, G.E. and Marshall, P., 1983, 'Attitudes and Experiences of some Young British Women entering Engineering Education and Training Courses', paper presented at the Girls and Science and Technology conference, Oslo, Sept.

City of Leicester Teachers' Association, 1987, *Outlaws in the Classroom: Lesbians and Gays in the School System*, C.L.T.A., Leicester

Clarricoates, K., 1983, 'Some Aspects of the "Hidden" Curriculum and Interaction in the Classroom', *Primary Education Review*, no.17, Summer, pp 10–14

Connell, R.W. et al, 1982, *Making the Difference: Schools, Families and Social Division*, Allen & Unwin

Connell, R.W., 1985, *Teacher's Work*, Allen & Unwin

Connell, R.W., 1983, *Which Way is Up? Essays on Class, Sex and Culture*, Allen & Unwin

Coote, A., 1980, 'Why Girls don't like Maths', *New Statesman*, 11 Jan

Cornbleet, A. and Sanders, S., 1982, *Developing Anti-sexist Initiatives* (DASI), ILEA/EOC

Crossman, F.M., 1984, 'Girl-talk – Teacher/pupil Interaction', paper presented at 'Girl-friendly Schooling' conference, Manchester Polytechnic, 11–14 Sept.

Crowther, R.D. and Durkin, K., 1982, 'Sex and Age-related Differences in the Musical Behaviour, Interests and Attitudes towards Music of 232 Secondary School Students', *Educational Studies*, Abingdon, Vol.8, no.2, pp 131–139

Cullen, M. (ed), 1987, *Women in Education*, Arlen, Dublin

Dale, R. et al (eds), 1981, *Education and the State*, Vol.2: *Politics, Patriarchy and Practice*, Falmer, Lewes

Davis, J. and Ticher, J., 1986, 'Can Girls Build or do they Choose not to? A Study of Girls and Boys using Construction Materials', *Primary Teaching Studies*, Vol.1, no.2, Feb, pp 28–36

David, M., 1986, *Child Care Policy: A Feminist Perspective*, HMSO

Davies, L., 1984, *Pupil Power: Deviance and Gender in School*, Falmer, Lewes

Deem, R., 1984, *Co-education Reconsidered*, Open University Press, Milton Keynes

Deem, R. (ed), 1980, *Schooling for Women's Work*, Routledge and Kegan Paul

Deem, R., 1981, 'State Policy and Ideology in the Education of Women, 1944–1980', *British Journal of Sociology of Education*, Vol.2, no.2, pp 131–144

Delamont, S., 1980, *Sex Roles and the School*, Methuen

Department of Education and Science, 1980, *Girls and Science: HMI Matters for Discussion*, HMSO

Dinitto, D., Martin, P.Y. and Harrison, D.F., 1982, 'Sexual Discrimination in Higher Education', *Higher Education Review*, Vol.14, no.2, Spring, pp 35–54

Driver, G., 1980, 'How West Indians do Better at School (especially the Girls)', *New Society*, January

Dubois, E. et al, 1985, *Feminist Scholarship: Kindling in the Groves of Academe*, University of Illinois Press

Dunlop, F., 1982, 'The Ideas of Male and Female: a Prolegomenon to the

Question of Educational Sex-bias', *Journal of Philosophy of Education*, Vol.16, no.2, pp 209–222

Dweck, C.S. and Bush, E.S., 1976, 'Sex Differences in Learned Helplessness', *Developmental Psychology*, Vol.12, pp 147–161

Dyhouse, C., 1981, *Girls Growing up in Late Victorian and Edwardian England*, Routledge and Kegan Paul

Dyhouse, C., 1977, 'Good wives and Little Mothers: Social Anxieties and the Schoolgirls' Curriculum, 1890–1920', *Oxford Review of Education,* Vol.3, no.1, pp 21–35

Eddowes, M., 1983, *Humble Pi: The Mathematics Education of Girls*, Longman

Eddowes, M. and Sturgeon, S.B., 1981, *Mathematics Education and Girls: A Research Report*, Sheffield City Polytechnic and the British Petroleum Company Ltd

Ennew, J., 1986, *The Sexual Exploitation of Children*, Polity Press

Equal Opportunities Commission,
    1981, *Education of Girls: A Statistical Analysis*
    1982, *Gender and the Secondary School Curriculum*
    1983, *Equal Opportunities in CDT*
    1983, *Equal Opportunities in the Classroom*, conference held 12 March 1983, Birmingham
    1983, *Girls and Girls' Only Schools*
    1983, *Information Technology in Schools*, L.B. Croydon
    1985, *Equal Opportunities and the School Governor*
    1985, *Equal Opportunities and the Woman Teacher*

EOC, Manchester (Contact them for details of new publications)

European Community Action Programme, 1985, *Action Handbook: How to Implement Gender Equality*, (Working document DOC: 05WDF85EN), IFAPLAN Programme Information Office, Brussels

Evans, J., 1984, 'Muscle, Sweat and Showers: Girls' Conceptions of Physical Education and Sport: A challenge for Research and Curriculum Reform', *Physical Education Review*, Vol.7, no.1, Spring, pp 12–18

Evans, T.D., 1982, 'Being and Becoming: Teachers' Perceptions of Sex-roles and Actions towards their Male and Female Pupils', *British Journal of Sociology of Education*, Vol.3, no.2, pp 127–143

Everley, B., 1983, 'Measures to reduce Sex-role Stereotyping in the Primary School', *Primary Education Review*, no.17, Summer, pp 13–15

Everley, B., Everley, M. and Oldham, P., 1981, 'Teachers Study Group on Sex Differences and the Curriculum', *Sheffield Educational Research Current Highlights*, no.3, August, pp 12–13

Fawcett Society, 1986, *Opening Doors: to Equality in Education and Training for Girls*, Fawcett Society

Fennema, E. and Ayers, J., 1984, *Women and Education: Equity or Equality?* McCutchan, Berkeley, CA

Fennema, E. and Peterson, P.L., 1986, 'Teacher-student Interactions and Sex-related Differences in Learning Mathematics', *Teaching and Teacher Eduction*, Vol.2, no.1, pp 19–42

Fennema, E. and Sherman, J., 1977, 'Sexual Stereotyping and Mathematics Learning', *Arithmetic Teacher*, Vol.24, no.5, pp 369–72

Fennema, E. and Sherman, J., 1978, 'Sex-related Differences in Mathematics Achievement and Related Factors: A Further Study', *Journal of Research in Mathematical Education*, Vol 9, pp 189–203

Fletcher, S., 1984, *Women First: The Female Tradition in Physical Education, 1880–1980*, Athlone

Flynn, P., 1986, *You're Learning all the Time: Women, Education and Community Work*, Spokesman Books, Nottingham

Foster, V., 1984, *Changing Choices: Girls, School and Work*, Hale & Ironmonger, Sydney

Fox, L.H., 1979, *Women and Mathematics: The Impact of Early Intervention Programs upon Course-taking and Attitudes in High School*, John Hopkins University, Baltimore

French, J., 1986, 'Gender and the Classroom', *New Society*, Vol.75, no.1210, 7 March, pp 404-406

French, J. and French, P. 1983, 'Gender Imbalances in the Primary Classroom: and Interactional Account', *Educational Research*, Vol.26, no.2, June, pp 127–136

Friesman, S., 1980, 'Gender, Class and Education', *Schooling and Culture*

Gaff, R., 1982, 'Sex-stereotyping in Modern Language Teaching: An Aspect of the Hidden Curriculum', *British Journal of Language Teaching*, Vol.20, no.2, Summer, pp 71–78

Gamma (Girls and Mathematics Association), 1985, *Bibliography*, GAMMA

Gamarnikow, E. et al (eds), 1983, *Gender, Class and Work*, Heinemann

Gates, B., Klaw, S. and Steinberg, A., 1979, *Changing Learning, Changing Lives: A High School Women's Studies Curriculum of the Group School*, Feminist Press, Old Westbury, New York

Gilbert, V.F. and Tatla, D.S. (comps), 1985, *Women's Studies: A Bibliography of Dissertations, 1870–1982*, (pp 28–93: Education), Blackwell, Oxford

Girls and Occupational Choice, 1984–1986, Working papers, University of London Institute of Education

Gray, J., McPherson, A. and Raffe, D., 1979, 'Boys and Girls Choose Different Subjects', *Educational Research*, Vol.21, no.3

Goldsmith, J. and Shawcross, V., 1985, *It ain't half Sexist, Mum: Women as Overseas Students in the UK*, WUS and UK Council on Overseas Student Affairs

Gorham, D., 1982, *The Victorian Girl and the Feminine Ideal*, Croom Helm

Griffin, C. and Barton L. (eds), 1985, *Typical Girls? Young Women from School to the Full-time Job Market*, Routledge and Kegan Paul

Griffiths, V., 1986, *Using Drama to get at Gender*, University of Manchester, Dept of Sociology

Hacker, R.G., 1986, 'Class, Gender and Science Teaching Processes', *European Journal of Science Education*, Vol.8, no.1, Jan–March, pp 57–71

Hannan, D. et al, 1983, *Schooling and Sex Roles: Sex Differences in Subject Provision and Student Choice in Irish Post-primary Schools*, Economic and

Social Research Institute, Dublin

Harding, J., 1979, 'Sex Differences in Examination Performance at 16+', *Physical Education*, Vol.14

Harding, J., 1983, *Switched off: The Science Education of Girls*, Longman

Harding, J., 1985, 'Girls and Women in Secondary and Higher Education: Science for only a Few', *Prospects*, (UNESCO) Vol.15, no.4, pp 553–564

Harding, J., 1986, 'The Making of a Scientist', *University Quarterly*, Vol.40, no.1, Winter, pp 55–62

Harlen, W., 1985, 'Girls and Primary-school Science Education: Sexism Stereotypes and Remedies', *Prospects*, (UNESCO) Vol.15, no.4, pp 539–551

Harvey, T.J., 1984, 'Gender Differences in Subject Preference and Perception of Subject Importance among Third-year Secondary School Pupils in Single-sex and Mixed Comprehensive Schools', *Educational Studies*, Abingdon, Vol.10, no.3, Oct., pp 243–253

Harvey, T.J., 1985, 'The Correlation between Mechanical Reasoning and Spatial Ability, for First-year Secondary School Boys and Girls: A Research Note', *Journal of Further and Higher Education*, Vol.9, no.2, Summer, pp 77–80

Harvey T.J. and Wilson, B., 1985, 'Gender Differences in Attitudes towards Microcomputers shown by Primary and Secondary School Pupils', *British Journal of Educational Technology*, Vol.16, no.3, Oct, pp 183–187

Haworth, G., Povey, R. and Clift, S., 1986, 'Girls and Engineering: Perceived Influences on Career Choice among Craft and Technician Engineers and Non–engineers', *British Journal of Guidance and Counselling*, Vol.14, no.2, May, pp 196–204

Hearn, M., 1979, 'Girls for Physical Science: A School-based Strategy for Encouraging Girls to Opt for the Physical Sciences', *Education in Science*, April

Hedge, A., 1985, *Gay Students at School*, ACE

Holland, J., 1986, 'Girls and Occupational Choice: In Search of Meanings', paper for Education and Training 14–18 conference, St Hilda's, Oxford, Sept

Holleran, P.R., 1984, 'Sex Equality as a Curricular Issue', *Higher Education Review*, Vol.16, no.3, Summer, pp 9–15

Hoste, R., 1982, 'Sex Differences and Similarities in Performance in a CSE Biology Examination', *Educational Studies*, Abingdon, Vol.8, no.2, pp 141–155

Hudson, B., 1985, 'Social Division or Adding up to Equality? Militarist, Sexist and Ethnocentrist Bias in Mathematics Textbooks and Computer Software', *World Studies Journal*, Vol.15, no.4, pp 24–29

Hughes, M. and Kennedy, M., 1985, *New Futures: Changing Women's Education*, Routledge and Kegan Paul

Hunt, F. (ed), 1987, *Women and Education 1850–1950*, Blackwell, Oxford.

Hutchins, G., 1984, 'Challenging Traditional Sex-role Stereotypes in Careers Education Broadcasts: The Reactions of Young Secondary School Pupils', *Journal of Educational Television*, Vol.10, no.1, March, pp 25–33

Inner London Education Authority, 1985, *Everybody Counts: Looking for Bias and Insensitivity in Primary Mathematics Materials*, ILEA

Inner London Education Authority, 1985, *Report of the Working Party on Single-sex and Co-education*, ILEA

Inner London Education Authority, 1985, *The English Curriculum: Gender*, ILEA English Centre

Inner London Education Authority, 1986, *Primary Matters: Some Approaches to Equal Opportunities in Primary Schools*, ILEA

Inner London Education Authority, 1986, *Secondary Issues? Some Approaches to Equal Opportunities in Secondary Schools*, ILEA

Inner London Education Authority, 1987, *Further Concerns: Some Approaches to Equal Opportunities in Further Education Colleges*, ILEA

Issues in Race and Education, 1984, 'Issues for girls', *Issues in Race and Education*, no.41, Spring

Jonathan, R.M., 1983, 'Education, Gender and the Nature/Culture Controversy', *Journal of Philosophy of Education*, Vol.17, no.1, July, pp 5–20

Jones, J. (ed), 1985, 'Sexism in Schools', *School Organisation*, Vol.5, no.1, Jan–March, special issue

Kalia, N., 1979, *Sexism in Indian Education: Lies we Tell our Children*, Vikas, New Delhi

Kant, L., 1982, 'Are Examinations up to the Mark?', *Secondary Education Journal*, Vol.12, no.2, June, pp 8–10

Kant, L. and Brown, M., 1983, *Jobs for the Girls*, School Curriculum Development Committee

Kelly, A., 1981, *The Missing Half: Girls and Science Education*, Manchester University Press

Kelly, A. et al, 1982, 'Gender Roles at Home and School', *British Journal of Sociology of Education*, Vol.3, no.3, pp 281–295

Kelly, A. and Smail, B., 1986, 'Sex Stereotypes and Attitudes to Science among Eleven-year-old Children', *British Journal of Educational Psychology*, Vol.56, no.2, June, pp 158–168

Kelly, A., Whyte, J. and Smail, B., 1984, *Girls into Science and Technology: Final Report*, University of Manchester, Dept. of Sociology

Kelly, P. and Elliot, C. (eds), 1982, *Women's Education in the Third World: Comparative Perspectives*, State University, New York

Klein, S. (ed), 1985, *Handbook for Achieving Sex equality through Education*, John Hopkins, Baltimore

Langland, E. (ed), 1981, *A Feminist Perspective in the Academy: The Difference it Makes*, University of Chicago Press

Lasser, C., 1987, *Educating Men and Women Together: Co-education in a Changing World*, University of Illinois Press

Leaman, O., 1984, *Sit on the Sidelines and Watch the Boys Play: Sex Differentiation in Physical Education*, Longman

Lees, S., 1983, 'How Boys Slag off Girls', *New Society*, 13 Oct

Lees, S., 1986a, *Learning to Love: How Girls become Wives*, Hutchinson

Lees, S., 1986a, *Losing out: Sexuality and Adolescent Girls*, Hutchinson

Liss, M.B. (ed), 1983, *Social and Cognitive Skills: Sex Roles and Children's Play*, Academic Press, New York

Lloyd, B. and Smith, C., 1985, 'The Social Representation of Gender and Young Children's Play', *British Journal of Developmental Psychology*, Vol.3, pt.1, March, pp 65–73

McRobbie, A. and Nava, M., 1984, *Gender and Generation*, MacMillan

McRobbie, A., 1978, *Jackie: An Ideology of Adolescent Femininity*, University of Birmingham, Centre for Contemporary Cultural Studies

Mahony, P., 1983a, 'Boys will be Boys: Teaching Women's Studies in Mixed-sex Groups', *Women's Studies International Forum*, Vol.6, no.3

Mahony, P., 1983b, 'How Alice's Chin really came to be Pressed against her Foot: Sexist Processes of Interaction in Mixed-sex Classrooms', *Women's Studies International Forum*, Vol.6, no.1, pp 1,07–115

Mahony, P., 1985, *Schools for Boys? Co-education Reassessed*, Hutchinson

Majumdar, P.K., 1983, *Faltering First Step: Reasons for Disparity of Sex-ratio in Primary Education Level: A Sociological Analysis*, Cosmo, New Delhi

Marland, M. (ed), 1983, *Sex Differentiation and Schooling*, Heinemann

Marshall, J., 1983, 'Developing Anti-sexist Initiatives in Education', *International Journal of Political Education*, Vol.6, no.2, Aug., pp 113–137

Martini, R., Myers, K. and Warner, S., 1984, *Is your School Changing?*, ILEA

May, N. and Rudduck, J., 1983, *Sex Stereotyping and the Early Years of Schooling*, University of East Anglia, Centre for Applied Research in Education

Mathematical Education Committee, 1986, *Girls and Mathematics*, The Royal Society

Meyenn, R.J., 1980, 'Schoolgirls' Peer Groups', in Woods, P. (ed), *Pupil Strategies*, Croom Helm

Michel, A., 1986, *Down with Stereotypes: Eliminating Sexism from Children's Literature and School Textbooks*, UNESCO, Paris

Millman, V., 1982, *Double Vision: The Post-school Experience of 16–19-year-old Girls*, Elm Bank Teachers' Centre, Coventry

Millman, V., 1984, *Teaching Technology to Girls*, Coventry Education Authority

Millman, V. and Weiner, G., 1985, *Sex Differentiation in Schooling: Is there Really a Problem?*, Longman

Murphy, R.J.L., 1982, 'Sex Differences in Objective Test Performance', *British Journal of Educational Psychology*, Vol.52, pt.2, June, pp 213–219

Myers, K. (ed), 1986, *Genderwatch! Self-assessment Schedules for Use in Schools*, Schools Curriculum Development Committee

National Association for the Teaching of English, Language and Gender Working Party, 1985, *Alice in Genderland: Reflections on Language, Power and Control*, NATE, Sheffield

National Association of Teachers in Further and Higher Education, 1980, *The Education, Training and Employment of Women and Girls*, NATFHE

National Association of Teachers in Further and Higher Education, National Union of Teachers and National Association of Schoolmasters and Union of

Women Teachers, *Sexual Harassment of Women Teachers*, NATFHE

Northam, J., 1982, 'Girls and Boys in Primary Maths Books', *Education 3–13*, Vol.10, no.1, Spring, pp 11–14

O'Donnell, C., 1984, *The Basis of the Bargain: Gender, Schooling and Jobs*, Allen & Unwin

OECD, 1986, *Girls and Women in Education*, OECD

Open University /ILEA, 1986, *Girls into Mathematics*, Cambridge University Press

Open University, 1981, 'Class, Gender and Education', (E353, units 10/11), Open University

Open University, 1983, 'Educating Girls', (U221, unit 13), Open University

Open University, 1984, 'Gender Differentiation in Schools', (E205, unit 26), Open University

Open University, 1984, Inequality: Gender, Race and Class', (E205, unit 27), Open University

Open University, 1984, 'Women and Education', (E205, unit 25), Open University

Open University, 1986, 'Race, Gender and Education Policy-making', (E333, module 4), Open University

Organisation of Women of Asian and African Descent, 1979, 'Black Women and Education', OWAAD conference papers, *Black Women in Britain Speak Out*, Women in Print

Orr, P., 1982, 'Sex Differentiation in the Curriculum', *Secondary Education Journal*, Vol.12, no.2, June, pp 3–5

Pain, C., 1980, 'Are we Providing Equal Opportunities? A Study of Sex-role Stereotyping in an Infant School', *Sheffield Educational Research Current Highlights*, no.2, Aug, pp 13–14

Paley, V.G., 1984, *Boys and Girls: Superheroes in the Doll Corner*, University of Chicago Press

Parker, F. and Parker, B., 1981, *Women's Education: A World View*, Vol.1: *Annotated Bibliography of Doctoral Dissertations*; Vol.2: *Annotated Bibliography of Books and Reports*, Greenwood, New York

Parmar, P., 1981, 'Young Asian Women: A Critique of the Pathological Approach', *Multiracial Education*, Vol.9, no.3, pp 19–29

Partington, G., 1976, *Women Teachers in the Twentieth Century in England and Wales*, NFER – Nelson, Slough

Payne, G., Cuff, E. and Hustler, D., 1984, *GIST or PIST: Teacher Perceptions of the Project 'Girls into Science and Technology'* (mimeo), Manchester Polytechnic

Pellow, E., 1984, 'Primary Science and Girls: The Need for Intervention', *Primary Education Review*, no.19, Spring, pp 15–16

Pepper, B., Myers, K. and Coyle–Dawkins, R., 1984, *Sex Equality and the Pastoral Curriculum*, ILEA

Pratt, J., Bloomfield, J. and Seale, C., 1984, *Option Choice: A Question of Equal Opportunities*, NFER – Nelson, Slough

Rendel, M., 1978, 'The Death of Leadership or Educating People to Lead Themselves', *Women's Studies International Quarterly*, Vol.1, no.3

Riding, R.J. and Armstrong, J.M., 1982, 'Sex and Personality Differences in Performance on Mathematics Tests in 11-year-old Children', *Educational Studies, Abingdon*, Vol.8, no.3, pp 217–225

Riding, R.J. and Boardman, D.J., 1983, 'The Relationship between Sex and Learning Style and Graphicacy in 14-year-old Children', *Education Review*, Vol.35, no.1, pp 69–79

Riley, K., 1981, 'Black Girls Speak for Themselves', *Multiracial Education*, Vol.10, no.3, pp 3–12

Robyns, J., 1977, 'Reproductive versus Regenerative Education: The Extension of English Education through Reference to Feminism', University of London Institute of Education, unpublished associateship report

Sadker, M., 1981, *Sex Equity Handbook for Schools*, Longman, New York

Safilios-Rothschild, C., 1981, *Sex-stereotyping in US Primary and Secondary Schools and Interventions to Eliminate Sexism*, Council of Europe, Strasbourg

Sexton, P., 1976, *Women and Education*, Phi Delta Kappa, Bloomington

Shakeshaft, C., 1987, *Women in Educational Administration*, Sage

Sharma, S. and Meighan, R., 1980, 'Schooling and Sex roles: The Case of GCE 'O' level Mathematics', *British Journal of Sociology of Education*, Vol.1, no.2, pp 193–205

Shaw, B., 1979, 'Sex Discrimination in Education: Theory and Practice', *Journal of Philosophy of Education*, vol.13

Sherman, J., 1980, 'Mathematics, Spatial Visualization and Related Factors: Changes in Girls and Boys Grades 8–11', *Journal of Educational Psychology*, Vol.72, no.4, pp 476–482

Sherman, J. and Fennema, E., 1977, 'The Study of Mathematics by High School Girls and Boys: Related Variables', *American Educational Research Journal*, Vol.14, pp 159–168

Shirt, K., 1979, 'Sexism', *Journal of Curriculum Studies*, Vol.11, no.3

Skaalvik, E.M., 1983, 'Academic Achievement, Self-esteem and Valuing of the School: Some Sex Differences', *British Journal of Educational Psychology*, Vol.53, pt.3, Nov, pp 299–306

Slater, F., 1983, 'Sexism and Racism: Parallel Experiences: An Exploration', *Contemporary Issues in Geography Education*, Vol.1, no.11, pp 26–31

Slayton, P. and Vogel, B., 1986, 'People without Faces: Adolescent Homosexuality and Literature', *English in Education*, Vol.20, no.1, Spring, pp 5–13

Smail, B., 1983, 'Getting Science Right for Girls', paper presented to the second International Conference on Girls and Science and Technology, Oslo, Norway

Smail, B., 1984, *Girl-friendly Science: Avoiding Sex Bias in the Curriculum*, Longman

Smock, A., 1981, *Women's Education in Developing Countries: Opportunities and Outcomes*, Praeger, New York

Solomon, B., 1985, *In the Company of Educated Women: A History of Women and Higher Education in America*, Yale University Press

Spare Rib, 1978, 'Back to School', *Spare Rib*, no.75

Spare Rib, 1983, 'Sexual Harassment of Girls and Women Teachers', *Spare Rib*, no.131

Spear, M., 1984, 'Sex Bias in Science Teachers' Ratings of Work and Pupils Characteristics', *European Journal of Science Education*, Vol.6, no.4, Oct–Nov, pp 369–377

Spender, D., 1980a, 'The Education Manacle', *Times Higher Education Supplement*, no.453, 10 July, p 14

Spender, D., 1980b, 'The Facts of Life: Sex-differentiated Knowledge in the English Classroom and School', *English in Education*, Vol.12, no.3

Spender, D. (ed), 1981, *Men's Studies Modified: The Impact of Feminism on the Academic Disciplines'*, Pergamon, Oxford

Spender, D., 1981, *The Role of Teachers: What Choices do they Have?*, Council of Europe, Strasbourg

Spender, D., 1982, *Invisible Women: the Schooling Scandal*, Writers and Readers Publishing Co-operative

Sprung, B., 1976, *Non-sexist Education for Young Children: A Practical Guide*, Women's Action, New York

Sprung, B. (ed), 1978, *Perspectives on Non-sexist Early Childhood Education*, Teachers' College Press, University of Columbia

Stanworth, M., 1983, *Gender and Schooling: A Study of Sexual Divisions in the Classroom*, revised edition, Hutchinson

Statham, J., 1981, 'A Review of Research on Sex-role Learning', *Early Childhood*, Vol.1, no.10, July pp 12–13

Steedman, C., 1982, *The Tidy House: Little Girls' Writing*, Virago

Steedman, J., 1983, *Examination Results in Mixed and Single-sex Schools: Findings from the National Child Development Study*, EOC, Manchester

Stones, R., 1983, *Pour out the Cocoa, Janet: Sexism in Children's Books*, Longman

Sutherland, M., 1981, *Sex Bias in Education*, Blackwell, Oxford

Sutherland, M., 1983, 'Women and Fair Shares in Education', *Education Today*, Vol.33, no.1, pp 60–68

Taylor, H. (ed), 1984, *Seeing is Believing: Teacher Investigations into Gender Differences in the Classroom*, Curriculum Development Study Unit, Brent

Taylor, H. (ed), 1985, *It ain't necessarily so: Studies in Schools' Construction of Female Gender Roles*, Curriculum Development Study Unit, Brent

Taylor, H. (ed), 1986, *Steps to Equality*, Curriculum Development Study Unit, Brent

Teaching London Kids, 1978, no.10, TLK

Tellis-Nayak, J.B., 1982, *Education and Income Generation for Women: Non-formal Approaches*, Indian Social Institute, New Delhi

Thompson, D.G., 1985, *As Boys Become Men: Learning new Male Roles: Curriculum for Exploring Male Role Stereotyping*, Irvington, New York

Thompson, J., 1983, *Learning Liberation: Women's Response to Men's Education*, Croom Helm

Trenchard, L., 1984, *Talking about Young Lesbians*, London Gay Teenage Group

231

Trevett, C., 1983, 'The Lady Vanishes: Sexism by Omission in Religious Education', *British Journal of Religious Education*, Vol.5, no.2, Spring, pp 81–83

Verinsky, P., 1984, 'In Search of a Gender Dimension: An Empirical Investigation of Teacher Preferences in Teaching Strategies in Physical Education', *Journal of Curriculum Studies*, Vol.16, no.4, Oct/Dec, pp 425–430

Walden, R. and Walkerdine, V., 1982, *Girls and Mathematics: The Early Years*, University of London Institute of Education

Walden, R. and Walkerdine, V., 1985, *Girls and Mathematics: From Primary to Secondary Schooling*, University of London Institute of Education

Walford, G., 1983, 'Science Textbook Images and the Reproduction of Sexual Divisions in Society', *Research in Science and Technological Education*, Vol.1, no.1, pp 65–72

Walker, S. and Barton, L. (eds), 1983, *Gender, Class and Education*, Falmer, Lewes

Walkerdine, V., 1981, 'Sex Power and Pedagogy', *Screen Education*, no.38, Spring, pp 14–25

Walkerdine, V. (ed), 1985, *Language, Gender and Childhood*, Routledge and Kegan Paul

Warren, H., 1984, *Talking about School*, London Gay Teenage Group

Warren, H. and Trenchard, L., 1985, *Talking About Youth Work*, London Gay Teenage Group

Weiler, K., 1987, *Women Teaching for Change: Gender, Class and Power*, Bergin and Garvey, South Hadley, Mass.

Weiner, G. (ed), 1985, *Just a Bunch of Girls: Feminist Approaches to Schooling*, Open University Press, Milton Keynes

Weiner, G. and Arnot, M. (eds), 1987, *Gender under Scrutiny: New Inquiries in Education*, Hutchinson, London

White, J., 1985, 'The Writing on the Wall: Beginning or End of a Girl's Career?', *Women's Studies International Forum*, Vol.9, no.5, pp 561–574

Whyld, J., 1983, *Sexism in the Secondary Curriculum*, Harper Row

Whyte, J., 1981, 'Are you Discriminating?', *Junior Education*, Vol.5, no.5, May, pp 10–11

Whyte, J., 1983a, *Beyond the Wendy House: Sex-role Stereotyping in the Primary School*, Longman

Whyte, J., 1983b, 'How Girls Learn to be Losers', *Primary Education Review*, no.17, Summer, pp 5–7

Whyte, J., 1983c, 'Non-sexist Teachers: Evaluating what Teachers can do to help Girls Opt into Science and Technology', proceedings of the 2nd International GASAT Conference, Gran, Norway

Whyte, J., 1984, 'Observing Sex Stereotypes and Interactions in the School Lab and Workshop', *Education Review*, Vol.36, no.1, Feb, pp 75–86

Whyte, J. 1985a, *Gender, Science and Technology: Inservice Handbook* Longman

Whyte, J., 1985b, *Girls in Science and Technology*, Routledge and Kegan Paul

Whyte, J. et al (eds), 1986, *Girl-friendly Schooling*, Methuen

Wickham, A., 1985, 'Gender Divisions, Training and the State', in Dale, R.

(ed), *Education, Training and Employment: Towards a New Vocationalism?*, Pergamon Press

Wickham, A., 1986, *Women and Training*, Open University, Milton Keynes

Widdowson, F., 1980, *Going up into the Next Class: Women and Elementary Teacher Training 1904–1914*, Hutchinson

Wilkinson, L.C. and Marrett, C.B. (eds), 1985, *Gender Influences in Classroom Interaction*, Academic Press, Orlando

Witcher, H., 1984, 'Responses to Gender Typification in the Primary Classroom', unpublished MEd thesis, University of Stirling

Wolfenden, M.H. and Pumfrey, P.D., 1986, 'A Review of Research: Students' Study Behaviour', *Educational Psychology in Practice*, Vol.1, no.4, Jan., pp 135–141

Women and Geography Study Group, 1984, *Geography and Gender*, Hutchinson

Women's Education Resource Group, 1987, 'Challenging Heterosexism', *Gen: Challenging Racism and Sexism in Education*, no.10/11, double issue

Women's National Commission, 1983, *Report on Secondary Education*, WNC's Recommendations on Secondary Education to the Secretary of State for Education and Science, Cabinet Office

Wright, A., 1985, 'The Education of Girls and Women: Primary Sources, no.3', *History of Education Society Bulletin*, no.36, Autumn, pp 27–30

Yeung, K., 1985, *Working with Girls: A Reader's Route Map*, 3rd edition, National Youth Bureau, Leicester

Feminism, women's studies, gender issues

Anzaldua, G. and Moraga, C. (eds), 1983, *This Bridge Called my Back: Writings by Radical Women of Colour*, Kitchen Table Press, New York

Arcana, J., 1983, *Every Mother's Son: The Role of Mothers in the Making of Men*, The Women's Press

Baehr, H., 1984, *Shut up and Listen: Women and Local Radio: A View from the Inside*, Comedia in assoc. with Boyars

Barrett, M., 1980, *Women's Oppression Today: Problems in Marxist Feminist Analysis*, NBL

Banks, O., 1981, *Faces of Feminism*, Robertson, Oxford

Beddoe, D., 1983, *Discovering Women's History: A Practical Manual*, Pandora

Beechey, V. and Whitelegg, E., 1986, *Women in Britain Today*, Open University Press

Bernstein, H., 1986, *For Their Triumphs and for Their Tears*, IDAF

Birke, L., 1985, *Women, Feminism and Biology: The Feminist Challenge*, Wheatsheaf, Brighton

Blagden, P., 1985, *Women's Studies: An examination of library use by researchers in the field with special reference to the Fawcett Library*, LLRS

Bleier, R., 1984, *Science and Gender: A Critique of Biology and its Theories*

233

on Women, Pergamon

Blunt, R. and Rowan, C. (eds), 1982, *Feminism, Culture and Politics*, Lawrence and Wishart

Bourne, J., 1984, *Towards an Anti-racist Feminism*, Institute of Race Relations

Bowles, G. (ed), 1984, *Strategies for Women's Studies in the 80's*, Pergamon

Bowles, G. and Klein, R.D. (eds), 1983, *Theories of Women's Studies*, Routledge & Kegan Paul

Brittan, A., 1984, *Sexism, Racism and Oppression*, Robertson, Oxford

Brock-Utne, B., 1985, *Educating for Peace: A Feminist Perspective on Peace Research and Action*, Pergamon

Bryan, B., Dadzie, S. and Scafe, S., 1985, *The Heart of the Race: Black Women's Lives in Britain* Virago

Carby, H., 1982, 'White Women Listen! Black Feminism and the Boundaries of Sisterhood', in *The Empire Strikes Back*, CCCS, Hutchinson

Cliff, T., 1984, *Class Struggle and Women's Liberation: 1640 to the Present Day*, Bookmarks, London

Coote, A., 1988, *Sweet Freedom: The Struggle for Women's Liberation*, Blackwell

Coote, A. and Gill, T., 1985, *Women's Rights: A Practical Guide*, Penguin

Coward, R., 1984, *Female Desire*, Granada

Coveney, L. et al (eds), 1984, *The Sexuality Papers: Male Sexuality and the Social Control of Women*, Hutchinson

Cowley, R., 1984, *What about Women: Information Sources for Women's Studies*, Fanfare, Manchester

Dale, J. and Foster, P., 1986, *Feminists and State Welfare*, Routledge & Kegan Paul

Daly, M., 1984, *Pure Lust: Elemental Feminist Philosophy*, The Women's Press

Davis, A., 1981, *Women, Race and Class*, The Women's Press

De Beauvoir, S., 1972, *The Second Sex*, Penguin

Delamont, S., 1980, *The Sociology of Women: An Introduction*, Allen & Unwin

Delphy, C., 1984, *Close to Home*, Hutchinson

Dickson, A., 1985, *The Mirror Within: A New Look at Sexuality*, Quartet

Dworkin, A., 1982, *Our Blood: Prophesies and Discourses on Sexual Politics* The Women's Press

Eagleton, M. (ed), 1986, *Feminist Literary Theory: A Reader*, Blackwell, Oxford

Eisenstein, H., 1986, *Contemporary Feminist Thought*, Allen & Unwin

Ellis, P. (ed), 1986, *Women of the Caribbean*, Zed

Ettore, E.M. (ed), 1980, *Lesbians, Women and Society*, Routledge & Kegan Paul

Evans, J. et al, 1986, *Feminism and Political Theory*, Sage

Evans, M. (ed), 1985, *Black Women Writers: Arguments and Interviews*, Pluto

Faderman, L., 1985, *Surpassing the Love of Men*, The Women's Press

Feminist Review, 1984, 'Many Voices one Chant: Black Feminist

Perspectives', *Feminist Review 17*, August 1984

Figes, E., 1986, *Patriarchal Attitudes*, Macmillan

Friedmann, S. & Sarah, E., (eds), 1982, *On the Problem of Men*, The Women's Press

Frye, M., 1983, *The Politics of Reality: Essays in Feminist Theory*, Crossing Press, Trumensburg, NY

Hall, R.E., 1985, *Ask any Woman: A London Enquiry into Rape and Sexual Assault*, Falling Wall Press, Bristol

Hartnett, O. et al (eds), 1979, *Sex–role Stereotyping*, Tavistock

Heron, L. (ed), 1985, *Truth, Dare or Promise: Girls Growing up in the Fifties*, Virago

Heron, L., 1986, *Changes of Heart: Reflections on Women's Independence*, Pandora

Holland, J. (ed), 1984, *Feminist Action*, Battle Axe

Home Office, 1975, *A Guide to the Sex Discrimination Act, 1975*, HMSO

Home Office, 1975, *White Paper Equality for Women*, HMSO

Hooks, B., 1982, *Ain't I a Woman: Black Women and Feminism*, Pluto

Hooks, B., 1986, *Feminist Theory: From Margin to Centre*, South End Press, Boston

Hull, G., Scott, P.B. and Smith, B. (eds), 1982, *All the women are White, all the Blacks are Men, but Some of us are Brave*, Feminist Press, Old Westbury, NY

Hunt, P., 1980, *Gender and Class Consciousness*, Macmillan

ISIS, 1983, *Women in Development: A Resource Guide for Organisation and Action*, ISIS, Geneva

Jackson, S., 1982, *Childhood and Sexuality*, Blackwell

James, S. (ed), 1985, *Strangers and Sisters: Women, Race and Immigration*, voices from the conference 'Black and Immigrant Women Speak Out and Claim Our Rights, 1982', Falling Wall Press, Bristol

Janssen-Jurreit, M., 1985, *Sexism: The Male Monopoly on History and Thought*, Pluto

Jeffreys, S., 1985, *The Spinster and her Enemies: Feminism and Sexuality 1890–1930*, Pandora

Joseph, G.I. and Lewis J., 1981, *Common Differences: Conflicts in Black and White Feminist Perspectives*, Anchor/Doubleday, New York

Klobenschlag, M., 1983, *Goodbye Sleeping Beauty: Breaking the Spell of Feminine Myths and Models*, Arlen House, Dublin

Kramarae, C. & Treichler, P. (eds), 1985, *A Feminist Dictionary*, Pandora

Kuhn, A. and Wolpe, A-M. (eds), 1978, *Feminism and Materialism*, Routledge & Kegan Paul

Lee, C., 1983, *The Ostrich Position*, Writers & Readers

London Feminist History Group, 1984, *Sexual Dynamics of History*, Pluto

London Rape Crisis Centre, 1984, *Sexual Violence: The Reality for Women*, The Women's Press

Marshall, M., 1985, *Breaking our Silence: An Introduction*, WEA

Martyna, W., 1980, 'Beyond the "He/Man" Approach: The Case for Non-sexist Language', *Signs*, 5, no.3, Spring

Mattelart, M., 1986, *Women, Media, Crisis: Femininity and Disorder*, Comedia

Mies, M., 1986, *Patriarchy and Accumulation on a World Scale: Women in the International Divisions of Labour*, Zed

Miller, C. and Swift, K., 1981, *The Handbook of Non-sexist Writing for Writers, Editors and Speakers*, The Women's Press

Mitchell, J., 1984, *Women: The Longest Revolution: essays on feminism, literature and psychoanalysis*, Virago

Moi, T., 1985 *Sexual/Textual Politics: Feminist Literary Theory*, Methuen

Morgan, R., 1984, *Sisterhood is Global: The International Women's Movement Anthology*, Anchor Press/Doubleday, New York

Morphy, L., 1984, *Pictures of Women: Sexuality: A Study Guide*, Pictures of Women Productions

Murray, Janet, 1984, *Strong-minded Women: and other Lost Voices from Nineteenth-century England*, Penguin

New, C. and Davis, M., 1985, *For the Children's Sake: Making Childcare more than Women's Business*, Pelican

Ni Chuilleanain, E. (ed), 1985, *Irish Women: Image and Achievement*, Arlen House, Dublin

Nicholson, J., 1984, *Men and Women: How Different are They?*, OUP

Oakley, A., 1985, *Taking it like a Woman*, Fontana

Pollert, A., 1981, *Girls, Wives, Factory Lives*, Macmillan

Reid, I. and Wormald, E. (eds), 1982, *Sex Differences in Britain*, Grant McIntyre

Rendall, Jane, 1985, *The Origins of Modern Feminism: Women in Britain, France and the United States, 1780–1860*, Macmillan

Roberts, E., 1984, *A Woman's Place: Oral History of Working-Class Women 1890–1940*, Blackwell

Roberts, H. (ed), 1981, *Doing Feminist Research*, Routledge & Kegan Paul

Root, J., 1984, *Pictures of Women: Sexuality*, Pandora in association with Channel 4

Rowbotham, S., 1977, *Hidden from History: 300 Years of Women's Oppression and the Fight against it*, Pluto

Rowe, M. (ed), 1982, *Spare Rib Reader*, Penguin

Sayers, J., 1986, *Sexual Contradictions: Psychology, Psychoanalysis and Feminism*, Tavistock

Segal, L., 1987, *Is the Future Female?: Troubled Thoughts on Contemporary Feminism*, Virago

Sichtermann, B., 1986, *Femininity: The Politics of the Personal*, Polity in association with Blackwell

Sivard, R.C., 1987, *Women . . . a World Survey*, World Priorities, Washington DC

Spender, D., (ed), 1983, *Feminist Theorists: Three Centuries of Women's Intellectual Traditions*, The Women's Press

Spender, D., 1980, *Man Made Language*, Routledge & Kegan Paul

Spender, D., 1983, *There's always been a Women's Movement this Century*, Pandora

Spender, D., 1985, *For the Record: The Making and Meaning of Feminist Knowledge*, The Women's Press

Stanley, L. and Wise, S., 1983, *Breaking out: Feminist Consciousness and Feminist Research*, Routledge & Kegan Paul

Statham, J., 1986, *Daughters and Sons: Experience of Non-sexist Childraising*, Blackwell

Steedman, C., 1986, *Landscape for a Good Woman: A Story of Two Lives*, Virago

Swindells, J., 1985, *Victorian Writing and Working Women*, Polity Press

Tate, C. (ed) 1985, *Black Women Writers at Work*, Old Castle Books, Harpenden, Herts

Thiam, A., 1986, *Black Sisters Speak out: Feminism and Oppression in Black Africa*, Pluto

Tuttle, L., 1987, *Feminist Encyclopedia*, Arrow

Vogel, L., 1984, *Marxism and the Oppression of Women: Towards a Unitary Theory*, Pluto

Whitelegg, E. et al (eds), 1982, *The Changing Experience of Women*, Martin Robertson in association with the Open University, Oxford

Women and Geography Study Group, 1984, *Women's Role in Changing the Face of the Developing World*: Papers for Discussion, University of Durham Geography Department

Women: A World Report, 1985, Methuen

Materials for the classroom: a selection

Adams, C., Bartley, R. and Loxton, C. (eds), 1985–1987, *Women in History* series: *Coalmining Women; From Workshop to Warfare; Under Control; Women as Healers; Women in Revolutionary Russia; The Women's Suffrage Movement*, Cambridge University Press

Barrett, S. et al, 1985, *South African Women on the Move*, Zed

Bell. R., 1981, *Changing Bodies, Changing Lives: A Book for Teens on Sex and Relationships*, Random, New York

Birmingham Film & Video Workshop, 1987, *Girl Zone*, (Video and teaching pack), Birmingham Film & Video Workshop

Brent, CDSU, 1985, *Working Now*, (pack: photos, leaflets, teachers' notes) Brent Curriculum Development Support Unit

British Youth Council, 1984, *Young Women*, (pack: leaflets and notes), British Youth Council

The Clarity Collective, 1985, *Taught not Caught: Strategies for Sex Education*, Learning Development Aids, Wisbech, Cambs

Connexions, 1985, *Girls Talk*: a linked video and educational package about sexism, (video and portfolio), Connexions, Newcastle-upon-Tyne

Cousins, J., 1988, *Make it Happy, Make it Safe: What sex is all about*; revised edition, Penguin

Coussins, J., 1979, *Taking Liberties*: a teaching pack for boys and girls on equal rights, Virago

Coventry Education Authority, Minority Group Support Service, 1986, *Harriet Tubman: Freedom Fighter*, (pack: charts, leaflets, transparencies, pamphlet), Coventry Education Authority

Coventry Education Authority, Minority Group Support Service, 1986, *Mary Seacole: Nursing Heroine*, (pack: charts, leaflets, transparencies, pamphlet), Coventry Education Authority

Hemmings, S. (ed), 1982, *Girls are Powerful: Young Women's Writing from Spare Rib*, Sheba

Hemmings, S. (ed), 1986, *True to Life: Writing by Young Women*, Sheba

ILEA, 1983, *Women in Construction* (video, posters, teachers' notes), ILEA

ILEA, 1984, *Women in Engineering* (video, posters, teachers' notes), ILEA

ILEA English Centre, 1985, *The English Curriculum: Gender: Material for Discussion*, ILEA

ILEA, 1988, *A Different Story: The Lives and Experiences of a Group of Young Lesbians and Gay Men* (video), ILEA

Jones, A., 1982, *Male and Female: Choosing your Role in Modern Society*, revised edition, Hobsons Press, Cambridge

Just Seventeen magazine readers, 1987, *Bitter-sweet Dreams: Young Women's own Stories*, Virago (Upstarts)

Lawson, L., 1985, *Working Women: A Portrait of South Africa's Black Women Workers*, Ravan, Johannesburg

Leigh, M., 1984, *Messages: A Booklet for use in Workshops and Seminars concerned with Sexism and the Development of Non-sexist Work with Young People*, British Council of Churches

McCaffery, J., 1985, *What about Women?*, John Murray

McRobbie, A. and McCabe, T. (eds), 1981, *Feminism for Girls: An Adventure Story*, Routledge and Kegan Paul

New Grapevine, 1984, 'The Grapevine Game (Sex and Sexuality)', (board game with pamphlet), New Grapevine

Owens, R., 1985, *Did your Granny have a Hammer? History of the Irish Suffrage Movement, 1876–1922*, (portfolio pack; leaflets, postcards, badge), Attic and Women in Community Publishing Course, Dublin

Poster Film Collective, 1982, *Between Future and Past* (poster pack and teachers' book), Poster Film Collective

Reading Matters 1986, *Proud to be a Woman still Fighting: Writing from Young Women in Haringey*, Reading Matters

Returned Volunteer Action, 1984, *Manomiya: A Discussion Game* (board game, leaflets, co-ordinator's notes), Returned Volunteer Action

Sandhu, R., 1986, *The Tech and Tools Book: A Guide to Technologies Women are using Worldwide*, International Women's Tribune Centre, New York

Seager, J. and Olson, A., 1986, *Women in the World: An International Atlas*, Pan

Sharpe, S., 1987, *Falling for Love: Teenage Mothers Talk*, Virago (Upstarts)

Spindler–Brown, A., 1983, *Women's Studies: A Resource Pack*, National Extension College, Cambridge

Szirom, T. and Dyson, S, 1986, *Greater Expectations: A Source Book for*

Working with Girls and Young Women, British edition edited by H. Slavin, Learning Development Aids, Wisbech, Cambs

Thompson, D.C., 1985, *As Boys become Men: Learning Male Roles: Curriculum for Exploring Male Role Stereotyping*, Irvington, New York

Thompson, J.L., 1987, *All Right for Some: The Problem of Sexism*, Hutchinson

Trades Union Congress, 1984, *Images of Inequality: The Portrayal of Women in the Media and Advertising: a TUC Report*, TUC

Trenchard, L., 1984, *Talking about Young Lesbians*, London Gay Teenage Group

Trenchard, L. and Warren, H. (eds), 1984, *Something to Tell You: The Experiences and Needs of Young Lesbians and Gay Men in London*, London Gay Teenage Group

Walker, D., 1986, *Gender Equality: An Effective Resource for Today's Classroom*, Learning Development Aids, Wisbech, Cambs

Walton, A., 1984, *Science and Engineering: It's a Woman's World Too*, LLRS

Watts, A. and Kant, L., 1986, *A Working Start: Guidance Strategies for Girls and Young Women*, Longman

Whyld, J., 1986, *When Bees Sting, They Die: Male Culture, Sexual Relationships and Aggression*, J. Whyld, Moorland House, Caisor, Lincs LN7 6SF

Journals: a selection

Aurora
PO Box 4
Liverpool L17 7EE

Cassoe Newsletter
7 Pickwick Court
London SE9 4SA

Everywoman
34a Islington Green
London N1 8DU

Feminist library and information
Centre Newsletter
Hungerford House
Victoria Embankment
London WC2N 6PA

Feminist Review
11 Carlton Gardens
Brecknock Road
London N19 5AQ

Gen: Challenging Racism and Sexism
in Education.
WedG, ILEA Drama & Tape Centre
Princeton Street
London WC1R 4BH

Manushi (New Delhi)
c/o 147 Grove lane
London NW3

Mukti (ceased publication 1988)
213 Eversholt Street
London NW1

Outwrite Women's Newspaper
Oxford House
Derbyshire Street
London E2 6HG

Spare Rib
27 Clerkenwell Close
London EC1R OAT

Trouble and Strife
P.O.Box MT16
Leeds LS17 5PY

WEG (Women's Equality Group)
Newsletter
(ceased publication 1988)
London Strategic Policy Unit
Middlesex House
20 Vauxhall Bridge Road
SW1V 2SB

Wires Newsletter
P.O.Box 162
Sheffield S1 1UD

Women's Studies International
Forum
Pergamon Press
Headington Hill Hall
Oxford OX3 OBW

Working with Girls
National Association of Youth Clubs
30 Peacock Lane
Leicester LE1 5NY
(ceased publication 1987)

Further Information

Publishers

A selection of British and Irish publishers, including feminist presses, community presses, and some mainstream publishers

Arlen House
Kinnead Court
12–16 South Cumberland Street
Dublin 2
Eire
tel: 0001 717383

Attic Press
44 East Essex Street
Dublin 2
Eire
tel: 0001 716367

Basil Blackwell
108 Cowley Road
Oxford OX4 1JF
tel: 0865 72214

Black Woman Talk
Box 32
190 Upper Street
London N1

Bloodaxe Books
P.O.Box ISN
Newcastle-upon-Tyne NE99 ISN
tel: 091 232 5988

Bowker Publishing Company
Erasmus House
58/62 High Street
Epping
Essex CM16 4BU

Brilliance Books
14 Clerkenwell Green
London EC1
tel: 01 250 0730

Bristol Broadsides
108a Stokes Croft
Bristol
BS1 3RU
tel: 0272 40764

Cambridge University Press
The Edinburgh Building
Shaftesbury Road
Cambridge CB2 2RU
tel: 0223 312393

Camden Press
43 Camden Passage
London N1 8EB
tel: 01 226 2061

Carmine Pink
4 Dashwood Road
Oxford OX4 45J
tel: 0865 771378

Centerprise
136 Kingsland High Street
London E8
tel: 01 254 9632

Change
29 Great James Street
London WC1N 3ES
tel: 01 405 3601

Falling Wall Press
75 West Street
Bristol B52 OBX
tel: 0272 559230

Falmer Press
4 John Street
London WC1N 2ET
tel: 01 405 2237

Franklin Watts Group
10 Golden Square
London W1R 3AF
tel: 01 278 6881

Harper & Row
28 Tavistock Street
London WC2E 7PN
tel: 01 836 4635

Harvester Press
16 Ship Street
Brighton
East Sussex BN1 1AD
tel: 0273 729 585

Lawrence & Wishart
39 Museum Street
London WC1A 1LQ
tel: 01 405 0103

Leeds Postcards
P.O.Box 84
Leeds LS1 4HU

Methuen Books
11 New Fetter Lane
London EC4P 4EE
tel: 01 583 9855

Only Women Press
38 Mount Pleasant
London WC1
tel: 01 837 0596

Penguin Books
27 Wrights Lane
London W8 5TZ
tel: 01 938 2200

Pluto Press
c/o Allison and Busby
6a Noel Street
London W1V 3RB
tel: 01 734 1498

Polity Press
108 Cowley Road
Oxford OX4 1JF
tel: 0865 72214

Peckham Publishing
13 Peckham High Street
London SE15
tel: 01 701 1757

Reading Matters
10 Lymington Avenue
London N22
tel: 01 881 3187

Sage Publications
28 Banner Street
London EC1Y 8QE
tel: 01 253 1516

See Red Women's Workshop
(posters)
90a Camberwell Road
London SE5

Serpent's Tale
27 Montpelier Grove
London NW5 2XD
tel: 01 267 1956

Sheba Feminist Publishers
10a Bradbury Street
London N16 8JN
tel: 01 254 1590

Stramullion
43 Candlemakers Row
Edinburgh EH1 2QB
tel: 031 228 6280

Tavistock
11 New Fetter Lane
London EC4P 4EE
tel: 01 583 9855

Verso
6 Meard Street
London W1V 3HR
tel: 01 437 3546

Virago Press
41 King William IV Street
London WC2
tel: 01 379 6977

Womenwrite Press
P.O.Box 77
Cardiff CF2 4XX
tel: 0222 496062

Women's Community Press
48 Fleet Street
Dublin 2,
Eire

The Women's Press
34 Great Sutton Street
London EC1V ODX
tel: 01 251 3007

Zed Books
57 Caledonian Road
London N1 9BU
tel: 01 837 8466

Resource lists

Cissy, 1987, 7+ *stories: An Annotated Booklist of about 100 Titles for Parents, Librarians and Teachers*, CISSY (Campaign to Impede Sex Stereotyping in the Young)

Feminism Book Fortnight, Annual List of Books, Feminist Book Fortnight Group

Feminist Library, Newsletter (includes list of books received), Feminist Library, A Woman's Place

Heffers Booksellers, 1986, *Women's Studies*: Heffers catalogue 224, Heffers, Cambridge

ILEA English Centre, 1987, *Gender: Resources for English*, ILEA

ILEA, 1986, *Positive Images:* A Resources Guide to Materials about Homosexuality, including Gay and Lesbian Literature for use by Teachers and Librarians in Secondary Schools and Further Education Colleges

Lavender Menace, *Independent Women*: A Women's Books Newsletter and Lavender Lesbian List, Lavender Menace, Edinburgh

Letterbox Library, Quarterly catalogues (of non-sexist and multi-cultural children's books), Letterbox Library

Silver Moon Bookshop, Quarterly booklist, Silver Moon

Sisterwrite Bookshop, Booklist *and* children's booklist, Sisterwrite

Organisations

Black Women's Centre
Mary Seacole House
41 Stockwell Green
London SW9
tel: 01 274 9220

Cassoe
7 Pickwick Court
London SE9 4SA
tel: 01 857 3793

Centre for Research & Education on Gender
University of London, Institute of Education
20 Bedford Way
London WC1H OAL
tel: 01 636 1500

CISSY (Campaign to impede sex stereotyping in the young)
177 Gleneldon Road
London SW6 2BX
tel: 01 677 2411

Equal Opportunities Commission
Overseas House
Quay Street
Manchester
M3 3HN
tel: 061 833 9244

Fawcett Library
City of London Polytechnic
Old Castle Street
London E1 7NT
tel: 01 283 1030

Feminist Archive
Bath University
Claverton Down
Bath BAZ 2AY
tel: 0225 312703

Feminist Audio Books
52/54 Featherstone Street
London EC1 8RT
tel: 01 251 2908

Feminist Book Fortnight Group
c/o Loddon House
Church Street
London NW8 8PX

Feminist Library & Information
Centre
Hungerford House
Victoria Embankment
London WC2N 6PA
tel: 01 930 0715

Gamma (Girls and Mathematics
Association)
c/o Girls and Mathematics Unit
University of London, Institute of
Education
58 Gordon Square
London WC1
tel: 01 636 1500 ext 496

Gemma
BM Box 5700
London WC1N 3XX

ILEA Gender Focus on Resources
Resources Library
Centre for Learning Resources
275 Kennington Lane
London SE11 5QZ
tel: 01 633 4204

Lavender Menance
11a Forth Street
Edinburgh EH1 3LE
tel: 031 556 0079

Lesbians in Education
c/o A Woman's Place
Hungerford House
Victoria Embankment
London WC2

Letterbox Library
(children's book club)
8 Bradbury Street
London N6
tel: 01 254 1640

London Lesbian & Gay Centre
68 Cowcross StreetLondon EC1M
6BP
tel: 01 608 1471

London Lesbian Line
52/54 Featherstone Street
London EC1
tel: 01 251 6911

London Rape Crisis Centre
P.O.Box 69
London WC1NX 9NJ
tel: 01 837 1600 (24 hr line)
  or: 01 278 3956

London Women's Centre
Wesley House
70 Great Queen Street
London WC2
tel: 01 430 1076

Manchester Women in Education
c/o 14 St Brendan's Road
Withington
Manchester 20

Northern Ireland Women in
Education
c/o 17 Ardmore Avenue
Ballynafeigh
Belfast 7
tel: 0232 646530

Rights of Women
52/54 Featherstone Street
London EC1
tel: 01 251 6577

Silver Moon Bookshop
68 Charing Cross Road
London WC2
tel: 01 836 7906

Sisterwrite Bookshop
190 Upper Street
London N1
tel: 01 226 9782

A Woman's Place
Hungerford House
Victoria Embankment
London WC2
tel: 01 836 6081

Women and Manual Trades
52/54 Featherstone Street
London EC1
tel: 01 251 9192

Women in Construction Advisory
Group
Southbank House
Black Prince Road
London SE1 7SJ

Women's Education Group
ILEA Drama & Tape Centre
Princeton Street
London WC1
tel: 01 242 6807

Women's Equality Group
London Strategic Policy Unit
Middlesex House
20 Vauxhall Bridge Road
SW1V 2SB
tel: 01 633 3645

Women's International Resource
Centre
173 Archway Road
London N6 5BL
tel: 01 341 4403

Young Lesbian Group
8 Manor Gardens
London N7
tel: 01 263 6270

Notes on the Contributors

Contributors to the 1980 Edition

Pippa Brewster, born in London in 1949, did a degree at Durham before entering publishing in 1971. Having worked as an editor with Routledge & Kegan Paul promoting feminist authors, she is now Publisher of Pandora Press.

Lou Buchan, born in Australia in 1946, has degrees from the University of Sydney and the University of New South Wales. She lives in Toronto where she is involved in the women's liberation movement and the Feminist Party of Canada. She taught for a number of years in secondary schools in Australia in both the private and state system and left teaching, disillusioned. She has two sons.

Katherine Clarricoates, born in Harrogate, brought up in Leeds, now lives in Hull. She has been an active member of the women's liberation movement since 1972 and completed her PhD on sexism in the primary school. She has many interests, from Arts and Crafts to writing, which she states is not really an interest, but a consuming need.

Madeleine Epstein, born in London in 1953, a graduate of London University and lecturer in English at a college of higher education, she has taught in a variety of schools. She has been involved in the women's liberation movement for some years and is interested in developing women's studies courses. She is a keen cook and gardener.

Stevi Jackson, born in Portsmouth in 1951. She has been teaching in Higher Education since 1975 and works at the Polytechnic of Wales. Has been involved in the women's liberation movement since her 1970 student days; now works with the South Wales Rape Crisis Group. While a research student at the University of Kent she conducted research on teenage girls' sexual attitudes and was involved in a campaign aimed at interesting girls in the women's movement.

Anne Lee, born in Nottingham in 1951. Anne Lee has worked in Hertfordshire schools applying the principles of group work to classroom practices. She is working on collaborative learning and literacy at the Centre for Urban Educational Studies and the Institute of Education, London University. Her main concern is to explore the potential available within the education system to respond to the linguistic and cultural resources brought to schools by females and males in the multicultural society in which we live. She is a keen writer and reader.

Irene Payne, was born in Liverpool in 1950 and has been a secondary school teacher in London for five years. She is involved in trying to challenge sexism in education both inside and outside the school by participating in various groups to devise strategies for education.

Marion Scott, was born in Worthing in 1953 and has been actively involved in the women's liberation movement. After post-graduate work at Sussex she became interested in education and teaches English in a London comprehensive. Her general interests include philosophy, literature and history.

Anne Whitbread, born in Birmingham in 1950. Anne Whitbread is an English teacher in a girls' comprehensive in Inner London. After graduating from York University in English and Sociology, in 1973, she taught in the Far East for three years. She is a part-time poet and illustrator. She was employed in a boys' school in London when she wrote her contribution to this book and is now grateful to be out of the front line. She is now committed to widening the horizons of the girls whom she teaches.

Patricia de Wolfe, born in London in 1946, became involved in the women's liberation movement in about 1974. Spent a long period as a student in Higher Education which provided a context in which feminist ideas could be worked out, although it also involved many contradictions, especially when Women's Studies was part of the curriculum. Now works at the Women's Research and Resources Centre and is trying to stay out of patriarchal education.

Contributors to the 1989 Edition

Sue Adler has lived in London since 1972. She is a librarian and has (almost) always worked in education – schools, colleges and teachers' centres. She was born in South Africa in 1948. Her commitment is to liberation, literacy and the connections between the two.

Grace Evans came to Britain from the USA in 1969 to complete secondary school. After reading Politics at the University of Reading and obtaining a Post Graduate Certificate in Education from Goldsmiths' College she became a teacher. While teaching she was closely involved with the work of the Afro-Caribbean Education Resource Porject (ACER) which produces anti-racist learning materials for use in schools. She was a full-time member of the Spare Rib Editorial Collective from 1984 to 1987, has taught courses for women for the Extra-Mural Studies Department of the University of London and at present works in the Women's Unit of Haringey Council.

Pat Mahony was born in Kent in 1943. For the past ten years she has been fortunate in working in the Post Graduate Secondary Education Department, Goldsmiths' College, amongst supportive colleagues. She has two daughters, both at a girls' comprehensive school which she with other parents successfully campaigned to save from amalgamation with a boys' school. She detests cooking and has almost realised one major ambition – to give it up.

Lorraine Trenchard received a blantantly racist, sexist and heterosexist 'education' in what was then Rhodesia. The experience of being a young lesbian at school and therefore an outsider provided enough of an impetus to enable her to question how much of what passed for education was in fact indoctrination. She has been in England since 1980, and has been involved in a variety of projects concerned with supporting young gay people.